# CALL TO ORDER

Sustaining Simplicity in Architecture

# CALL TO ORDER

## Sustaining Simplicity in Architecture


**Edited by**
Carie Penabad

**Preface by**
Rodolphe el-Khoury

**Introduction by**
Carie Penabad

**Essays by**
Jean Francois Lejeune
Esteban Salcedo
Katherine Wheeler
Steven Fett
Edgar Sarli
Adib Cúre

**Interviews with**
Matteo Ghidoni
Nader Tehrani

**Postscript by**
Elizabeth Plater-Zyberk

**Editorial Assistants**
Aigerim Amirova
Sophie Juneau
Claire Morris
Minhae Shim Roth

School of Architecture **University of Miami**



OSCAR RIERA OJEDA
PUBLISHERS

# Contents


## 01. Preface
Rodolphe el-Khoury
06

## 02. Introduction
Carie Penabad
08

## 03. Essays
*A Short History*
Jean Francois Lejeune
16
*New Order. New Wave*
Esteban Salcedo
30
*Drawing Order*
Katherine Wheeler
38
*Call to Order Exhibition*
Curators: Steven Fett and Edgar Sarli
44
*Vernacularology*
Adib Cúre
50

## 04. Featured Projects
66

## 05. Conversations
Matteo Ghidoni
404
Nader Tehrani
414

## 06. Round Table Discussion
Young Architects Symposium
420

## 07. Postscript
Elizabeth Plater-Zyberk
426

01.

# Preface

Rodolphe el-Khoury

In 2014, the University of Miami School of Architecture launched the Tecnoglass Lecture Series, a public program that includes lectures, interviews, mini-symposia, and exhibitions, all curated around an annual theme that is of particular relevance to the School. The inaugural 2014-15 series, titled CALL TO ORDER, and suggesting a re-grouping and a re-grounding upon the foundations of the discipline, celebrates the history of the school while clarifying its renewed purpose in an international arena. It is inspired by "Rappel à l'ordre," the post WWI European movement that rejected the extreme tenets of the avant-garde and its praise of disruption, machinery, violence and war, in favor of continuity and rational sobriety.

The series looks at an international group of architects and thinkers who are ostensibly rehearsing the ethos of the 1960s and 1970s when architects and thinkers converged in their resistance to what they saw as an erosion of the discipline by the social sciences and other centrifugal influences, re-grouping around the principal of autonomy.

CALL TO ORDER examines similarly resistant practices in the contemporary architectural scene that reinvest in restraint, simplicity, and rational order but without holding on to disciplinary autonomy. They build upon enduring foundations but only to project architecture into an expanded and enriched territory. The book surveys this contemporary condition in the context of a long historical trajectory to tease out and articulate a cultural project that is relevant to the ongoing architectural debate.

02.

# Introduction

Carie Penabad

Newport Street Gallery, London, Caruso St John Architects, 2015.

*"Simplicity must not be taken to be the synonym of 'poverty,' or to mean a retrogression. Simplicity progresses in the same way as refinement…"*
*Jean Cocteau, Call to Order*

*"Be not afraid of being called un-fashionable."*
*Adolf Loos*

A group of emerging architectural practices appear to have a renewed interest in fundamentals, simplicity, history, precedent, and typology, evoking more established approaches to architectural design. These practices are seemingly wary of the allure of the new and skeptical of the notion that every building must be invented from scratch, as a unique response to particular conditions. They challenge the double tyranny of program and diagram that have come to dominate the design process today; instead, their works rely on a broad understanding of typology for a looser—and therefore more sustainable—fit between program and form. Invested in building techniques that are culturally relevant as much as performative, these approaches capitalize on the intelligence sedimented in building morphologies that have evolved internationally over millennia to tackle the challenges of the environment and sustainability.

*Call to Order*, a year-long series of public programs and an accompanying exhibition at the University of Miami School of Architecture during the 2014–15 academic year, was the School's inaugural public investigation under the leadership of Rodolphe el-Khoury, who was appointed dean in July 2014. Through the programs and an exhibition, the School examined whether these new currents were isolated visual and formal manifestations of a style or if this new generation was expanding upon their predecessors' Call to Order with a relevant cultural project that could shape a new direction for the thinking and practice of architecture today. [1]

The dialogue generated by these activities has been thoughtful, invigorating, and is ongoing. With this publication, we are encouraging an expansion and deepening of the conversation. It is our hope that readers are intrigued and stimulated by the work presented here, and that the discussion grows. The University of Miami School of Architecture is particularly suited to have initiated this exploration, as it has traditionally had a commitment to the study of cities and to promoting an international discourse around the core elements of history, morphology, order, and simplicity. The programs and this volume signal a renewed commitment to these foundational principles, while expanding the discourse to include a broader and more inclusive notion of how these elements shape the thinking of architecture and cities today.

The essays collected here offer varying perspectives. Jean-François Lejeune provides a historical context for an understanding of what we mean by a Call to Order. His essay outlines how the early 20th century witnessed a move away from the avant-garde in art and architecture, coupled with an embrace of the principles of classicism and the rediscovery of the vernacular. These developments were due in part to a reaction against the machine and technology, both viewed as abetting the mass violence associated with World War I, as well as the perceived excesses of avant-garde modernism. This shift was not solely associated with conservative dictatorial regimes, but also resonated internationally with protagonists of modernity in both Europe and America. This reframing illustrates how the Call to Order was more open, more democratic, and more complex than many contemporary critics care to acknowledge. Moreover, LeJeune's essay demonstrates how this sensibility was not strictly opposed to modernism, but rather attempted to achieve a synthesis between modernity and tradition, a combination probably best illustrated in the work of leading Italian architects such as Gio Ponti and Adalberto Libera.

*"New Order, New Wave"* by Esteban Salcedo is distinctly different in style and tone. In contrast to the historical framework set forth by Lejeune, Salcedo more narrowly focuses on a new generation of architects working in and around Belgium whose work conforms to what he describes as a new *rappel à l'ordre* (call to order). Salcedo deliberately omits mentioning architects or their buildings by name. Rather, he refers to the group as New Wave architects and establishes an analytical structure based on sensibilities linked broadly to contemporary culture, including presentation, context, the idea of authorship, and the tension between production and consumption.

Salcedo makes reference to creative processes in art, music, philosophy, and film to draw analogies to the design methodologies employed by the New Wave architects. He describes this new generation as both curators and *bricoleurs* (craftsmen, tinkerers), capable of researching, assembling, and repurposing references to produce new and unexpected systems of organization.

Shifting to the visual material assembled here, Steven Fett and Edgar Sarli, who curated the *Call to Order* exhibition held at the University of Miami School of Architecture Glasgow Hall in Spring 2015, describe that project. The firms whose work was showcased are primarily emerging practices, such as the constellation of figures that have coalesced around the *San Rocco* journal, including Salottobuono and 2A + P/A as well as Pezo Von Ellrichshausen, Productora, Adrian Phiffer, and Cúre & Penabad. This work was displayed alongside more established voices, including Nader Tehrani of NADAA, OFFICE Kersten Geers David Van Severen, MOS Architects, and Johnston Marklee. Interestingly, even the more recognized firms in the show have limited built works. Their contributions to the world of architecture have been made largely through the power of their drawings and competition entries.

For the purposes of the exhibition, this latter observation afforded a criteria for selection and display in a limited physical space. For the book, we expanded the list to include the distinguished offices of Caruso St. John and Sergison Bates, as well as several emerging figures including Laurent de Carriere. While varied with regards to architectural output and ideology, this group shares certain sensibilities with the work gathered for the *Call to Order* exhibition. Viewing this extended grouping highlights that this new current is not merely an isolated formal manifestation but a broader search for a relevant architectural project that desires to shape a new direction for the thinking and practice of architecture today. Moreover, the architectural community has recognized these efforts as a relevant means of producing architecture. Most recently, Caruso St. John's Newport Street Gallery in London was awarded the 2016 RIBA Sterling Prize for best building of the year. This prestigious recognition signals that this way of making architecture is no longer unfashionable or the output of a rear guard, but rather a central player in the shaping of the contemporary city, particularly as it relates to works that do not seek immediate iconographic recognition, but are meaningfully rooted in the everyday life and material culture of the city.

Returning to the exhibition essay, Fett and Sarli outline the organizational structure of the show and highlight certain sensibilities that loosely bind the works together, including an interest in history, form, type, and meaning. These characteristics can be seen as both an inherent critique of the reliance on the diagram to describe and embody the complex realities of architecture and as a reaction to the neo-modernist fervor to uphold the tyranny of the new, producing a contempt of history that leads to a dissolving of architectural literacy, or at the very least, to the reduction of references deemed acceptable by certain modernist canons. The works assembled reveal a more open-minded attitude towards history that is more all-encompassing and simultaneously more personal and intuitive.

The majority of the projects display an intense commitment to the discipline of architecture, its material culture, and constructional conventions. Numerous works rely ostensibly on simple geometric forms for their architectural expression. This formal output does not appear to be solely guided by economy, but rather by a process of distillation that seeks to reduce the work to its most fundamental aspects.

Quite the opposite of simplification, distillation is the search for quintessence. As in the process of making wine, distillation extracts the essential characteristics, resulting in an outcome that could not be further reduced without being compromised. These distilled forms emerge from an understanding of architectural tradition interpreted in its broadest and most holistic sense. The significance of tradition that informs contemporary expression is described by T. S. Eliot in the following passage from "Tradition and the Individual Talent" in *The Sacred Wood*; although nominally intended for writers, his argument applies to any field with a history: *"Tradition is a matter of much wider significance. It cannot be inherited, and if you want it you must obtain it by great labour. It involves, in the first place, the historical sense, which we may call nearly indispensable to anyone who would continue to be a poet beyond his twenty-fifth year; and the historical sense involves a perception, not only of the pastness of the past, but of its presence; the historical sense compels a man to write not merely with his own generation in his bones, but with a feeling that the whole of the literature of Europe from Homer and within it the whole of the literature of his own country has a simultaneous existence and composes a simultaneous order. This historical sense, which is a sense of the timeless as well as of the temporal and of the timeless and of the temporal together, is what makes a writer traditional. And it is at the same time what makes a writer most acutely conscious of his place in time, of his contemporaneity."*

*Call to Order* Poster, University of Miami School of Architecture Tecnoglass Lecture Series, 2015-2016.

Seen through this lens, the works showcased in *Call to Order* demonstrate an understanding that the discipline of architecture has a language and a grammar of form making, and that contemporary works can participate in this broader lineage without the feelings of anxiety associated with a historicist discourse. The larger goal is the acquisition of architectural knowledge capable of being translated into the creation of new buildings and places of identity and wholeness.

As stated earlier, many projects in the exhibition are unbuilt. As such, drawings play a critical role in representing and projecting the work. "Drawing Order" by Katherine Wheeler asserts the importance of architectural representation in a rapidly evolving digital age and the power of drawing as an autonomous pursuit, capable of advancing architectural discourse alongside or often beyond the built work. Her essay focuses specifically on the drawings of the *Call to Order* exhibition, placing them within the greater lineage of architectural representation. She highlights the prevalent use of orthographic projection and axonometric drawing and points to the ways that specific works on display use these recognized conventions to new effect in their ability to communicate and represent architectural ideas.

Adib Cure's essay entitled Vernacularology, describes a series of studios currently being offered at the University of Miami School of Architecture that elaborate on themes associated with the Call to Order. The selection of student drawings illustrates a commitment to the fundamentals of the discipline and the pursuit of an architecture reflective of place.

Conversations with Nader Tehrani, Dean of the Cooper Union School of Architecture and principal of NADAAA, conducted by el-Khoury, and with Matteo Ghidoni, editor of *San Rocco* journal and founder of the research and design collaborative Salottobuono, which I conducted, follow the more formal essays and serve as a spontaneous record of the conversations that ensued as part of the year-long thematized lecture series. Broader themes surface as part of these discussions, including: the engagement with and transformation of type; the notion of formal innovation stemming from vernacular building traditions; the role of drawing as both the site of invention in design and as an act of construction; the critical role of collaboration in contemporary architectural production; and perhaps most importantly, the role of curation and the desire to establish what is fundamental in a work of architecture.

Elizabeth Plater-Zyberk's postscript marks both a physical and metaphorical transition for the University of Miami School of Architecture from her eighteen-year tenure as dean to el-Khoury's appointment. Plater-Zyberk points to the longstanding interest in both the rational and the vernacular at the School of Miami and the overarching interest to create an architecture of place, rooted in both the realities and opportunities of a given material context. Her piece provides a brief historical narrative of the School while placing the work within a broader global context. Moving forward, a continued search for what is fundamental, and thus timeless in architecture, and a continued commitment to the city present a robust and optimistic agenda for the future.

1 The series of events was conceived and organized by the public programs committee at the University of Miami School of Architecture, chaired by Adib Cúre, with committee members Germane Barnes, Roberto Behar, Jacob Brillhart, Steven Fett, Eric Firley, Jose Gelabert-Navia, Jean-François Lejeune, Edgar Sarli, and Allan Shulman.

03.

# Essays

Jean Francois Lejeune
Esteban Salcedo
Katherine Wheeler
Steven Fett & Edgar Sarli
Adib Cúre

# A Short History

## Jean Francois Lejeune

*"However remote in time events thus recounted may seem to be, history in reality refers to present needs and present situations wherein those events vibrate."*[1] *Benedetto Croce*

*"The Enlightenment, as Kant said, means daring to know. It is the leave-taking of man from his childhood. From this point of view, the Enlightenment requires, today as in the past, to choose one's camp, and to confide in humanity, in knowledge, and in progress. Mankind must save itself, and certainly, never ever, will it be the work of a God. We need Knowledge, truth, and reality will be required. Not to accept them, as did the post-modern philosophical and political populism, is to follow the alternate path, always possible, that the Grand Inquisitor offers: it means to follow the way of the miracle, of the mystery, and eventually of the authority of power."*[2] *Maurizio Ferraris*

At the end of WWI, Italian culture and architecture, best represented before 1914 by the loud and provocative manifestos of Marinetti and the Futurists, moved dramatically away from this destruction-loving avant-garde and its infatuation with war, machine, and technology. A large group of artists—Mario Sironi, Duilio Cambellotti, Fortunato Depero among others—embraced a return to the principles of classicism as carrier of universal beauty but also the rediscovery of the vernacular, in particular the Mediterranean one, as a source of a new "primitivism."[3] The art periodical *Valori Plastici*, launched by Mario Broglio in 1918, became the primary vector of this *return to order* and its reformist anti-futurist and anti-bolshevist program. In its pages, Alberto Savinio, Giorgio De Chirico, and Carlo Carrà advocated a "metaphysical classicism."[4] The movement resonated strongly across Europe and particularly in Paris, with Paul Valéry's *Eupalinos ou l'architecte* (1921), the poetic call to order by Jean Cocteau, *Rappel à l'ordre* (1926), and Pablo Picasso's shift from Cubism to a new classicism.[5]

*Figure 1* Cover of *Valori Plastici – Rassegna d'Arte*, III, nº 5, 1922

In Spain, the major protagonists of Catalan modernity, industrialist Eusebi Güell and philosopher Eugeni D'Ors, embraced a cultural and political project for Catalonia—Noucentisme—that would be based upon the return to a Mediterranean classicism dominated by the Greek ideal as "a metaphor of progress, sea, commerce and opening of the borders."[6] In France and Italy as well, the "myth of the Mediterranean" would exercise a notable magnetic force on the literary, artistic, and architectonic debates and works until the early 1940s.[7] Across Europe and beyond their stylistic identities, these forms of "return to order" or rather *Realisms between Revolution and Reaction* embraced the return to the figure and the real, but also expanded their field of representation to the modern urban landscape and its present and future conflicts.[8]

### ***North - South***

Although it was launched as a direct reaction to the traumas of the war and to the perceived excesses of avant-garde modernism, the contemporary *return to order* in architecture has more often than not been associated with the conservative and dictatorial regimes that used and manipulated the original ideas in favor of nationalistic causes in Italy, Germany, Russia, and in the early years of Franco's Spain. Yet, the movement was at once more open, more democratic, and more complex in terms of its premises, sources, and production. On the one hand it had its equivalent in democratic Scandinavia with the Nordic Classicism epitomized by Gunnar Asplund, Sigurd Lewerentz and others like Ivar Tengbom, as well as in North America with the abstract classicism that characterized the Depression era under the impulse of architects and educators such as Paul Cret. On the other hand, the *return to order* did not strictly oppose modernism but attempted to expand the language of classicism by renewing its primary tenets associated with rhythm, proportions, and composition. Return to order meant to achieve a dialectic synthesis between tradition and modernity—a strategy that was best illustrated in Italy in the works of Novecento architects Giovanni Muzio and Gio Ponti, and the most notable Rationalist, Giuseppe Terragni, Adalberto Libera, Giuseppe Vaccaro, and Luigi Moretti.

*Figure 2* Luigi Filocamo. *Giovanni Muzio dialoga con Vitruvio*, 1940. Behind Muzio, one recognizes, from bottom to top: Università Cattolica (Milano), Arengario, Santuario di Sant Antonio (Cremona) and Torre del Palazzo del Governo (Sondrio). © Archivio Muzio

Following WWI, the Novecento movement in Milano challenged the Beaux-Arts eclecticism that had dominated the beginning of the century with an abstract classicism

*Figure 3* Gruppo Urbanisti Romani (GUR). Central piazza of Sabaudia in the late 1930s, with city hall in the background. © Archivio Fotografico Touring Club Italiano

best exemplified by the works of Gio Ponti, and especially Giovanni Muzio and his built Milanese manifesto, the Cá Brutta (1922).[9] In 1926-27 the *Gruppo Sette*—which included Luigi Figini, Guido Frette, Sebastiano Larco, Giuseppe Pagano, Gino Pollini, Carlo Enrico Rava, Giuseppe Terragni and Ubaldo Castagnoli (replaced the following year by Adalberto Libera)—issued four manifestos on architecture that advocated "clarity, revision and order." They promoted the rationalism of Le Corbusier but argued that it should be mitigated by tradition and history:

*"Nothing hinders us from admiring the backgrounds of Giotto... the architectural marquetry of Francesco di Giorgio and the wood engravings of Serlio, and to understand the rhythm, the almost Greek purity of certain factories with walls of glass. There is no incompatibility between our past and our present. We do want to break with tradition; it is tradition which transforms itself, and assumes new aspects, few people recognize it."*[10]

In 1930s Rome, even more than in Milan where it was first influential in the preceding decade, the Metaphysical painting of Giorgio de Chirico, Carlo Carrà, and Mario Sironi was literally constructed in major urban and architectural projects such as the Città Universitaria, the Foro Italico, the E42 (now EUR) district, and the new towns of the Pontine Marshes. De Chirico himself was very aware of the connection of painting to architecture as he wrote in *Valori Plastici*:

*"In the construction of the city, in the architectural form of the houses, the squares, the gardens, the public promenades, the ports, and the train stations, etc., can be found the fundamental elements of a great metaphysical aesthetic...."*[11]

The "metaphysical" squares of Littoria, Sabaudia, Aprilia, and others in Pomezia and Guidonia opened to the landscape and the rural environment, thus reflecting another critical element of De Chirico's vision:

*"The landscape, framed in the arcade of a portico, as in the square or the rectangular of a window, acquires a major metaphysical value, as it solidifies and becomes isolated from the space that surrounds it. So, architecture completes nature."*[12]

To be sure, Italian architecture and urbanism of the interwar period never really embraced the International Style, its uniform approach to technology, and its predominantly anti-urban agenda. The northern tenets were contested on various grounds that included nationalism, tradition, climatic conditions, and constructive tectonics—the wall of the southern vernacular versus the wood-based post and beam of the northern one. In other words, as I argue throughout this essay, the post-1918 *return to order* in the field of architecture and urbanism corresponded to a moment or period when the South challenged the northern visions of architectural progress.

Italian architects were not alone to adopt that critical stance. At the beginning of the 1930s, Le Corbusier's epistemological shift from his machine-oriented modernism of the early 1920s to a southern version where the vernacular substituting for the discursive role played by the machine was also a direct response to a series of events, both personal and international, that put his original concept into crisis. On the one hand, it reflected the intellectual consequence of losing the competition for the Palais des Nations in Geneva (1928). On the other hand, the Great Depression, the critique of industrial capitalism, as well as the rise of Nazism in Germany made modernist arguments dangerously ambiguous. The impact of these events coincided with Le Corbusier's first meeting with the young José Luis Sert in Barcelona in 1932 and the subsequent journey aboard the ship Patris II from Marseilles to Athens to host the CIAM IV (1933) at which German architects were noticeably absent. Sert's later writings regarding vernacular and modernity made this southern global positioning clear:

*"Technically, modern architecture is mostly a discovery of the Nordic countries. Yet, spiritually, it is the "style-less" Mediterranean architecture which has influenced this new architecture. Modern architecture is a return to the pure, traditional forms of the Mediterranean. It is a victory of the Latin Sea.*[13] *[...] The pure functionalism of the 'machine à habiter' is dead.... Architects and theorists, above all Germanic, carried functionalist experiments to absurd extremes."*[14]

*Figure 4* Mario Sironi (with Giuseppe Terragni). Study perspective for the main façade (Via dei Fori Imperiali) of the Palazzo del Littorio, solution A, Roma, 1934. © Andrea Sironi-Straußwald & Romana Sironi

### *Continuità* & *Tendenza*: the Order of the City

The postwar period was equally complex and fractured in spite of the apparent and often self-proclaimed victory of the International Style and its Anglo-Saxon partisans. In France, Auguste Perret—whose all-concrete Musée des Travaux Publics, initiated in 1937 but only completed after WWII, was the most powerful representative of the French *return to order*—was finally given the opportunity to build the urban ensembles that he imagined in the 1920s.[15] The reconstruction of Le Havre that he directed from 1944 was an outstanding post-war example of postwar urbanism based on neo-classical principles of architecture and urban design, the systematic utilization of a modular grid, and the innovative exploitation of concrete.[16] Likewise, the reconstruction of the Vieux Port of Marseille by Fernand Pouillon can be considered a major example of the continuity of classicism in post-WWII France. It points to the reality of "another mass housing modernism," whose feasibility Pouillon demonstrated in direct opposition to the industrial lobby of concrete. For him, stone, wood and other traditional materials—combined with concrete if necessary—were not only compatible with mass housing but also highly competitive on an economic basis. The social housing districts that he conceived and erected in the 1950s on the hills overlooking Algiers brought about the symbiosis of the modern conception of housing with the recuperation of the antique know-how of the Mediterranean. Seen in its context, the Square of the Two Hundred Columns in the district *Climat de France* was unabatedly modern. At the same time, Pouillon transformed the working class district into a Mediterranean Acropolis.[17]

*Figure 5* Fernand Pouillon. Model of the housing district *Le Climat de France* with the Square of the 200 Columns, Algiers, 1955-57. © Archives Fernand Pouillon, Association Les Pierres Sauvages de Belcastel.

In Algiers, as in the housing projects on the periphery of Paris, Pouillon used modern typologies including the *immeuble-barre* and the tower. Not only did he successfully integrate those neighborhoods within their urban and landscape contexts, but also, through a careful study of proportions both in facades and in *plan masse*, he was able to create the harmonious and modern public spaces that distinguish his *grands ensembles* in Algiers and Paris.[18]

In post-1945 Italy, Neorealism in literature, cinema, and eventually architecture and urbanism was not only a reaction to the excesses of symbolism and classicism during the Mussolini period, but also to Futurism and rationalism. The 1950s INA-Casa social neighborhoods of Rome—Tiburtino and Tuscolana as the most exemplary—as well as La Martella in Matera (1952-54) deployed a modernized vernacular architecture coupled with Camillo Sitte-based urban design tenets.[19] Their organic design and rural references and techniques demonstrated—in the words of Carlo Aymonino—"an accentuated pursuit of the 'picturesque.'" Facades, roofs, exterior balconies and stairs "reinforce their character of being constructions that have risen spontaneously at successive moments in time."[20] As such they stood in stark contrast with much of the European—especially British, Dutch and German—technologically driven reconstruction and architectural culture.

At the end of 1953, Ernesto Nathan Rogers, a member of the Milanese group BBPR, became the new editor of *Casabella* and changed its title to *Casabella Continuità*. In his first editorial, Rogers argued for continuity with the work of the prewar editors Pagano and Persico, and hence continuity "not only with the most recent heritage of the Modern Movement, but with its deeper roots (the work of the proto-Modern), and even with the whole arch of the history of architecture."[21] The entire history of the city was at the core of this program, from antique and medieval times to, perhaps more surprisingly, the city of the 18th and 19th century of which Milan and Turin were rich examples and that young professionals like Aldo Rossi started to study and write about. As Manuel López Segura wrote, *"any architect, not blinded by the avant-gardist cries against the historical city, had to be touched by the arcades, the galleries and the profound shadowed entrances open to the cortile; that is, by an urbanity conveying an extraordinary civic sense, a deep espressione di civiltà (expression of civility)."*[22]

Around 1959-60, the British critic and writer Reyner Banham, whose image of Italy remained molded by the technological futurism of Antonio Sant'Elia and friends, launched a "North-South" confrontation between *Architectural Review* and *Casabella Continuità*.[23] The argument was the clamorous completion of the Milanese Torre Velasca (BBPR, 1950-58) and the following publication in *Casabella Continuità* of a series of "neoliberty" projects by Roberto Gabetti and Aimaro d'Isola. About the Torre Velasca, Banham attacked "the ex-modernists who have abandoned the accepted moral, social, and mechanical imperatives of the modern movement, and gone native in the thickets of *gusto, cultura, storia*, and so forth...." Furthermore, he violently criticized the architecture of Gabetti and d'Isola, to which Rogers reacted by calling the British critic the "defender of the refrigerators." [24]

However, the battle was essentially an architectural one and it is Aldo Rossi who would eventually and resolutely shift the discussion toward the morphological and typological reading of the city. Rossi presented his first projects at the 13th Triennale of Milano of 1964 and two years later Marsilio published *L'architettura della città*. The book and other writings emphasized concepts such as the permanence of the urban plan, developed the typological studies of his master Saverio Muratori, introduced the reader to the thesis of Maurice Halbwachs on *Collective Memory*, and initiated the rehabilitation of Socialist-Realist urban works such as the Stalinist-influenced Karl-Marx-Allee in former East Berlin.[25] Formed around Rossi in the mid-1960s, *La Tendenza* referred to a collective of architects, "who invoke the memory and history of their discipline, which is in turn conceived as a scientific and autonomous domain."[26] Inspired by structuralism and militant social criticism, Rossi and his friends refused both avant-garde and utopia, while initiating a political and critical architecture engaging with the real. This new "Realism" searched for the formal constants in the history of architecture and observed in the city and its structural organization—typology and morphology—the very essence of reality. The concept of type developed by Aldo Rossi and Rafael Moneo on the basis of Quatremere de Quincy's definition became the fundamental tool of both analysis and design:

*Figure 6* Mario Ridolfi, with L. Quaroni, C. Aymonino, C. Chiarini, M. Fiorentino, F. Gorio, M. Lanza, S. Lenci, P.M. Lugli, C. Melograni, G.C. Menichetti, G. Rinaldi, M. Valori. Houses with outdoors gallery, District INA-Casa Tiburtino, Roma, 1950-56. © Archivio INA-Casa

*Figure 7* BPPR Architetti, Torre Velasca, Milan, 1951-58. Photo Jean-François Lejeune

*"We are impervious to the accusations of historicism; we have simply snatched elements from the history of architecture to propose them anew as a driving force. History is viewed from the perspective of struggle and not as the mere relation of facts.... The coherence of typologies within an architectural project is the ultimate goal towards which we are working. That is the project."*[27]

Less obvious, particularly within the American reading of Rossi's works, were the political motivations that he followed as a member of the political left to develop his theory, and that Pier Vittorio Aureli has put forth:

*"Rossi's elaboration of an autonomous architecture coincided with his proposal of a theory of the city capable of challenging what he saw in the early 1960s as capitalism's new form of urban project: its totalistic planning of the city, with its concomitant celebration of technology. For Rossi, the premise of a contemporary theory of the city should be the city as a site of political choices—as a concrete geography of places irreducible to the totality and continuity of urbanization."*[28]

Moreover, from this standpoint, *"only an analysis of architecture could reveal the city's imminent separateness, that is, its constitution of parts not reducible to the common denominator of technological development."*[29] Typology meant *the return to the order* of the city as a means of resistance to and escape from the capitalist technocratic and essentially suburban concepts of industrialized and object-based approach to urban development.

The same year 1966 saw the publication, on the other side of the Atlantic, of Robert Venturi's *Complexity and Contradiction in Architecture*. Under the patronage of the Museum of Modern Art in New York, the book became, in Vincent Scully's analysis, the indispensable complement of Le Corbusier's *Toward a New Architecture* (1923): "The older book demanded a noble purism in architecture, in single buildings and in the city as a whole; the new book welcomes the contradictions and complexities of urban experience at all scales."[30] Venturi's inspiration did not come from Le Corbusier's Greek temple, but from "the urban facades of Italy, with their endless adjustments to the counter-requirements of inside outside and their inflection with all the business of everyday life."[31] Yet, the true forerunner of an American call to order was Jane Jacob, whose masterpiece *The Death and Life of Great American Cities* (1961) had opened the way for the preservation movement and explicitly confronted the assumptions of modern urban renewal operations and suburbanization trends in the country.

**Call to *Urban Order* beyond Italy**

Rossi's theses about the city, urban form and typology had a major and long-lasting impact on the European scene. They brought along a fundamental rejection of the urban tenets of the Modern Movement and, under various forms, labels and formats, were instrumental in changing the course of urban design and bringing a call *to urban order*. Following the post-Civil War classical period, modernism returned to Spain in the early 1950s through the advocacy of a modern vernacular whose use extended from the individual house to the urban and rural environment. José Antonio Coderch, Miguel Fisac, Alejandro de la Sota, and José Luis Fernández Del Amo were the actors of a movement sustained by the theoretical contributions of Fernando Chueca Goitia's *Invariantes castizos de la arquitectura española* (1947) and the *Manifiesto de la* Alhambra (1952).

In the 1970s, Manuel de Sola-Morales, Rafael Moneo, and the periodical *2C–Construcción de la Ciudad* brought typological studies to the forefront of research and practice. Its direct application was seen in Barcelona under the leadership of Oriol Bohigas and culminated in the program of public spaces and block-based urban housing of the Olympic games of 1992. Likewise, in post-Salazar Portugal, Fernando Távora (who was one of the initiators of the *Inquérito à Arquitectura Regional Portuguesa*), Alvaro Siza, and Nuno Portas were all major actors and promoters of the SAAL program (Serviço Ambulatório de Apoio Local), which made direct use of typological research in the design and construction of social housing neighborhoods.[32]

In 1977, *Architecture d'aujourd'hui* published its issue 190 dedicated to *Formalisme/Realisme*. Supporting his thesis with projects from Aldo Rossi, Massimo Scolari, Raimund Abraham, Rob Krier and Leon Krier, chief editor Bernard Huet advocated the "realism" of the Tendenza, i.e., the importance of history, and the reconstruction of the discipline of architecture within its own reality:

*"[To be a realist] is to take reality in order to transform it politically. It is not to impose a new way of life to the residents, but to offer them the typologies that they expect... It is not to create meaning which the greatest number cannot understand, but to deploy common sense."*[33]

In Belgium, Maurice Culot published, along with Leon Krier, *Rational Architecture – The Reconstruction of the European City* (1978)—a seminal work that collected projects by a diverse group of neo-rationalist architects that included Rossi, Grassi, Scolari, Huet, O.M.A., Linazasoro, Van Eyck, Ungers, and Sola-Morales. Based in Brussels, the Reconstruction movement and its strategy of "counter-projects" exhibited at the 1980 Biennale of Venice within the *Strada Novissima;* transforming the dynamics of modernization of the European capital: *"Countless images of restored neighborhoods and rebuilt landmarks were disseminated, canalizing a longing for a lost conviviality. The images entrenched themselves in the collective imagination and caused the city to be seen as a living fabric, which had to be sewn back together, in close consultation with its inhabitants, through a succession of small-scale operations."*[34]

*Figure 8* José Luis Fernandez del Amo. Colonization village El Realengo, 1957. Photo Joaquin del Palacio Kindel. © Servicio Historico, COAM Madrid

*Figure 9* Alvaro Siza. Street in the SAAL housing district Quinta da Malagueira, Évora, Portugal, 1977-1998. Photo Jean-François Lejeune

*Figure 10* Cover of *Architecture d'aujourd'hui*, n° 190, Paris, 1977

*Figure 11* Aldo Rossi. Sketches for the School of Architecture at the University of Miami, 1987. © University of Miami School of Architecture

Realism or Rational Architecture was the main engine of the work realized in Berlin by the promoters of the *Internationale Bauaustellung Berlin* (IBA) held in the still-divided city in 1984-87. Under the direction of Vittorio Magnago Lampugnani, Josef Kleihues, Rob Krier, and Hardt-Waltherr Hämer, IBA 84-87 deployed a multi-thronged strategy of urban renewal that included sustainable renovation of existing housing, in-fill housing, and construction of entire urban blocks within the urban tradition of the $18^{th}$ and $19^{th}$ century.

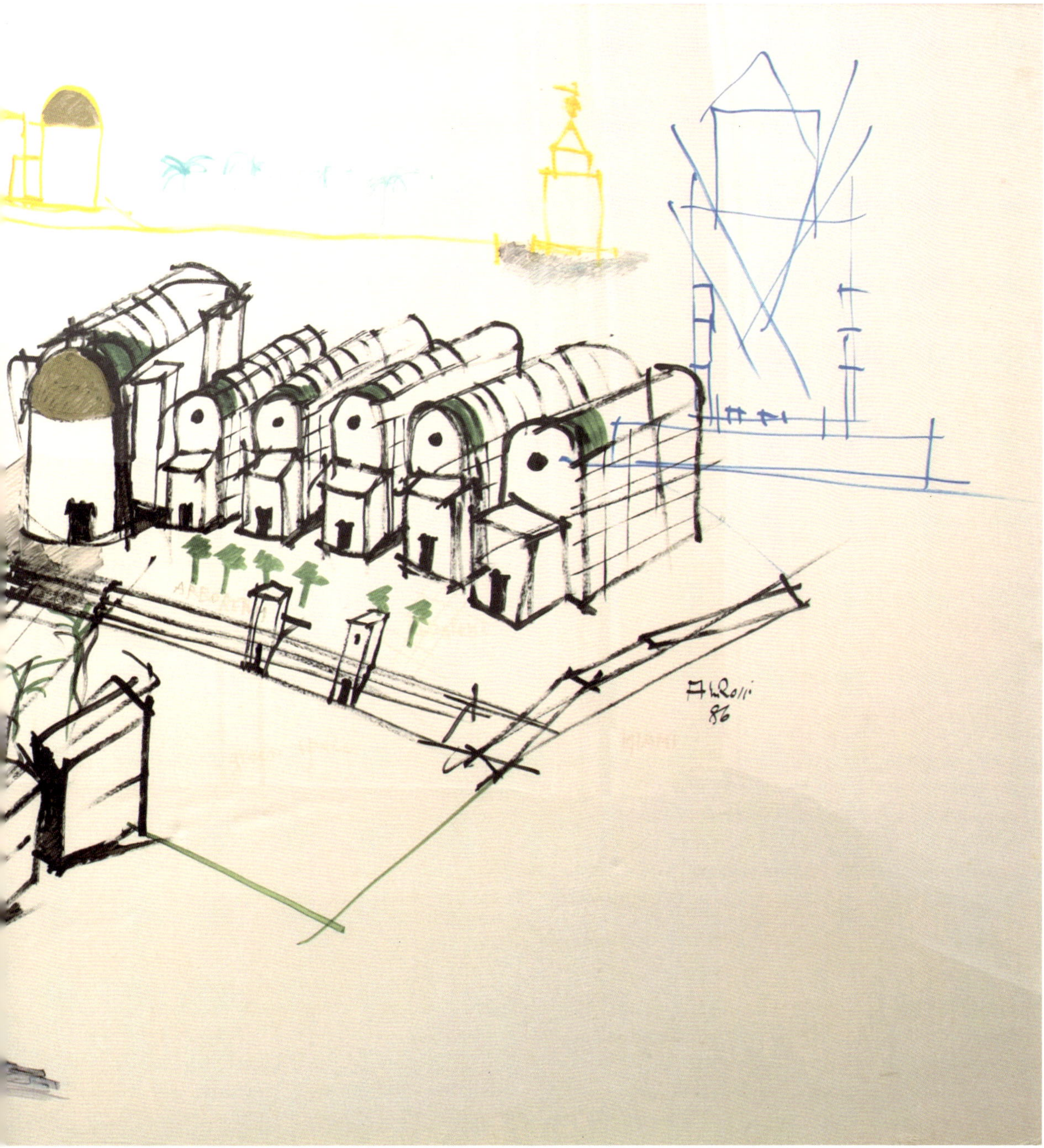

In the United States, the Institute of Architecture and Urban Studies, its leader Peter Eisenman, and members such as Machado and Silvetti and Agrest and Gandelsonas were instrumental in introducing the writings and projects of Aldo Rossi and La Tendenza, even though the American edition of *The Architecture of the City* was issued late in 1982.[35] At the same time, the Institute's periodical *Oppositions* published from 1973 to 1984 made available, for the first time in English, important historical texts among which the four manifestos of the *Gruppo Sette* mentioned at the beginning of this essay. It is thus to the Institute that Italian Rationalism and the extraordinary group of architects ranging from Pagano to Figini & Pollini to Libera to Terragni became emblematic references of an alternative to the historicist postmodernism that was increasingly dominating the American scene. In 1991, historian Thomas Schumacher made an important connection between the contemporary debates and the architectural spirit of the 1930s in his monograph about Giuseppe Terragni:

*"Significantly, many of the architectural values and directives that have been brought into question in the last two decades, in the wake of the postmodern reaction to modernism, are the same values and directives that some Italians questioned during the twenties and thirties. Revisionist histories have been written to "correct" the excesses of the polemics of orthodox modernism from almost all European countries... This book is one of them."*[36]

He also published the astonishing drawings of the *Danteum* project by Terragni and his collaborators (1938), perhaps the greatest example of *architecture parlante*. Contrary to the formalist, a-contextual and mostly Como-based analysis of Peter Eisenman, Schumacher emphasized Terragni's links to typology and literature, to modernity and tradition, to technology in service of tectonics and materiality—in brief, an architect anchored in both classical and vernacular sides of *mediterraneità*. More than in Como, the lesson of Terragni in Rome was that modernity and the city did not have to be antithetical, but was in fact complimentary.[37]

### Maurizio Ferraris and the *Nuovo Realismo*

With La Tendenza and its international offshoots, the pendulum of architecture and urban thinking had shifted to the South. The 1998 MoMA exhibition and catalogue *Deconstructivist Architecture* marked the beginning of a formidable reaction coming from the North, a reaction that once again emphasized the autonomy of the architectural object in front of its context and had as its leaders Coop Himmelblau, Peter Eisenman, Frank Gehry, Zaha Hadid, Rem Koolhaas, Daniel Libeskind, and Bernard Tschumi.

Since then and in absence of a genuine social and/or political agenda, the Northern-based contemporary avant-gardes have been progressively swallowed by capitalist globalization and their shock value degraded for profit and instant media abuse. Along with the theory of deconstruction, the introduction of parametric design had a nefarious influence on the acknowledgement of typology. The theoretical escape from the essence of the discipline toward other fields resulted, more often than not, in sensationalism, in the solitude of the iconic object, and in a succession of consumerist images. As Elia Zenghelis, one of the founders of the Office for Metropolitan Architecture (O.M.A.), wrote in 2007, *"the self-indulgence of the contemporary Star Architect only contributes to the visual and environmental pollution created by the current economic power of pluralism, of which he is only the slave."*[38]

In December 2012 a conference and exhibition took place in Turin and Naples, Italy, under the title *"Nothing is gained by theorizing alone: New Realism and Architecture of the City."* The initiative was a follow-up of the publication earlier that year, by Italian philosopher Maurizio Ferraris, of the *Manifesto del Nuovo Realismo*.[39] Ferraris's manifesto aims at reorienting the philosophical field from deconstruction

*Figure 12* Giuseppe Terragni, with Antonio Carminati, Pietro Lingeri, Ernesto Saliva, Luigi Vietti and the collaboration of Marcello Nizzoli and Mario Sironi. Perspective of the Palazzo del Littorio, solution A, Roma, 1934. © Francesco Fattori (digital model), under the direction of Flavio Mangione, Luca Ribichini, Attilio Terragni, CE.S.A.R/ Università della Sapienza Roma

and doubt to the reality of the real. Its author analyzes how the postmodern philosophers from Jean-François Lyotard and Jacques Derrida onwards have, along with the distrust toward progress and the argument of the end of ideologies, brought forward the concept of the relativity of truth, arguing like Nietzsche that *"There are no facts... only interpretations."*[40] This evolution, he demonstrates, has led to a dangerous revival of populism where facts and reality are constantly trampled under the leaden weight of modern mass and social media.

The exhibition and conference argued that architecture has to go back to the reality of the physical world and, first and foremost, of *"the city as the finest human construction starting from a profound knowledge of its structure, its contradictions and problems to propose an adequate advancement and transformation."*[41] If Rossi's and the neo-Rationalists's emphasis on morphology and typology—the Architecture of the City—was the means of resistance to indiscriminate urban and regional development, the progressive return of typology on the urban and architectural scene can be seen as the logical reaction of a new generation of architects in front of the hyper-capitalistic and globalizing homogenization of real estate, architecture, and urban planning. To some extent one can argue that the emphasis on the real brought by Ferraris's philosophical position has the potential to bring typology back again to the forefront of theory and practice. Not only typology, but even more importantly, the ecology of the site, the neighborhood, the city, the region and the territory as the contemporary elements of the real that should and must influence a truly sustainable conception of architecture, the city, and landscape as urbanism.[42]

*Figure 13* Uwe Schröder, Residential building, Bonn, Germany, 1996-2000. Photo Peter Oszvald. © Uwe Schröder Architekt, Bonn

In contrast with this philosophical and disciplinary position, the lament of Patrick Schumacher reacting to the awarding of the 2015 Pritzker Prize to Alejandro Aravena, reads like a sad and desperate swan song:

*"The Pritzker Prize mutates into a prize for humanitarian work. The role of the architect is now 'to serve greater social and humanitarian needs' and the new Laureate is hailed for 'tackling the global housing crisis' and for his concern for the underprivileged. Architecture loses its specific societal task and responsibility, architectural innovation is replaced by the demonstration of noble intentions and the discipline's criteria of success and excellence dissolve in the vague do-good-feel-good pursuit of 'social justice'... I would not object to this year's choice half as much if this safe and comforting validation of humanitarian concern was not part of a wider trend in contemporary architecture that in my view signals an unfortunate confusion, bad conscience, lack of confidence, vitality and courage about the discipline's own unique contribution to the world."*[43]

1 Benedetto Croce, *History as the Story of Liberty*, London: G. Allen and Unwin, 1941, p. 19.
2 Maurizio Ferraris, "Il ritorno a un pensiero forte," *La Repubblica*, 8 August 2011.
3 Virgilio Marchi, "Primitivismi capresi," *Cronache d'attualità* 6-10, 1922, pp. 49-51.
4 The first to call for a return to order and to make the connection between order and classicism was the Futurist artist Gino Severini, who, as early as 1917, advocated a return from cubism to classicism. In 1921 he published his ideas in his book *Du Cubisme au Classicisme*.
5 See Gérard Monnier, "Un retour à l'ordre: architecture, géométrie, société," Le retour à l'ordre dans les arts plastiques et l'architecture, 1919-1925, St-Etienne, Université de St-Etienne, pp. 45-54.
6 Josep Rovira, *José Luis Sert: 1901-1983*, Milan: Electa, 2000, p. 197.
7 See Jean-François Lejeune and Michelangelo Sabatino, *Modern Architecture and the Mediterranean: Vernacular Dialogues and Contested Identities*, London: Routledge, 2010; and in particular the essay by Benedetto Gravagnuolo, "From Schinkel to Le Corbusier: The Myth of the Mediterranean in Modern Architecture."
8 From the title of the 1980 exhibition in Paris *Les Réalismes entre revolution et réaction 1919-1939*, Paris: Centre Pompidou, 1980.
9 Fulvio Irace, *Giovanni Muzio, 1893-1982*, Milano: Electa, 1994.
10 Gruppo Sette, "Architecture" (1926) and "Architecture (II): The Foreigners" (1927), in *Oppositions*, Fall 1976/6, pp. 89-102. Quote on p. 90.
11 From Carlo Fabrizio Carli, "La koiné metafisica. Novecentismo, Razionalismo, Futurismo nelle Città nuove pontine," *Metafisica costruita. Le città di fondazione degli anni Trenta dall'Italia all'Oltremare*, Milano: Regione Lazio & Touring Club Italiano, 2002, p. 36.
12 Ibidem.
13 José Luis Sert, "Raíces mediterráneas de la arquitectura moderna," *A.C.* 18, 1935; reprinted in Antonio Pizza, *J.LL.Sert and the Mediterranean*, Barcelona, Col.legi d'Arquitectes de Catalunya, 1997, p. 217.
14 José Luis Sert, "Arquitectura sense 'estil' i sense 'arquitecte'", *D'Aci i d'Allà* 179, Dicembre 1934; reprinted in Antonio Pizza (ed.), *J.LL.Sert and the Mediterranean*, p. 210.
15 See Jean-Louis Cohen and Vanessa Grossman (eds.), *France 101 bâtiments 1914-2014 – La modernité, promesse ou menace?*, Paris: Institut français d'architecture, 2014.
16 Long neglected or eclipsed in favor of more radical projects such as Le Corbusier's, Le Havre is now inscribed on the UNESCO World Heritage List.
17 Alberto Ferlenga, "Fernand Pouillon (1912-1986)", *The New City: Modern Cities*, Miami/New York: University of Miami School of Architecture/Princeton Architectural Press, 1996, pp. 71-93.
18 Adam Caruso and Helen Thomas (eds.), *The stones of Fernand Pouillon: an Alternative Modernism in French Architecture*, Zürich: GTA Verlag, 2013; Bernard Félix Dubor, *Fernand Pouillon: architetto delle 200 colonne*, Milano: Electa, 1987.
19 See Stephanie Zeier Pilat, *Reconstructing Italy: the INA-Casa Neighborhoods of the Postwar Era*, London: Ashgate, 2014. Also see Mario Ridolfi, *Manuale dell'architetto* (1945-46), which illustrated traditional and vernacular techniques for modern construction.
20 Carlo Aymonino, "Storia e cronaca del Quartiere Tiburtino," *Casabella-continuità* 215 (April–May 1957), p. 20, quoted by Bruno Reichlin, "Figures of Neorealism in Italian Architecture (Part 1), *Grey Room* 05, Fall 2001, p.85.
21 Ernesto Nathan Rogers, Editorial, *Casabella-continuità* 199 (December 1953/ January 1954), pp. 2-3. The four partners of BBPR were Gianluigi Banfi, Lodovico Barbiano di Belgiojoso, Enrico Peressutti, and Ernesto Nathan Rogers.
22 Manuel López Segura, "Neoliberty & co.: The *Architectural Review* against 1950s Italian Historicism," *Cuadernos de Proyectos, ETSAM* 4, p. 137.
23 Reyner Banham, "Neoliberty: The Italian Retreat from Modern Architecture," *Architectural Review* 125, April 1959, pp. 230-235. Also see Matthew Critchley, "Continuity or Crisis? A brief history between the polemics of Aldo Rossi and Reyner Banham,"http://www.aaschool.ac.uk/downloads/WritingPrize/2013Shortlist/MatthewCritchley.pdf (last accessed May 23, 2016).
24 Reyner Banham, "Milan: the Polemical Skyline," in *The Listener*, September 1 1960, p. 338, quoted by Matthew Critchley, p. 39. See Reyner Banham, "Neoliberty: The Italian Retreat from Modern Architecture," *Architectural Review* 225, April 1959, pp. 230-235. And the response by Ernesto Rogers, "L'evoluzione dell'architettura: Risposta al custode dei frigidaires, *Casabella-continuità* 228, June 1959, pp. 2-4.
25 Maurice Halbwachs, *La mémoire collective*, Paris: Presses Universitaires de France, 1950. In English, *On Collective Memory*, Chicago: University of Chicago Press, 1992.
26 Alfred Pacquement, "Preface," in Frederic Migeyrou, *La Tendenza – Italian Architecture 1965*-1985, Paris: Centre Pompidou, 2012, p. 8.
27 Frédéric Migayrou, "La Tendenza: Historical Backlash (L'histoire en retour)" in *La Tendenza* catalogue, p. 21, quoted from Aldo Rossi, *Architettura razionale*, Milano: FrancoAngeli, 1973, p. 18. Also see Rafael Moneo, "On Typology," *Oppositions*, n° 13, 1979 and Quatremere de Quincy, *Dictionnaire historique d'architecture*, Paris, 1825.
28 Pier Vittorio Aureli, *The Project of Autonomy: Politics and Architecture within and against Capitalism*, New York: Princeton Architectural Press, 2008, p. 97.
29 Pier Vittorio Aureli, p. 62.
30 Vincent Scully, "Introduction," in Robert Venturi, *Complexity and Contradiction in Architecture*, New York: The Museum of Modern Art, 1966, p.10.
31 Ibidem.
32 The Inquérito was a multi-volume research and publication about vernacular architecture and urbanism in Portugal. Started in 1955, it was eventually published in 1961. Also see Delfim Sardo, *The SAAL Process: Architecture and Participation 1974-1976*, Montréal: Centre Canadien d'Architecture, 2015.
33 Bernard Huet, "Formalisme et Réalisme," *Architecture* d'aujourd'hui 190, April 1977. Also see Jean Clair (ed.), *Les Réalismes, 1919-1939*, Paris: Centre Georges Pompidou, 1980.
34 Maurice Culot, *Rational Architecture – The Reconstruction of the European* City, Brussels: Archives d'architecture moderne, 1978; Géry Leloutre and Iwan Strauven, "Brussels-Europe: An Aporia?" in *Brussels: A Manifesto. Towards the Capital of Europe*, Rotterdam: NAi Publishers/Berlage Instituut, 2007, p. 217.
35 Remarkably, Colin Rowe, who was a major instigator of a return to typology and the history of the city from Cornell University, did not mention Aldo Rossi or any actor of La Tendenza in his book (with Hans Kollhoff), *Collage City*, Cambridge: The MIT Press, 1978. Rowe was an early member of the Institute but left after disagreements with Eisenman.
36 Thomas Schumacher, *Surface and Symbol: Giuseppe Terragni and the Architecture of Italian Rationalism*, New York: Princeton Architectural Press, 1991, p. 15.
37 See Flavio Mangione, Luca Ribichini, and Attilio Terragni, *Giuseppe Terragni a Roma*, Roma: Prospettiva, 2015.
38 Elia Zenghelis, "For a New Monumentality," in *Brussels: A Manifesto*, p. 231.
39 Maurizio Ferraris, *Manifesto del Nuovo Realismo*, Roma-Bari: Laterza, 2012. See the digital catalogue at http://labont.it/wordpress/wpcontent/uploads/2012/10/Turin_Naples_program.pdf (last accessed March 15, 2017).
40 Friedrich Nietszche, *Frammenti postumi*, 1885-1887, quoted by Ferraris, *Manifesto del Nuovo Realismo*, p. 9.
41 *Nuovo Realismo e Architettura della* Città, digital edition, p. 16.
42 Globally, the New Urbanism Movement could be referred to the thesis of new realism. Also see Charles Waldheim, *Landscape as Urbanism: A General Theory*, Princeton: Princeton University Press, 2016.
43 See https://www.facebook.com/patrik.schumacher.10/posts/10207222111024032 (last accessed March 15, 2017).

# New Order. New Wave.[1]

**Esteban Salcedo**

In recent years, a new generation of architects has achieved international acclaim for a body of work that conforms to a new *rappel à l'ordre*. This article will attempt to draw a critical cartography that charts the course for the development of their architecture. This new generation, principally situated in and around Belgium, is not monolithic in character or in ideology; and while there exists certain formal similarities, the more meaningful overlaps occur with regards to common interests and sensibilities.

Classification serves to sketch a map or to draw schematic lines with which to orient and help chart a journey through a fictional plane. But in reality, a map is not a territory. It is at best a distortion and a schematic reduction of reality. First there are things described that are not designated on a map, making the document incomplete. Second, maps quickly become obsolete because the reality they depict is rapidly changing. Similarly, the territory of architecture is always richer, full of nuances and varying realities that are difficult to generalize and assemble in this reduction that we "will draw." Yet, we will not stop trying to outline the map because it allows us to move forward and orient ourselves within the territory of architecture, even if it is not a consistent and timeless representation, but a vast territory dotted with tools that can be structured in different ways by the reader.

Let me explain further.

The more evident approach to analyze this generation of architects refers to something that makes them haughty, distant and cold: *hardcore*.[2] On the other hand, this initial impression coexists alongside an eloquent ambiguity that unveils a more critical space to explore the less obvious aspects of the work, defined here as *new wave* (NW). Those aspects are related to an atypical scope of references, a determined commingling with other disciplines, and a personal reading of historical topics transferred to the present. This new wave will be described from the point of view of architecture as a discipline but without referring to specific buildings or references. Rather it will structure a framework for analysis centered on a panorama of cutting edge attitudes linked more broadly to contemporary culture.

*Figure 1* Barragán's turntable at his house. Picture took by Cerith Wyn Evans. In *El aire es azul. Reflexiones sobre arte y arquitectura en torno a Luis Barragán* by Hans Ulrich Obrist and Pedro Reyes. 2006

*Figure 2* Vynil-book, The Curves of the Needle by Cerith Wyn Evans. 2005

## The Curves of the Needle[3]

In 2003, the British architect and artist Cerith Wyn Evans was invited by the Barragán Foundation to pay tribute to the deceased architect. On that occasion, Wyn Evans pointed to the sonic potential of Barragan's architecture. He observed that the rooms of Barragán's own house served as sonic platforms for a variety of technological equipment that the architect had collected throughout his lifetime and on which he played his extensive record collection. Wyn Evans listed the records in the collection and then selectively played them on gramophones found throughout the Casa Barragán. The recordings served as an audio-visual meditation for the exhibition *The Air is Blue* and were later documented in the record/book entitled *The Curves of the Needle.*[4]

Wyn Evan's recordings of selected tracks were mixed with the ambient sound of the house and played to accompany his series of photographs of Barragán's residence, studio, and garden. The project carefully unfolds one story atop another, providing an abbreviated history of music during the beginnings of its technical reproducibility, producing a complex image-sound arrangement and parallel narration about the art of listening.

For Wyn Evans, the selection process and recording sessions became an "*other technological file assigned to the house, and very specific, to its architecture.*"[5] His research of Barragán's record collection and the thousands of exploratory photographs became a project of the recovery of interstitial spaces, simultaneously providing a more complete picture of Barragán's physical building and audio archive.

The work of artists such as Wyn Evans or Ignasi Aballí, through his *Listados*[6], focuses on perception and the problems derived from it: the presentation, the context, the notion of author, the nature of the work and the tension between production and consumption, serving as a *means* to initiate a critical approach to the work described herein (NWMA).[7]

*Figure 3* List of Barragán's vinyl records by Cerith Wyn Evans. In *El aire es azul. Reflexiones sobre arte y arquitectura en torno a Luis Barragán* by Hans Ulrich Obrist and Pedro Reyes. 2006

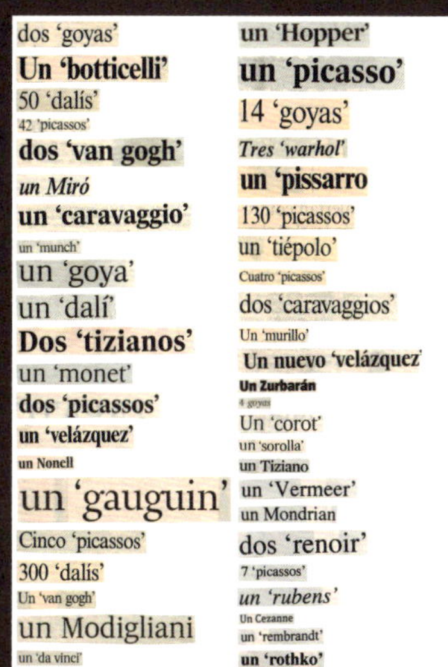


*Figure 4* *Listados*. Ignasi Aballí. 2011

*Figure 5* The Sound of Belgium. Documentary directed by Jozef Devillé. 2012

*Figure 6* Sound of Belgium CD Compilation. 1989

*Figure 7* The Belgian pavilion by OFFICE KGDVS at the 2008 Venice Biennale Architecture. Bas Princen. 2008

### A new sound for a new city

For electronic music lovers, the 80s began with a great loss. Ian Curtis, leader of Joy Division, committed suicide on May 19, 1980, ending the belligerent howls of a reactionary generation against the limited future prospects provided by the musical genre known as Punk. In his last compositions it is evident that Curtis' desire was to move beyond the limitations of the genre and advance towards something more striking and individual, inaugurating his own farewell space of possibilities described by critic Simon Reynolds, as *Post Punk* (or *Afterpunk*): *"An artistically expansive cultural current constantly changing in a spirit of change and political-cultural idealism that permeated to the bone to a young generation eager for change."*[8]

Curtis' death left a great void, but what followed is deeply linked to his investigations. His influences can be heard in historic and contemporary references including the lyrics of Antonin Artaud's randomness, J.G. Ballard's techno barbarism or Burroughs' *Wild Boyhood*[9], whom Curtis met at a public appearance at the Brussels' Club Plan K in October 1979.[10] These examples contain key ingredients for the building of a New Order, or at least a new idea of order that articulated the individual's resistance to the common with the search for an end to the continuous tension between omnipotence and abjection. This new idea of order became most evident in the work of New Order, the band formed by the remaining members of Joy Division marking the beginning of the so-called *New Wave* with its eclectic mix of sounds and styles that had its roots in earlier decades. The party of programmed sounds, eclectic mixes and environmental sequences, as shown in the documentary *The Sound of Belgium*[11], invaded Belgium in the late eighties in the form of what is now called *New Beat*. This new sound had unexpected success—albeit short lived—which left a mark on a new generation of Belgium youth.

### After the party[12]

Published in 2005, volume 67 of the Dutch architectural journal *OASE* offers a selection of articles and interviews about the end of what has been called *SuperDutch*[13], or the willful superficiality of Dutch design in the late 90s. This change was produced by a complex amalgam of coincidences including: a post-ideological approach to government with a clear acceptance of economic liberalism and a lack of urban/architectural commissions, a waning architectural debate, a frustration with the architectural utopias of the 90s, and the crisis of a self-centered discipline. As articulated by architect and educator Pier Vittorio Aureli, *"once it became clear that this branding of Dutch architecture was nothing more than a grouping together of things without a serious critical vision, it ended with a feeling of dissatisfaction, a feeling that something is really missing."*[14] This view was strengthened by a lack of convincing, controversial or critical statements that have the capacity of generating discourse.

Despite the seeming negativity, younger generations began to understand that this situation might create a positive momentum: "Instead of just embracing the many mutations of late-capitalism—as an alibi for innovative architecture—they should start to question the imperial logic of late-capitalism and develop alternatives[15]" for a new discipline. As enunciated by architects André Kempe and Oliver Thill:

*"The party is over and architecture should strive to fundamentally new approaches. If the ambitious young architects wishing to operate in other ways underground and are still part of a reality defined economically, they must find a fundamentally new approach."*[16]

Their strategies for the "After the Party" architect are structured around the following topics: Economic Technology, Prefabricated Elements, *Objets Trouvés*, Deep Building Systems and Serial Production, Typical Plan Independence from the Program and

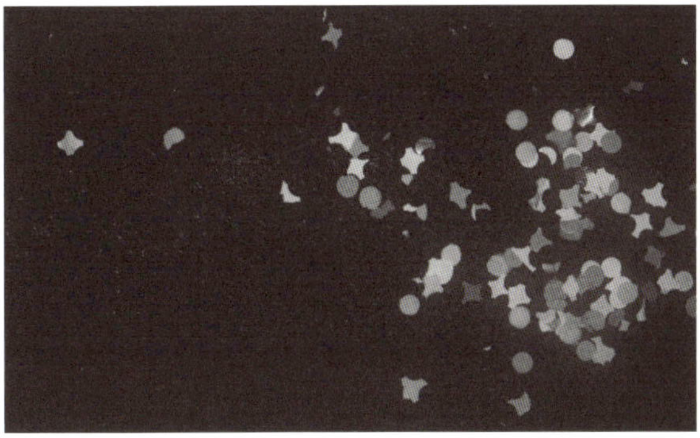

*Figure 8* ' Untitled, rock diary' by Hedi Slimane. 2007

*Figure 9 The Archduke Leopold Wilhelm in his Picture Gallery in Brussels.* David Teniers II. 1650

'*As-It-Is*'-The Poverty Label, unveiling an updated version of pragmatism based on two main ideas: manipulation or *typological correction,*[17] and an advanced concept of economy (even if precarious).

The first topic, Economic Technology, is generated from an understanding of the need to disassociate typological devices and program. The NW architect creates a distance between the program and the container to advance architectural ideas; they put their trust in what they have called *Architecture without Content*[18], an academic program that is based on typological transfers as a vehicle of architectural invention and exploration beyond programmatic constraints.

*"When looking at a program brief without prejudice, we can conquer new degrees of freedom, renouncing a functionalism of inert spaces as an organizational argument"*[19]. As such the work of an NW architect has more to do with the ability to reinvent the variables with which architecture will face future changes.

The French sociologist, philosopher and cultural theorist, Jean Baudrillard identified this process as the displacement from a structure of collocation or composition, where objects describe "the limits of a symbolic configuration"[20] with their presence, "a system where what was formerly an object to be exhaustively defined with exclusive attention becomes a mere trigger of phenomena."[21]

Following the modern notion of "enframing" (Gestell) coined by Martin Heidegger, NW architects encourage us to see objects in our world in terms of how they can serve us. The focus shifts to a definition of limits and interstitial spaces between forms. This is where the perception of phenomena is produced.

Beyond an appreciation for technique, their work leads them to discard any material system that is superfluous. Or rather, nothing is regarded as a figure or element to be perceived preferentially, but as background to be confronted. As a result, neither technique, material, object nor form plays a central figurative role. Nothing commands a level of heightened definition. Everything is blurred in favor of a densely stimulated space, conveniently *enframed*. Thus, the elements of this system are absolved from any imposing aim: they do not mark or fix the way this new spatial system is perceived or what and how it should be used. It is precisely for this reason that they avoid a direct relationship between space and use, with the exception of a few links, sufficiently intense to facilitate or enable certain activities before others.

As a result, each project is developed as an *autonomous* structure that defines its architectural characteristics. The program is distinctive in so far as it can be easily inserted, with its own structural logic, into the project.

Another fundamental topic pointed out by Kempe and Thill is that of Economy. This category has a greater variety of connotations, especially those that result from an understanding of the profession as a precarious balance between resources and exigencies. This reality is compounded by the speed of events in contemporary society, making efficiency a necessity.[22]

Intentionality is in many ways an economic conception. In this context, the term 'economically' refers to the production and distribution of scarce resources and the handling of them in an opportunistic and frugal manner. It is understood as a topic that offers limits to find unexpected but timely solutions, or as a vehicle for radical ways to revolutionize a number of seemingly untouchable conventions.

Haste forces us to act quickly and to use or repeat what we know. The basis of what we call wild appropriationism (not necessarily postmodern) celebrates the efficiency and optimization of material resources, frugality, simplicity, conventionality of techniques and

*Figure 10* *Warburg, Atlas Mnemosyne.* Board 79, 1929

*Figure 11* André Malraux among the photographs for 'Les Voix du Silence', 1951

*Figure 12* Weegee and his collaborator Mel Harris, 1952

resistant languages, and the dominion of sociological and technological themes to the domain of architecture.

**Wild appropriationism**

At the beginning of his 1962 book, *La pensée sauvage*[23] Claude Levi-Strauss describes the primitive basis of thought as the process that explains the transition from nature to civilization. "The savage thought" he writes, "is neither the mind of savages nor that of primitive or archaic humanity, but rather the mind in the wild...."[24]

For the NW architect, *Bricolage* is the means by which the untamed mind brings order to things. It is a means of operating with economy. Hence the *bricoleur* employs what is at hand, because it is all that he has. The material is not related to the immediate project because it is itself the result of previous constructions. Levi-Strauss refers to this material as "pre-constrained." The architectural critic Irenée Scalbert[25] has highlighted the figures of James Stirling and even Le Corbusier as *bricoleur* architects.

In the words of the American philosopher Richard Rorty, this capacity could be defined as *pragmatic imagination*, or, the ability to reassemble elements from the past (both near and distant) into new organizations; and, in so doing, endow them with new potential. For the *bricoleur*, the task is to identify ways to resituate oneself vis-à-vis these 'objects' and see them as 'forms' in relief or counterpoint to their functionality.[26] In this context, it is possible to describe NW architects as assemblers of techniques, projects, words, images, theories, etc. With an apparent distancing from reality, they operate on a theoretical plane that exacerbates the intellectual potential of a project to later reinsert it in the present.

In this primitive state of thought between economy and instability, the role of the architect is transformed into that of a selective collector that reassembles elements from the near and distant past to construct a new vision of the world.

In "*The System of Collecting,*" Baudrillard defines the behavioral patterns of the collector as "*accumulation, ordering and aggressive conservation*"[27] coming to personify objects and even identifying with them. These phases can be applied to the working methodology of the NW architect.

Similar to the Surrealists who believed that objects in the world possessed a certain but unspecifiable intensity that had been dulled by everyday use, NW architects mean to reanimate this dormant intensity, by bringing attention to the matter that makes up their world. André Breton's maxim, "Beautiful as the chance encounter of a sewing machine and an umbrella on an operating table"[28] describes the work as an expression of the belief that simply placing objects in an unexpected context reinvigorates their mysterious qualities.

But we could go further and rediscover the art of collecting as something that goes beyond the appreciation of objects and becomes a search for meaning in the foundations or core of the discipline.

**The death of the author, the birth of the curator**

The idea of collecting can hardly be separated from its organizational structure - the archive. The concept of archive, such as the *Atlas Mnemosyne*[29] sets the archive-memory relationship as deeply linked to the ideas of origin and order or to authenticity and authorship. In *Mal d'archive, une impression freudienne*[30], Derrida traces 'archive' to *archeion,* the ancient Greek word for the residence of superior magistrates (the archons). In French, *mal d'archive* contains the concept of both illness and evil. For Derrida, there is something morbid and sinister at the core of the archival impulse: "It is to have a compulsive, repetitive, and nostalgic desire. To return to the origin, the most archaic place of absolute commencement."[31] Derrida relates this compulsion to the Freudian death drive or the death of the author.

As described by Derrida, this return to the origin accepts criteria that have been used for nearly two centuries: the genius of authenticity, metaphysical transcendentalism, classification, difficulty of execution, manual dexterity etc., no longer operational for current cultural conformations related to immediacy, obsolescence and bordering territories with art. Moreover, it implies the capacity to accept the crisis of the traditional models of categorization and authorship, as understood in the past. In *What is an author?* Foucault says he does not want to be asked who he is nor to be demanded to be always the same. He writes to lose his identity, to be another in the act of being himself while writing, "In writing, the point is not to manifest or exalt the act of writing, nor is it to pin a subject within language; it is, rather, a question of creating a space into which the writing subject constantly disappears."[32]

As pointed out by the composer and musician Brian Eno, with the death of the author, we are faced with the appearance of a new figure: the curator: "Curatorship is arguably the big new job of our times: it is the task of re-evaluating, filtering, digesting, and connecting together. In an age saturated with new artifacts and information, it is perhaps the curator, the connection maker, who is the new storyteller, the meta-author."[33] In a 1995 interview with Wired magazine, Eno characterized the contemporary artist as a "connector of things" versus a creator. This is why the curator, the editor, the compiler, and the anthologist have become such big figures.

*Figure 13* Picture took by the author at OFFICE KGDVS Studio, 2014

The term 'curator' derives from the Latin word for guardian, someone who ensures order, and originally had an ecclesiastical meaning, referring to low ranking priests responsible for the care of souls. In the late seventeenth century, it began to refer to the custodian of a library, museum or archive or any type of collection maintained by a cultural-heritage institution.

Nicolas Bourriaud, coiner of controversial concepts like *post-production*[34] and *altermodern*, argues that today creativity involves "strategies of mixing and combining products." He upholds the DJ as the model for contemporary practices: "DJs don't engage in quotation, citation or even referencing; they just 'wander' through history and take whatever they need. This method might look like postmodernism, but the mindset is different. Citation implies deference to authority, to the Old Masters and their Masterpieces."[35]

This reasoning invites us to think of the NW architect as the commissioner of his/her own archive; a curator who sequences, edits, frames, and finally "activates" the results, not unlike a DJ in the production of an event. DJs have at their disposal all the necessary archival material to post produce at will, operating on the principle of "relational aesthetics."[36] For this to function it is not enough to acquire distance from the unsubtle processes of identification and avoid the imperative formal and technical mechanisms of using the latter. Instead it becomes necessary to skillfully detect the more fertile strains of contemporary culture, while having a profound knowledge of the history of the disciplne.

In their hands, the traditional work of the architect is disrupted and altered into an intense investigation, recognition and reformatting of the medium. The NW architect shares the potential for offering a precise X-ray of determinant factors of contemporary culture: technique, economy, politics, and their impact on the collective. For them, the project determines, preserves,

*Figure 14* Picture took by the author at OFFICE KGDVS Studio. 2014. It shows a board from A Grammar for the City Competition by Office KGDVS and DOGMA. 2005

*Figure 15* Picture took by the author at 51n4e Studio

and transmits within the public domain, something that the collective should remember even if is not a finished architectural product but a cultural contribution.

### The project as Research

The NW Architect engages a project as a research endeavor, not merely understood as the discovery of facts, but as the production of a discourse beyond operational or instrumental issues.[37] This idea depends on an understanding of the project as a model of reality to test a specific situation by using a set of given tools.

Despite their similarities, each NW project is an individual entity, a body of research that is no longer about searching for true principles or beliefs, but about how to produce the necessary tools for constructing the work. Thus design signifies the refining of working methods and the building of an archive. It becomes a deliberate, selective, and controlled form of behavior from which certain themes, images or references surprisingly emerge. In this way, the act of design implies a detachment from the need for different methods appropriate to the particular nature of each distinct object and involves a more fluid relationship to the present, where any act of research is undertaken and is directed towards how to see and respond to the emergence of things for which we have yet to develop the right tools. Seen through this lens, the relationship to the future is transformed. The latter ceases to be the object of our imagination or prediction. It is remixed. Moreover, a more pragmatic way of confronting the future appears, one that is related to the present via those multiple futures that have yet to be imagined, because we are in the act of making them a reality or inventing them.

We might infer that the NW architect's project is a work of *re-territorialization*, a re-weaving of beliefs and desires where renovation assumes importance and inherited ideas are superimposed upon current ones "through new word usage, the invention of neologisms and the linking of hitherto non-related conditions."[38] The NW architect emerges from a triangular relationship between research, teaching and practice. In the end, the thinking and making of architecture extends beyond the acquisition of wisdom or practical ability attained during its conception, to connect the work itself to academia, personal writings, and the public realm, thus re-describing the technical and cultural context of architectural practice.

### Trainspotters

In Britain, the term trainspotter is used to describe an individual whose energy is spent in stockpiling what appears to be meaningless data. The term gained universal recognition through the publication of Irvine Welsh's novel, *Trainspotting*[39], made into a film by Danny Boyle, whose characters became obsessed with the consumption of information with no apparent outcome or purpose. However, this seemingly futile phenomenon is closely related to the productive way that knowledge is acquired in the field of electronic music, specifically the New Beat. Learning is conducted in "live" sessions through intense and critical observation, where the tricks of the trade are passed down from mentors to apprentices. Observation is valued as the pedagogical basis of a movement that recognizes the creative potential inherent in the act of observing, naming and organizing. *Learning from looking at buildings*[40] is the application of this concept for the NW architect. Adopting an obsessive and autonomous trainspotter mentality, they amass enormous collections of references and exhaustive information about publications, works, and authors. This form of collecting goes hand in hand with creation and the legitimation of critical discourses that construct canons, genealogies, practices, and a new order.

*Figure 16* Skanderberg Square project, 51n4e. 2009

*Figure 17* Cedric Price's project for a university in motion, the Potteries Thinkbelt, 1964

1 Despite the fact that this article does not focus on a particular office or specific project, it gathers the impressions collected during trips made by the Emerging Practices research group from ETSAM Madrid to Brussels and London respectively. During those trips, visits were made to the architectural offices of OFFICE KGDVS, 51N4E, DOGMA, XDGA in Brussels and Tony Fretton, CARUSO St JOHN, Sergison Bates, and David Chipperfield in London.

2 ARCH+ 214: *Hardcore-Architektur 1 - Das nicht gehaltene Versprechen / ARCH+ 215: Hardcore-Architektur 2 - Politik versus Form*. Verlag Aachen: GmbH, 2014.

3 Cerith Wyn Evans. *The Curves of the Needle*. Berlin: Bawag Contemporary, 2006.

4 Hans Ulrich Obrist and Pedro Reyes. *El aire es azul. Reflexiones sobre arte y arquitectura en torno a Luis Barragán*. México: Trilce Ediciones, 2006.

5 Ibidem.

6 Ignasi Aballi. *Listados*. Bilbao: Belleza infinita, 2011

7 North Western Metropolitan Area. In AURELI, Pier Vittorio. *Brussels: A Manifesto Towards the Capital of Europe*. Rotterdam: NAi Publishers, 2007

8 Simon Reynolds. *Rip it Up and Start again: Post Punk, 1978-1984*. London: Faber & Faber, 2005.

9 William S. Burroughs. *The Wild Boys: a Book of Dead*. New York: Grove press, 1971.

10 John Savage. *So this is Permanence: Joy Division Lyrics and Notebooks*. London: Faber & Faber, 2014.

11 Jozef Deville and Pablo Eekman. *The Sound of Belgium*. Brussels, 2012.

12 Kersten Geers and David Van Severen. *After the party*. 2G N.63 OFFICE Kersten Geers David Van Severen. Barcelona: Gustavo Gili, 2012

13 Bart Lootsma. *Superdutch: New Architecture in the Netherlands*. New York: Princeton Architectural Press, 2000

14 Joachim Declerck and Dries Van De Velde. "From Realism to Reality. A Future for Dutch Architectural Culture. A Conversation with Pier Vittorio Aureli and Roemer van Toorn." In OASE 67: After the Party. Dutch Architecture 2005. Rotterdam: NAi Publishers, 2005.

15 Atelier Kempe Thill. *New discipline*. In OASE 67: *After the Party. Dutch Architecture 2005*. Rotterdam: NAi Publishers, 2005.

16 Ibidem.

17 Juan Herreros. *Correcciones Tipológicas*. MPAA 7-ETSAM. Madrid. 2015.

18 Geers, Kersten; Kritis, Joris; Pancevac, Jelena; Piovene, Giovanni; Rodet, Dries and Zanderigo, Andrea. *Architecture Without Content*. London: Architectural Association, 2015.

19 Juan Herreros. "Nada excepcional" in El Croquis 177-178. Madrid: El Croquis, 2015.

20 Jean Baudrillard. *The System of Objects*. London: Verso, 1968.

21 Ibidem.

22 Esteban De Backer. *Efficiency as Necessity. A Conversation with Kersten Geers. An Economy of Means*. ARPA Journal 03. New York: Columbia GSAPP, 2015.

23 Claude Lévi-Strauss. *The Savage Mind*. Chicago: The University Chicago Press, 1966.

24 Ibidem.

25 Irénée Scalbert. "The Architect as Bricoleur" in *Candide* 4. Aachen: RWTH, 2011.

26 Richard Rorty. *Contingency, Irony and Solidarity*. Cambridge: Cambridge University Press, 1989.

27 Jacques Derrida. *Archive Fever: a Freudian Impression*. Chicago: The University Chicago Press, 1996.

28 Jean Baudrillard. *The System of Objects*. London: Verso, 1968.

29 Aby Warburg. *Atlas Mnemosyne*. Madrid: Akal, 2010.

30 Jacques Derrida. *Archive Fever: a Freudian Impression*. Chicago: The University Press, 1996.

31 Ibidem.

32 Michel Foucault. "What is an author?" in Faubion, James. *Aesthetics, Method, and Epistemology*. New York: The New York Press, 1999.

33 Simon Reynolds. *Retromania: Pop Culture's Addiction to Its Own Past*. London: Faber & Faber, 2011.

34 Nicolas Bourriaud. *Postproduction - Culture as Screenplay: How art reprograms the world*. Berlin: Sternberg press, 2005.

35 Ibidem.

36 Nicolas Bourriaud. *Relational Aesthetics*. Dijon: Les Presses du Réel, 1998.

37 Joachim Declerck and Dries Van De Velde. "From Realism to Reality. A Future for Dutch Architectural Culture. A Conversation with Pier Vittorio Aureli and Roemer van Toorn" in *OASE* 67: *After the Party*. Dutch Architecture 2005. Rotterdam: NAi Publishers, 2005.

38 Richard Rorty. "Inquiry as Recontextualization" in *Objectivity, Relativism, and Truth: Philosophical Papers*. Cambridge: Cambridge University Press, 1991.

39 Irvine Welsh. *Trainspotting*. London: Secker & Warburg, 1993.

40 Jonathan Sergison and Stephen Bates. "Learning from Looking at Buildings" in *Papers II*. Barcelona: Gustavo Gili, 2007.

*Figure 18* Capture from Trainspotting movie by Danny Boyle. 1996

# Drawing Order

## Katherine Wheeler

"All images have a pre-history in other images," wrote the historian of science Klaus Hentschel, and the drawings in the University of Miami Call to Order exhibition in the fall of 2015 are no exception.[1] The drawings acknowledge generational and pedagogical genealogies as they take their place within the larger trajectory of architectural drawing's lineage. Spanning from Arquitectonica's works of the late 1970s to the present day works of the "Young Ancients," the architects use typical drawing types to new effect in their attempts to communicate architecture. The drawing types—plan, section, elevation, axonometric, and perspective—settle clearly within standard architectural drawing conventions, yet many drawings show the architects' playfulness and an awareness of drawing's limitations.

With roots stretching back before the Renaissance, the most fundamental architectural drawing type is the orthographic drawing—the plan, elevation, or section. While there are many extant examples of orthographic drawings prior to the 15th century, the standardization of orthographic practices did not begin until the Renaissance, and medieval architectural drawings occasionally show plan and elevation simultaneously. In the 9th-century Plan of St Gall, for example, the cloister arcades are shown as though "lying down," combining the elevation and the plan. By the 20th century, these inconsistencies were gone, and the rules of orthographic drawing were the basis of architectural training in both books and formalized education. It seems that there would be little that an architect could do to present his work differently within the confines of this drawing type, but it is the inherent confines that can create ambiguities and multiple readings when exploited. The most obvious of these limitations is orthographic drawing's inability to present the entire picture in one drawing. A plan simply cannot describe an entire project, as the vertical characteristics are unknown, and likewise, the elevation on its own tells nothing of the plan and interior configuration. Multiple drawings must be taken together for the design to be fully understood. Shortcomings can become strengths in the right hands, and the architect can intentionally create uncertainty for a desired effect.

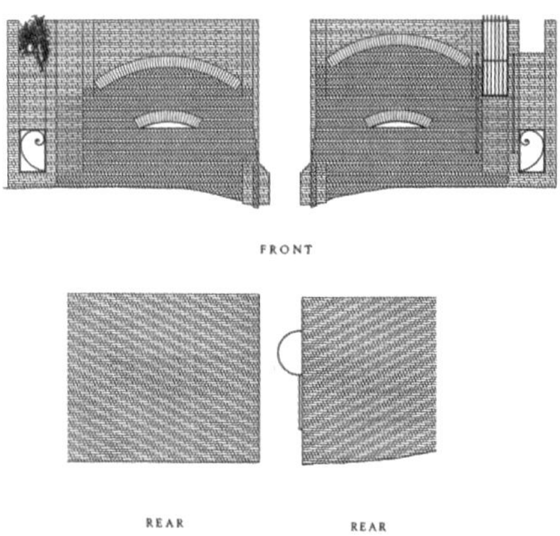


*Figure 1* Elevations. Taberna Ancipitas Formae, Machado Silvetti

Machado Silvetti Architects' drawings for Garden Folly, Taberna Ancipitis Formae, 1983, exploit the orthographic drawing's ambiguities. The nine elevations of the two cubes when unfolded create masks; mute faces of brick arched "eyebrows," two slotted "eye" windows, and golden section "ears" (Figure 1). Not immediately legible in three dimensions, the mask is only revealed when the elevations are laid out in a certain order. The elevation mask hides the interior of the folly, leaving it up to the plans to reveal the geometric games and dualities of the two intersecting cubes of air and water. The orthographic sections, thick-walled containers that open to the sky, are equally obtuse games of grids that also require the plans to make them legible. Machado Silvetti creates a game of peek-a-boo by playing with orthographic drawing's limitations to create intentional ambiguities and multiple readings.[2] Likewise, in their drawings of the Djerba House, Machado Silvetti uses orthographic drawing as a narrative revelation of the project (Figure 2). The crisp, black lines of the plans present the geometries, axes, and material thicknesses with precision, but the plan holds double readings of the central space as open to the sky or enclosed. The hand-colored elevations in subtle beige tones against a blue sky reveal the project as a twisting nautilus form, almost completely blind on the exterior, with exquisitely placed, punched openings. In this series, the sections reveal the hidden spaces contained within the mute shell with their shadows enhancing the building's quality of space within its shell-like exterior. Each of the drawings is complete in itself as a mode of representation, but each drawing can only tell one portion of the story of the building. Machado Silvetti's awareness of both the power of the orthographic drawing and its limitations heightens the reading of their projects.

*Figure 2* Elevation, Djerba House, Machado Silvetti

An intriguing variation on the orthographic drawing that also occurs in the exhibit is the unfolded plan with elevations, also called the "developed elevation" or "laid-out elevation."[3] This drawing type has its roots in the 18th century in the drawings of British architects such as Robert Adam (1728-1792) and Isaac Ware (1704-1766), who were exploring new ways to present interior decorative schemes. Ware described this unique drawing type as when "[t]he four sides of the room being laid down on paper, with the space or proportion of the floor between, the figure represents at once to the eye the whole and its several parts: they are easily seen to be uniform or disagreeable; fancy can at pleasure raise them perpendicularly, and see the room in miniature, divested of its ceiling."[4] The developed elevation treats the floor and adjacent walls as having one continuous design intent, thus emphasizing the surfaces as just that, surfaces: flat, yet contiguous canvases for which lace-like plaster ornament became the connecting element from one plane to the next, the walls and the floor or ceiling. While essentially orthographic, and therefore representing spatial relationships, the historian Laura Jacobus notes that these drawings are primarily topographic in that their main concern is typically that of surface, an approach that is both embraced and rejected in its use in the Call to Order exhibit.

The Miami firm R&R Studio exploits this duality of orthography-topography—or space and surface—of the developed elevation in its proposal for Valby Square, Copenhagen, 2009 (Figure 3). Here, the designers, Roberto Behar and Rosario Marquardt, used the developed elevation to present an exterior space, treating the facades lining the square as interior surfaces, complete with striped, colorful "wallpaper." The selection of this drawing type reinforces their idea of the square as a "room" in a way that the accompanying perspectives do not, aligning with the drawing type's initial intention and strengths.

2A+P/A also uses the developed elevation; however, its emphasis is not on surface or the enclosure of space but instead as an unfolding of an enclosed form (Figure 4). The inspiration for the project is Ettore Sottsass's "Monumental Architecture," a drawing of a black vaulted form with curiously placed openings. 2A+P/A has accentuated the ambiguities in Sottsass's drawing in scale, function, and interior by trying to solidify and reimagine it as a villa on the beach. What would typically be elevations splayed out from the plan are instead sections, subverting the drawing type's ability to connect surfaces together as the inserted grid structure intervenes. The flatness the developed elevation typically conveys is lost, although the reading of the drawing as though the "walls" could simply be folded up to create the room remains. What would be missing, however, would be the inserted grid structure. The result, therefore, is a drawing that is as deliberately mysterious as Sottsass's original.

A variation on orthographic drawings came with the advent of the elevation oblique. The elevation oblique, can be understood as referring back to pre-Renaissance drawings like the Plan of St Gall, prior to strict graphic conventions, in that it tries to represent two drawings—the plan and the elevation—simultaneously. Revived in the 1970s with Postmodernism, the elevation oblique became a favorite mode of representation to show the character of architectural context. DPZ's drawing of Migrant Farmworkers' Housing, Florida, 1995, for example, shows the trees and the facades of the houses in elevation while the "ground" remains in plan with the rows of dirt brown dots of plantings (Figure 5). The effect is almost folk or naïve in style, perfectly capturing the project's duality of informality of life within the formality of the grid.

The elevation oblique is also a bridge to one of the most popular drawing types in the exhibit, the axonometric and its many variants. As the historian Massimo Scolari points out in his in-depth study on this form of "anti-perspective," the axonometric and oblique have been common forms of representation for centuries, although their use in professional architectural circles is much shorter.[5] Borrowed from engineering drawing methods developed in the 18th and 19th centuries, particularly the isometric drawings of William Farish (1759-1837), the axonometric combines the strengths of both the orthographic and the perspective drawing in that it is measurable on three axes.[6] The selection of axonometric as a drawing type within architecture also brings to mind the early 20th century avant-garde movements such as El Lissitzky's Prouns, Theo van Doesburg and the De Stijl movement, and theosopher-designer Claude Bragdon.[7] The scholar Yves Alain Bois has pointed out that the power of the axonometric is that it is "reversible; it tears free of the ground...facilitating aerial views."[8] The axonometric separates the object of study from its context, both the physical context of the building or project as well as the context of traditional architectural drawing representation. Axonometry was revived in architecture in the 1970s as a means to explore architecture beyond its contemporary condition, although this has yet to be acknowledged in the scholarship.

Aldo Rossi's large freehand isometric drawing for an addition to the University of Miami School of Architecture (unbuilt and ultimately designed by Leon Krier) shows the ability of this drawing type to present "urban" space created by the relationships of architectural forms. The viewpoint hovers above the buildings,

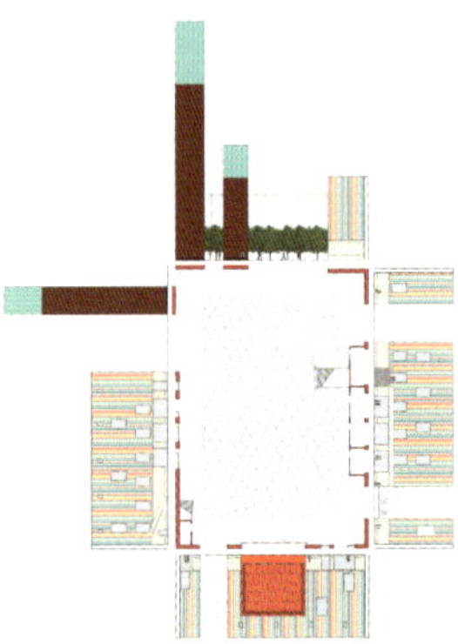

*Figure 3* Composite Drawing. Valby Square, R&R Studios

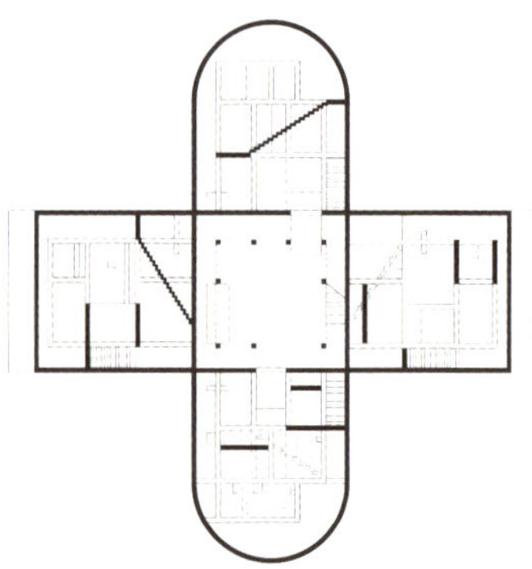

*Figure 4* Composite Drawing. House from Sottsass, 2A+ PA

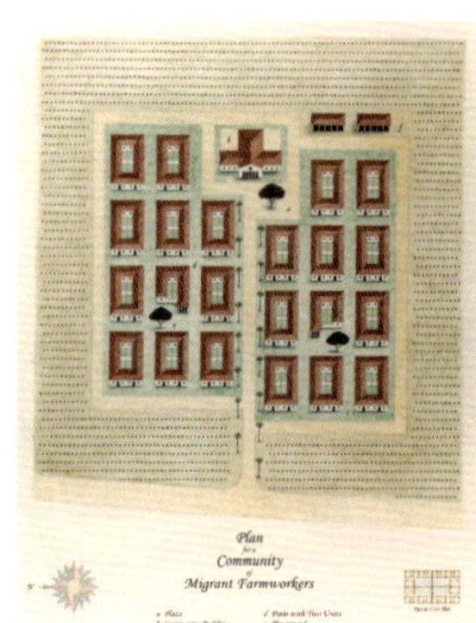

*Figure 5* Axonometric. La Estancia, DPZ

*Figure 6* Axonometric Drawing. Imperial, Arquitectonica

*Figure 7* Axonometric. MOS Architects Retail No 1

typical of isometrics, which facilitates the reading of an inherent order of compositional axes and repeated forms, creating a miniaturized example of Rossi's urban theories. As a drawing type, the isometric allows the three dimensionality of the forms and the plan to be seen simultaneously, while still inviting the viewer's imagination to place himself within the drawing as he would within a perspective. But the detached viewpoint of the isometric implies a scientific rigor in its precision, as it isolates the architectural objects. The space created is then both no place and everyplace, as the use of isometric promises a utopia, a place that had it been rendered in perspective would have been almost too real. Instead, it is just out of reach.

Often the axonometric, as a scientific or technical drawing used in detailed analysis, is completely without context, isolating the object of study like a moth pinned to a white board. Arquitectonica's drawing of the Imperial, Miami, 1984, for example floats alone in space. This building could be anywhere or nowhere. The drawing does not reveal cardinal orientation, and it is not clear how the building addresses Biscayne Bay, or what the red wall on the far side of the building might be facing (Figure 6). A singular corner of the plinth reaches out to hold a circular pool, the only "ground" available, and the slab above hovers over it protectively. A new "ground"—Corbusian to be sure—is visible on the roof and compliments the elevated angle of the axonometric which focuses attention on the roof-scape's parallel rows of trees, elongated linear pool and yellow sculptural form. The effect is otherworldly and sterile, distinctly outside of the mundane everydayness of an urban context and all its messiness.

There is also an otherworldliness and lack of context in MOS architects' drawing of a Retail Space in Miami which has reduced the project down to two planes—the façade and sidewalk—to create an exterior space (Figure 7). The drawings' boldness of colors and patterns gives an order that the dizzying lines on the zebra-striped pavement and the dancing grid of windows denies. Again, the unrealistic vantage point high above the project forces the imagination to work harder to place one's self within it, but there is no other drawing type which could so clearly emphasize the relationship between the two planar surfaces of facade and sidewalk.

The more common—and more historically contentious—alternative to the axonometric for the depiction of architecture three dimensionally is the perspective, which marries art and science, image and mathematics. Invented as a mathematical projection in the Renaissance and first used by painters, Alberti and Rafael considered it an inappropriate drawing type for architects because, unlike orthographic drawings, it could not be measured. Perspective was also a way of organizing the world, and it is no coincidence that Renaissance architecture is almost inherently perspectival (think of Brunelleschi's work at San Lorenzo, Florence). 19th century architects, however,

*Figure 8* Night view drawing, Pink House, Arquitectonica

*Figure 9* Perspective, color pencil drawing, Babylon, Arquitectonica

thought the perspective was problematic and tried to ban it from architectural competitions, because it had the ability to seduce and deceive.

Some of the perspectives gathered for the Call to Order exhibit are artistic and painterly in their approach, creating illustrations that appear to be part of a larger narrative and not merely renderings for a project. Arquitectonica's three perspectives of the Pink House, 1976, by Laurinda Spear, for example, present a different narrative of Miami from that of the bright sun and heat; instead, it is a Miami of warm, dark evenings punctuated by shooting stars (Figure 8). The placement of the primary wall parallel to the picture plane flattens the perspective and reinforces the architecture's theatrical effect. Interestingly, the Pink House perspectives with their higher than eye level vantage point have the same distant and isolated qualities of an axonometric, with the viewer separated from the space portrayed. Arquitectonica's colorful exterior perspective of the red-stepped Babylon, Miami, 1977, presents a project against a night sky gradated from the brightness of the city lights to an inky darkness with a sliver moon (Figure 9). The row of spherical, un-Miami looking, treetops buffer the building from the viewer, while in the foreground the blue waterline of Biscayne Bay wriggles past. Like the Pink House perspectives, the use of thick, rich, colors flatten the reading of the building against the background. There are no people and few architectural clues to give scale, leaving the project in a netherworld. The perspective presents the building as self-contained and separated from its context, allowing its system and rationale to stand independent from the city. Arquitectonica uses perspectives in these projects to isolate the building and to engage the imagination through a playful use of color, setting a stage for a new reading of the building.

The distance between the drawing and the viewer that is evident in the works of Arquitectonica and other firms, tends to disappear with the use of the computer as a rendering tool which can place the viewer within the project more directly. Nadaa's use of the computer for perspective in their design of a retreat in New Hampshire creates renderings that include the viewer, complete with wisps of smoke rising from a fire as the circular walls surround (Figure 10). But they also use the computer analytically, taking the information input and creating a section perspective that is skewed and partially rendered, while clearly dismissing a sense of realism (Figure 11).

Damiani Ngo Phiffer's (DNP) quirky rendering of a proposed interior of a cargo ship retrofit as the Guggenheim Helsinki places the viewer in a room as the head of a man peeks up from a hole in the floor (Figure 12). The realistic rendering of surfaces, the lack of a frame around the drawing, the florescent lights and shiny ductwork running towards and supposedly behind the viewer, and the curious figure of the man with his fingers gripping the edge of the hole, engage the imagination and force the mind into creating stories and reasons for him to be there.

The firm's sense of whimsy is also evident in their collage "Parkscape," where a giant shuttlecock lands amongst a stand of trees near a group of people sitting in a circle. The realism of the photograph and the absurdity of the scalar difference show how the computer can effectively generate collage. OFFICE Kersten Geers David Van Severen also uses collage to represent the Agricultural School in Leuven, Belgium, 2014 (Figure 13). The collage shows the exposed concrete wall parallel to the picture plane, which reinforces the wall's importance in the project, as the adjacent surfaces appear to fold and turn away forcefully. The focus on the wall reveals it as the primary organizational element in the building, a planar spine which holds the two spaces—interior and exterior—

together. Collage is not a common mode of architectural representation, although there are certainly notable exceptions, the most famous being those of Ludwig Mies van der Rohe, who used collage and perspective to create the impression of what would occur within his taut structural grids. Examples such as the collage for the George Schaeffer Museum, Germany, 1960-63 and the famous collage of the Chicago Convention Center, 1954, which is little more than three photographic textures to represent crowds of people, the walls, and the space frame, show how Mies saw texture—of material and people—as central to the designs. But the Mies collages might be a bit too stern as precedents for DNP and OFFICE, who might be looking more towards the comic book quality of the 'zines of Archigram or the photographic manipulations of Superstudio.

Representation—drawing and its siblings, painting and collage, whether done by hand or computer—is at the heart of the practice of architecture. Drawing is inherent in the art of architecture, yet not dependent on the laws of physics, budgets of clients, or constraints of contractors. The drawings are the raw product of the architect and are engaging works in themselves. Their conventions and limitations pull at the corners of how architects present their work. Ultimately the drawing is autonomous. It has the power to reveal which might be sensed but not fully comprehended without the drawings' omniscient view. The drawing also allows the architect to contribute to the architectural discourse without having to wait for a building to be built. The drawing is potent but not permanent. It might outlive a project, but could just as easily be wadded up and tossed away.

*Figure 10* View of courtyard. New Hampshire, NADAAA

*Figure 11* Section Perspective. New Hampshire, NADAAA

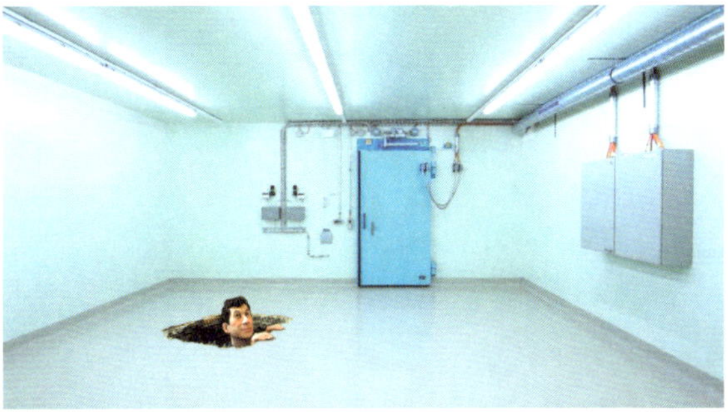

*Figure 12* Temporary Exhibition Room, rendering. Guggenheim Museum, Damiani Ngo Phiffer

*Figure 13* Collage. Agriculture School, Office KGDVS

1 Klaus Hentschel, *Visual Cultures in Science and Technology. A Comparative History* (Oxford: Oxford University Press, 2014), 72.
2 One interpretation of this peek-a-boo by Farés el-Dahdah highlights the folly as an object for erotic adventure. See Farès el-Dahdah, "The Folly of S/M, *recto-verso*," *Assemblage* 18 (August 1992), 6-19.
3 Laura Jacobus, "On 'Whether a man could see before him and behind him both at once': The role of drawing in the design of interior space in England c. 1600-1800," *Architectural History*, v. 31 (1988), 148-59+. See also, Robin Evans, "The Developed Surface," in *Translations from Drawing to Building and Other Essays, AA Documents* (London: Architectural Association, 1997), 194-231.
4 As quoted in Jacobus, 155.
5 Massimo Scolari, *Oblique Drawing: A History of Anti-Perspective* (Cambridge, MIT Press, 2012).
6 Yves Alain Bois, "Metamorphosis of Axonometry," *Daidalos* (1981), 54.
7 Bois, 40-58. See also Claude Bragdon, *The Frozen Fountain: Being Essays on Architecture and the Art of Design in Space* (1928; reprint New York, 1970).
8 Bois, 56.

## Curators: Steven Fett & Edgar Sarli

Twenty years after the release of Vincent Scully's "Between Two Towers," the seminal publication of drawings from the University of Miami's School of Architecture, an exhibition entitled "Call to Order" lined the walls of the Irving Korach Gallery. The exhibition was curated along two parallel walls: the first displaying a collection of historical projects from the late 1970s through the early 90s by University of Miami faculty members, related associates, and mentors, whose work helped establish an identity for a new school of architecture in Miami. This work served as a backdrop and a counterpoint to a variety of themes that have resurfaced in the current architectural discourse including the renewed interest in history, type, form, and meaning.

The second wall assembled a diverse group of contemporary Western architects whose work is both ideologically and formally varied but which ostensibly displays an interest in what could be described as a return to order. The work does not adhere to a common ideology; has no defining manifesto; and is not representative of any singular school of thought. Nevertheless, when viewed collectively a number of sensibilities emerge that loosely bind the work together. These include: the search for order through the use of simple geometric forms; the preoccupation with the relationship between graphic representation and theoretical intent; the reliance on collage as a primary means of representation; the use of repetitive compositions to convey symbolic meaning, and the search for a redefined relationship between architecture and the city.

Figure 1 Model. Djerba House, Machado Silvetti

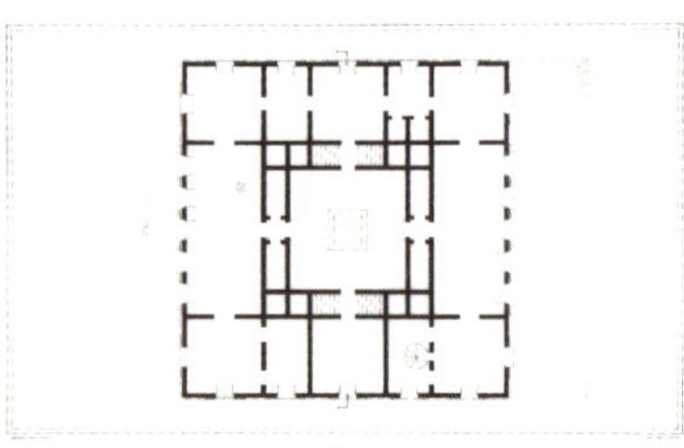


Figure 3 Plans. Ca'Ziff, DLGV

Common between the two walls is an interest in the architectural movements of the late 1960s and 1970s; most notably, the rationalism of La Tendenza emerges as an important reference for both, albeit with different theoretical and formal outcomes.

### The Work

One of the earliest projects exhibited on the historical wall is the Djerba House in Tunisia, designed by Rodolfo

Figure 2 Loggia elevation. Photograph by Elizabeth Felicella, Ca'Ziff, DLGV, demolished 2016

Machado and Jorge Silvetti, both former visiting critics at the University of Miami. The house connects to its vernacular neighbors through its massing, texture, and proportion of window to wall. The main elements of the composition, the "cubic" core and the spiraling staircase, could be found in the existing fabric of the island, yet the clashing monumental scale of the stair juxtaposed to the cube is decidedly more Roman, elevated to receive the breezes off the Mediterranean, or from what was once called "Mare Nostrum." (Figure 1)

Ten years later, and located on the shore of Miami's Biscayne Bay, Ca'Ziff by De La Guardia Victoria Architects, references Mediterranean and Venetian models. (Figure 2) The atrium, the generator and organizer of the Pompeiian house, here is contained within a square plan, comprised of single and double cubed rooms, unquestionably reminiscent of a Palladian Villa. (Figure 3) Opposite the main house, a two story rectangular building, crowned by a loggia, is composed of severely abstracted architectural elements, recalling twentieth century Italian rationalist architecture.

Figure 4 Sketch. University of Miami School of Architecture. Aldo Rossi, 1987

Members of La Tendenza, comprised of noteworthy architects, painters and theorists, the likes of Giorgio Grassi, Massimo Scolari and Aldo Rossi, participated in the academic life of the University of Miami during the late eighties and early nineties. Moreover, the School of Miami found a hero in Rossi, inviting him to design a new school of architecture in 1987. (Figure 4) (Image: Rossi SoA) The drawings along the historical wall of the exhibition are a direct result of this influence. The works are hand – drawn, rigorously labored, intentionally naïve and symbolically charged; and without exception, they are depicted orthographically rather than in perspective.

Scully, who taught history at the University of Miami from 1992-2005, suggested that this drawing approach was more influenced by the flatness of the medieval, "pre-Rafaelite," Italian painters than those who would follow.[1] The method places emphasis on the intrinsic characteristics of the objects depicted, rather than the way they would look from an arbitrarily fixed point of view. This method of representation was in sharp contrast to the more conventional approach adopted by most schools of architecture from the beginning of the twentieth century, which more closely followed Erwin Panofsky's models of visual representation set forth in his 1924 essay, "Perspective as Symbolic Form."[2]

Figure 5 Day view. (Photograph by courtesy of Pezo Von Ellrichshausen, Meri House), Pezo Von Ellrichshausen

The contemporary collection of projects shares a genesis of design firmly rooted in the use of ordinary, platonic structures, and deceptively simple buildings that originate from rational geometric forms. This approach not only links the oeuvres of the different architects visually, but also theoretically, as the ubiquitous forms in their tool boxes hold intrinsically significant meaning and architectural power. Consistency in the use of Platonic geometries is even pursued in cases when programmatic requirements suggest a more informal arrangement. Such is the case in the Meri House by Pezo Von Ellrichshausen with its rigid yellow board and batten façade set against an undulating Chilean backdrop. (Figure 5) The work is reminiscent of Scully's description of the solemnity of a Greek temple within the landscape as the "shapes brought the human presence into a new, fundamentally dramatic dialogue with the land."[3] Ten identical rooms, square in plan, sheltered by an ample horizontal overhang, achieve a high degree of visual tension between the natural world and architecture's realm of geometry and abstraction.

Figure 6 Aerial rendering. OFFICE 15: Border Crossing. Office KGDVS

The Border Garden project by OFFICE Kersten Geers David Van Severen, in collaboration with Wonne Ickx, sets a simple rectangular volume at the border crossing between Mexico and the US. This precisely defined figure is composed of a perimeter wall that encloses a dense grid of palm trees. The image is striking as the overall composition clearly demarcates an ordered, hypostyle, palm court amidst a barren and inhospitable landscape. With only a few compositional elements, the project manages to transform a space of passage into an oasis.

The persistent use of geometric restraint is willful and could be seen as a direct reaction to the excesses associated with parametric architecture. However, it does not appear to be guided solely by aesthetic preferences but also by an understanding of propriety and economy that re-establishes architecture's social and cultural power in the shaping of cities. This last observation has been elaborated at length by the Italian architect and theoretician, Pier Vittorio Aureli in his book The Possibility of an Absolute Architecture.

Once again – and to varying degrees – this new generation is influenced by the post-war, modern Italian Rationalist movement, La Tendenza and its interest in the link between graphic representation and theoretical intent. The rhetoric behind this collection of contemporary drawings is not to photo-realistically predict, but rather to search for something more meaningful, tied to the context of place, often, metaphysically. (Image: Copenhagen)

In his time, E.H. Gombrich, expressed concern that the persuasive skills of the artist might be abused to pander to the lower faculties of the soul.[4] Facing the newest generation of architectural thinkers exhibited in Call to Order is the temptation to indulge in the spectacular shape - making capabilities of advanced computer software and digital fabrication. Yet, this new group engages technology differently, relying on computer generated collage and basic tonal coloring techniques to produce drawings with sobering flatness. (Figure 7). The idea that this approach to architecture and drawing is inherently a reaction against the conventional form of persuasive illustration, i.e. the photo-realistic rendering, is secondary. Rather, the search for Beauty can be found in the historic archetype, producing rational, honest forms without ingratiation. This ongoing intellectual counterpoint is ultimately searching for a deeper connection to the primitive, which is viewed as the purest and most memorable form of architectural expression. (Figure 6) (Image: OFFICE)

The Maria Grazia Cutuli School in Afghanistan by 2A + PA exemplifies another recurring characteristic of the contemporary works exhibited - the daring use of color. Lapis lazuli blue, a hue prized since antiquity for its intense color, is used for the building walls and carmine red for the window mullions

Figure 7 Collage. Delta Rjeka, Salottobuono

Figure 8 Aerial view. Maria Grazia Cutuli, 2A+PA

Figure 9 Harbour presence, rendering. Guggenheim Museum, Damiani Ngo Phiffer

and doors. The effect is striking, producing a polychromatic compound set in sharp contrast to the neutral ochres of the surrounding landscape. (Figure 8) Lilac is the color chosen by Damiani Ngo Phiffer to give character and noticeability to their proposal for the Guggenheim Helsinki. The project repurposes an existing cargo ship and transforms it into a floating museum. By painting the ship in a single, unified color, the authors transform the reading of the subject, providing the vessel with a new identity. (Figure 9)

Figure 10 Elevation. Retail No 1, MOS Architects

Figure 11 Collage. Design District, Johnston Marklee

Figure 12 Collage. Agriculture School, Office KGDVS

Figure 13 Rendered elevation. House of the Arts and Culture, Productora

Repetition is deployed as a fundamental compositional device for both striking visual effect and to convey symbolic meaning. MOS Architects' façade design in Miami's Design District, plays on the idea of thickness versus thinness by creating a façade made of deeply recessed marble veneer panels punctuated by a repetitive grid of rotated square windows arranged as if in a state of collapse. The unexpected composition produces a façade that oscillates between order and potential chaos. (Figure 10)

The exhibition also included a second façade project for the Miami Design District by the office of Johnston Marklee. Inspired by the formal repertoire of the Italian rationalist movement, the project reinterprets the classical elements of the colonnade through the use of modern materials. Here the repetitive concave columns are clad in a reflective metal that mirrors the light, the sky, and the landscape of the surrounding context, producing a kaleidoscope of reflections that de-materializes the building's surface, while maintaining the overall order of the original form.

OFFICE Kersten Geers David Van Severen's Agricultural school building, situated on the outskirts of Leuven, is organized into two simple masses: a five - storey rectangular classroom building intersected by a lower horizontal volume housing the sports hall. The façade of the main building is strictly composed with a series of repetitive horizontal windows that correspond to the classrooms beyond. A single opening interrupts the overall composition and registers a large covered space located at the intersection of the two volumes. This outdoor room opens up to frame a view of the city of Leuven in the distance. In this way, the project acts as a metaphorical gateway to the city beyond.

Yet another example of the power of repetition in the construction of the work is Productora's House of Art and Culture in Beirut. The project develops a clear volume wrapped in a monumental peristyle composed of three perimeter layers of columns that syncopate according to the particulars of the given site. The overlapping of vertical elements produces a rhythmic composition that is at once familiar and new.

A variety of projects search for a redefined relationship between architecture and the city that can be illustrated at several scales. For instance, CÚRE & PENABAD's MDO retail store faces the street with a double height, quasi-blank wall giving it a bold, unexpected presence in one of Miami's most unmemorable areas. The subtle angle that indents and proclaims the store's entrance contrasts with the unmarked, suburban character of its neighbors, making MDO a memorable incident in the city. Contrarily, R&R Studios' urban intervention in Copenhagen searches for its identity analogously. Slender towers composed of brick bodies and copper tops define a new city square of colossal scale. The proposal stems from a careful study of the architectural, historical, and cultural context of place and time. It establishes a symbiotic dialogue with the city, harmoniously coexisting with its surroundings and enhancing the city's emblematic skyline.

Figure 14 East elevation. (Photograph by Steven Brooke) MDO, Cúre & Penabad

Adrian Phiffer's Europan 13 Competition prize-winning entry, explores the resilience of urban forms across time, a discussion that is all too often forgotten in the discussions that shape the form of the contemporary city. The project, set in Nacka, Stockholm, Sweden, utilizes the varying plateaus of the site to develop distinct urban moments that vary in character and type. Here, forms are not the direct result of any specific or singular program; rather, resilient types are utilized to develop a flexible structure that permits adaptability in the face of an uncertain economic and urban future.

Figure 15 Perspective. Valby Square, R&R Studios

In the end, the work displayed in the Call to Order exhibition is not a comprehensive representation of a new style but rather a glimpse into a new sensibility that extends beyond mere curiosity. The work does not set out to create a new architectural movement but rather advances a consciousness about the current state of the discipline that extends beyond a single region, forming an unintended and perhaps uneasy alliance of individuals. Nevertheless, the exhibit highlights a renewed faith in a view of architecture that strives for order amidst tangible and contradictory forces. Will this sensibility signal a shift in architectural culture? Perhaps it is to early to tell as the majority of the work on display is paper architecture, yet translated to building.

Figure 16 Site model. The Ends of the CIty - European 13 Competition, Office of Adrian Phiffer

1 Vincent Scully, *Between Two Towers: The Drawings of the School of Miami* (New York: Montacelli Press, 1996)

2 Erwin Panofsky, *Perspective as Symbolic Form* (New York: Zone Books, 1991)

3 Vincent Scully, Architecture the Natural and the Manmade (New York: St. Martin's Press, 1991)

4 Richard Woodfield, "The Primitive and its Value in Art," in *The Essential Gombrich: Selected Writings on Art and Culture* (Hong Kong: Phaidon Press, 1996), 299.

*Vernacularology*

## Adib Cúre

***Vernacular (noun): using a language or a dialect native to a region or country rather than a literary, cultured, or foreign language of, relating to, or characteristic of a period, place, or group; especially: of, relating to, or being the common building style of a period or place.***

***Vernacularology (noun): a branch of knowledge that observes, studies and documents the ordinary, colloquial, and oftentimes enigmatic artifacts particular to a given place.***

Palo Bonito, Las Flores, Barranquilla, Ana Gueracao and Lauren O'Halloran, Vernacularology studio, spring 2015

While uniformity has become the global standard and placelessness is now an integral part of our everyday lives, the pedagogy that shapes the direction of a series of studios at the University of Miami School of Architecture is conceived otherwise. The Vernacularology studios, explore the potential to create drawings, spaces, and buildings of cultural specificity where tradition and invention, the colloquial and the academic, the regional and the universal participate in the composition and construction of the contemporary city.

Vernacularology aims to understand the relevant cultural, morphological, typological, and constructive aspects of regional architectural form in search of what is elemental and significant. It does not limit itself to the vernacular architecture and urbanism of the distant past but is intrigued by contemporary solutions that are the products of current cultural, economic, and political circumstances. As such, investigations range from the study of thatch and wood *bohios*, to the analysis of informal settlements in Latin America. While formally and culturally distinct, these subjects exemplify the search for what is most essential, and thus most resilient in architectural form.

The role of the vernacular, and in particular, the influence of popular culture in the shaping of cities and architecture, has been an exceptionally strong tradition at the University of Miami School of Architecture. The projects produced in the series of Vernacularology studios stem from drawing traditions that emerged at the School in the 1990s, just as digital technologies were beginning to replace the time-tested conventions of architectural representation. Some of the most evocative drawings of this period are recorded in Vincent Scully's book Between Two Towers. However, the production of drawings and projects that came to define the School of Miami, as described by Scully, did not end with the publication of the book, but rather continued, nearly uninterrupted in the work of a variety of studios, including the Open City Studio and the first-year core design and drawing courses.[1]

The pedagogical structure of the Open City Studio was inspired by a course taught by Ernesto Rogers at the Polytechnic University of Milan entitled: *The Stylistic and Constructive Characteristics of Monuments*. Rogers' conception of monument stemmed from the etymological origins of the latin word *monere,* which means to remind. In this sense, the term monument had little to do with the conception of high art versus low art or public versus private. Rather it was understood as an artifact, capable of revealing, through its architectural form, a particular people, place, and time. [2]

Rogers' course was structured in two parts: the first was a documentation exercise that analyzed and drew fragments of cities, neighborhoods, and buildings, followed by a project that projected the lessons of the first exercise in the production of a new work of architecture. This structure underscores Rogers' commitment to the role of continuity in architecture as described in his seminal essay, *Continuity or Crisis* (1957). For Rogers, the concept of continuity implied change within the order of a tradition. [3]

Evident in the explanation that follows, the Open City Studio curriculum, added the compositional drawing to the documentation and project. This drawing had the capacity to describe more precisely the American circumstance and was more closely aligned to Latin American artistic traditions that did not abandon the figure in pursuit of modernity, relying on folklore for inspiration as in the case of Fernando Botero and Frida Kahlo in painting or Gabriel Garcia Marquez in literature. The compositional drawing re-assembled the objective elements of documentation, highlighting the salient cultural, urban, and architectural elements that defined a given place.

For nearly three decades, Open City Studio students have examined diverse communities and cultures globally and have described these experiences by way of drawing. Like no other activity in the study of the built environment, the act of drawing describes the shared fundamental qualities of settlement and reveals the constituent formal and visual components inherent in the idea of community and place.

After visiting numerous American and European cities including: Cartagena, Rome, Lisbon, and Stockholm, the Open City Studio shifted its attention to Asia, more specifically the architecture and culture of Japan. These visits were transformative, both in my teaching and in my practice, and exposed me to the rich lineage of the *observationists* and their "obsessive fixation on what's right there, on finding, identifying, collecting, and classifying phenomena in the streets with an entomologist's eye for minute detail." [4]

A kinship with Terunobu Fujimori and Genpei Akasegawa, founders of the Street Observation Society, emerged. They, along with the members of the Society, came together to search for moments of beauty found in ordinary, everyday places. The groups' activities were primarily a fusion of two complementary approaches to looking at the city including: historical fieldwork and the analysis of overlooked buildings throughout urban Japan; and the Dadaist sensibility of identifying and categorizing readymade objects lying latent in the streets of Tokyo.

Vuela Cometa Vuela, Washing station, Las Flores, Barranquilla, Nicki Gitlin and Andrea Gonzalez-Rebull, Vernacularology studio, spring 2015

Vuela Cometa Vuela, Light Court, Las Flores, Barranquilla, Nicki Gitlin and Andrea Gonzalez-Rebull, Vernacularology studio, spring 2015

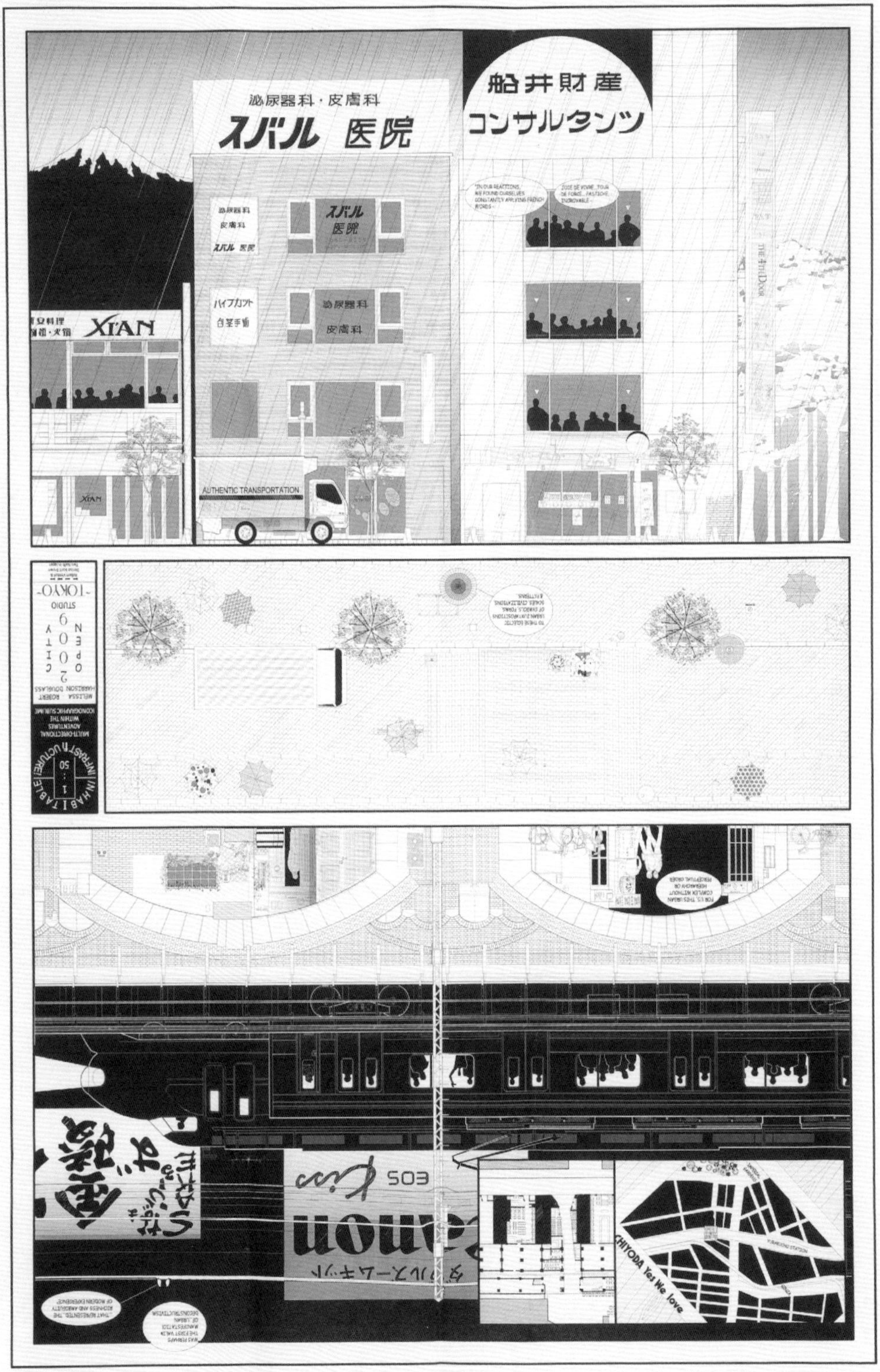


Ginza Infrastructure, Melissa Brillhart and Robert Douglas, Open City Studio, Tokyo 2009

Their interests dovetailed with my own; and I came to understand the quasi - scientific approach towards the study of everyday objects not as an esoteric pursuit but as a meticulous search for identity and character. [5]

Returning to Miami, after numerous visits to Japan, I, alongside Carie Penabad, developed the first Vernacularology studio, focusing on the study of vernacular urbanism in the Global South, more specifically the architectural and urban patterns of Latin America's informal settlements. Since 2008, we have traveled to various Latin American cities with students to learn first-hand about the urban and architectural patterns that define these places as well as the cultural context in which they develop. As explained by Robert Venturi and Denise Scott Brown, "Learning from the existing landscape is a way of being revolutionary for an architect. Not the obvious way, which is to tear down Paris and begin again, as Le Corbusier suggested in the 1920s, but another, more tolerant way; that is to question how we look at things."[6]

In this spirit, we ask students to look indiscriminately at a given place and to understand its cultural context, geographic circumstance, and natural setting, as critical elements that have a defining influence on the configuration and constitution of the work to be produced. Through on-site fieldwork, we meticulously record the existing conditions of the site, both through analog and advanced digital techniques. This documentation effort is not limited to the study of urban design and architecture but extends itself to include culture, oral traditions, folklore, geology, light, shadow, flora and fauna. The documentation is then translated into the production of critical drawings that underscore a phenomenological approach to architecture and inform the development of new architectural and urban design projects.

The drawings, a few depicted here, illustrate these new proposals in context. In the Vernacularology studios, we explore a variety of drawing techniques. We believe in drawing as a means of acquiring architectural knowledge, and are interested in recording the often-times overlooked aspects of place associated with light, shadow, and color. In part, the construction of these drawings informs and highlights our preoccupation with creating works of architecture, both in teaching and in practice, that are sensitized to the particulars of place and time. The drawings challenge the division of high art and popular culture and promote a more fundamental understanding of place that includes the relevance of type, the notion of permanence, the idea of craft, and dare I say, the pursuit of beauty.

1 Here I am referring directly to the 'Drawing and Place' exercises developed for the first year studio in collaboration with Professors Jorge Hernandez and Teofilo Victoria.
2 Aldo Rossi described the content and structure of Rogers' course to Teofilo Victoria, founder of the 'Open City Studio', and Roberto Behar upon his visit to the University of Miami School of Architecture in 1989.
3 Ernesto N. Rogers "Continuity or Crisis?" The Royal Architectural Institute of Canada 393rd ser. 35.5 (1958): 188-89. Originally published in Italian as "'Continuità o Crisi?,'" in Casabella Continuità, n. 215 (April-May 1957) p. 3-4.
4 Jordan Sands. "Open Letter to Gary Thomasson" in *Hyperart: Thomason* by Genpei Akasegawa, Kaya Press, Department of American Studies and Ethnicity, University of Southern California, 2010, p. 392.
5 Daniell, Thomas. "Just Looking, The Origins of the Street Observation Society," *AA Files* 64, Architectural Association School of Architecture, 2012, p. 60-68.
6 Robert Venturi, Denise Scott Brown, Steven Izenour. *Learning from Las Vegas*, Cambridge: MIT Press, 1972, p.3.

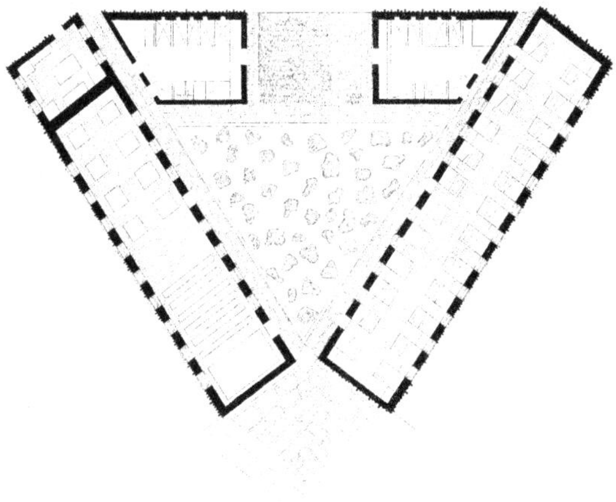

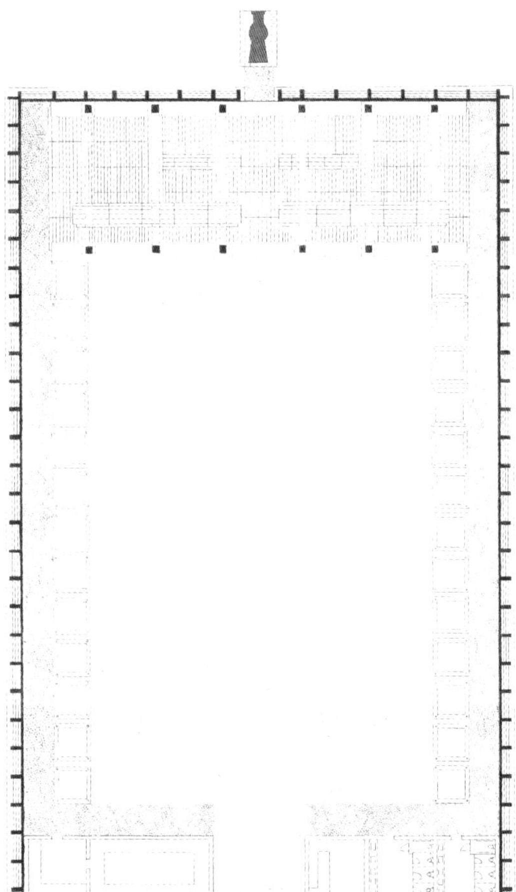

*Top* Troop 7 Boyscout camp, Matheson Hammock, Sofia Kiblisky, plan, pencil on vellum, first year design studio, fall 2016 / *Center* Troop 7 Boyscout camp, Matheson Hammock, Channing Washlesky, plan, pencil on vellum, first year design studio, fall 2016

*Top* Troop 7 Boyscout camp, Matheson Hammock, Sofia Kiblisky, basswood model, first year design studio, fall 2016 / *Center* Troop 7 Boyscout camp, Matheson Hammock, Channing Washlesky, basswood model, first year design studio, fall 2016

Fishery, view and longitudinal section, Las Flores, Barranquilla, Michael O'Neil, Vernacularology studio, spring 2012

Fishery, view and plan, Las Flores, Barranquilla, Michael O'Neil, Vernacularology studio, spring 2012

Fishmarket, Las Flores, Barranquilla, Jose Sarmiento, Claudia Noval, Alexandra Goldstein, Vernacularology studio, spring 2012

Vuela Cometa Vuela, View from the Magdalena River, Las Flores, Barranquilla, Nicki Gitlin and Andrea Gonzalez-Rebull, Vernacularology studio, spring 2015

*This and following page* Vuela Cometa Vuela, Composite drawing, Las Flores, Barranquilla, Nicki Gitlin and Andrea Gonzalez-Rebull, Vernacularology studio, spring 2015

04.

# Featured Projects

68 **CARUSO ST JOHN ARCHITECTS**
*Chiswick House Café*
*Newport St. Gallery*
*Europaallee Baufeld E*
*Bremer Landesbank*

92 **2A + P/A**
*Sottsass's House*
*Maria Grazia Cutuli School*
*Bamiyan Culture Center*
*Nine Square School*
*Le Ciel Bleu*

114 **CÚRE & PENABAD**
*MAG Headquarters*
*Oak Plaza*
*MDO*

136 **OFFICE OF ADRIAN PHIFFER**
*Bauhaus Atlas*
*Helsinki Guggenheim*
*The Ends of the City*
*Superflat*
*The New Museum of Ethnography*
*Urban Apparatus*

170 **SERGISON BATES ARCHITECTS**
*Welcome Centre and Offices*
*City Library*
*Care Home, Huise-Zingem*

182 **JOHNSTON MARKLEE**
*Miami Design District*
*Vault House*
*Chile House*

202 **KHOURY LEVIT FONG**
*Courtyard Mat: SEEH*
*Warp + Woof: The Museum of Underwater Antiquities*

212 **MACHADO SILVETTI**
*The Ruth and Elmer Wellin Museum of Art*

220 **NADAAA**
*New Hampshire Retreat*
*Ordos 20+10*

238 **OFFICE KERSTEN GEERS DAVID VAN SEVEREN**
*OFFICE 90: Agricultural School*
*OFFICE 15: Border Crossing*
*OFFICE 35: Cité de Refuge*
*OFFICE 57: Central Park Turnhout*
*OFFICE 51: 25 Rooms (Villa in Ordos)*
*OFFICE 73: Garden Residence*
*OFFICE 126: Centres for Traditional Music*

256 **PEZO VON ELLRICHSHAUSEN**
*Meri House*
*Guna House*
*Solo House*

276 **R & R STUDIOS / ROBERTO BEHAR & ROSARIO MARQUARDT**
*Valby Square*
*Rosario Library*

284 **PRODUCTORA**
*House of Art and Culture*
*Pavilion for the Culture Fair 2014*
*Central Library*
*Thermal Park in Dolores*
*Contemporary Art Museum*
*CAF Headquartes*

322 **CAVEJA STUDIO**
*Ampliamento Cantina Valpolicella Negrar*
*Nuovo Science Centre di Città della Scienza*

330 **LAURENT DE CARNIÈRE**
*Perpendicular - Guggenheim Museum Helsinki*
*Morland - Port Vertical Metropolitain*
*Terra Incognita*

346 **UHO**
*City of Students*
*Lake Park entrance*
*16 family housing*
*Public Library*

364 **SALOTTOBUONO**
*Delta and Porto Baros Area*
*Civic Center*

372 **MOS**
*House No. 2 (Floating House)*
*Store No. 1 (Miami Facade)*
*House No. 8 (Ramp Hill)*

384 **JAIME CORREA & ASSOCIATES**
*Mobile Stage*
*Red Square*

390 **LOEB SARLI ARCHITECTS**
*Tirana*
*KJPK*

398 **LEDERER RAGNARSDÓTTIR OEI**
*'Annexe to the annexe' of the Sparkasse*

# CARUSO ST JOHN ARCHITECTS

London, United Kingdom

### Chiswick House Café

*London, United Kingdom, 2006–2010*

The new café is part of the regeneration of the life of the Gardens, and has been designed as a meeting place, a kind of social hub for the park. It is sited between Chiswick House and the Italian Garden, at the confluence of several busy paths, and the temple-like form of the building is a response to this central situation. The arcaded elevations on three sides make a special place to gather, to enjoy the scenery and look out for your friends. The lawns around the café and the new adjacent playground provide outdoor playspace for more energetic members of the family, while others can enjoy sitting out in the sun with their tea and cake.

Chiswick House and its gardens, as well as being one of London's loveliest parks, were the site of very important artistic innovations in architecture and landscape design. To make a new building here is a once-in-a-lifetime opportunity. The design is more elegant and classical than most park cafés, which are more usually rustic, informal or housed in converted out-buildings. The atmosphere of the new cafe responds to the picturesque grandeur of Burlington and Kent's vision, with its references to the ruins, the shapely trees and the vistas in the Campagna around ancient Rome. Just like the classical pavilions that form focal points for scenes within the Georgian garden, the new café is a white pavilion that draws the eye and makes a composition with the surrounding trees.

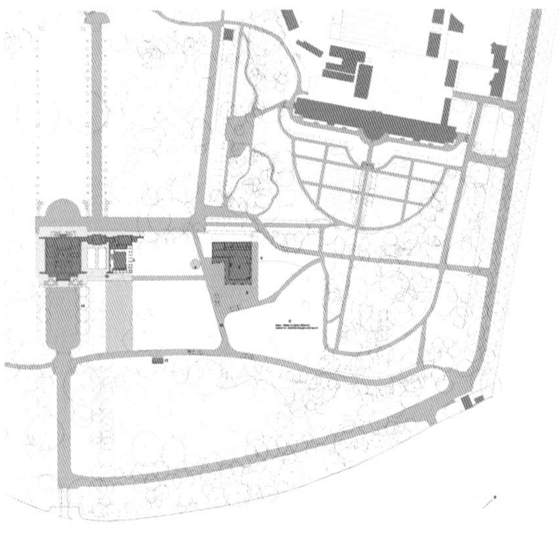

The project has involved careful consideration of the site of the building, and its effect on the parkland around it. The site is immediately adjoining Kent's gardens, where Burlington's Jacobean house and stables were once located. There was a smaller café from the 60s here before, which stood further to the south and was more isolated from the gardens around by dense evergreen woodland. Trees have been removed and the area feels more connected to the rest of the park. The new café with its southern aspect can now be seen from a distance as you approach it, between the rounded shapes of mature chestnut and willow trees.

At the center of the café is a large glazed room, which seats up to 80 people. The wide aspect from here includes newly opened-up views back to the portico of the House. A much larger number of people can also sit outside, on the forecourt and within the arcade which wraps around the façade. The wide piers of the arcade chase each other around the perimeter of the plan, to give a slightly labyrinthine effect that encloses the café interior. The piers are made of stacked blocks of Roachbed Portland stone. Its wild fossils and deep cavities are miniature versions of the primitive rockwork in the grottos that were popular in 18th century English gardens.

The scale of the arcade and its smooth masonry finishes refer to more recent Italian architectures. In particular, the arcades of 19th century Turin that are beautiful, cool places to take your lunch in summer, and Milanese cafes from the 1950s, where material luxury, and a sophistication in how masonry and metal are put together, make elegant places to sit and have a coffee.

Client: English Heritage.
Photography: Hélène Binet.

*Opposite page* Site plan / *Above* Exterior view / *Below left & right* Colonnade

*Above* Colonnade/ *Below* Ground floor plan & Interior / *Opposite page* Colonnade

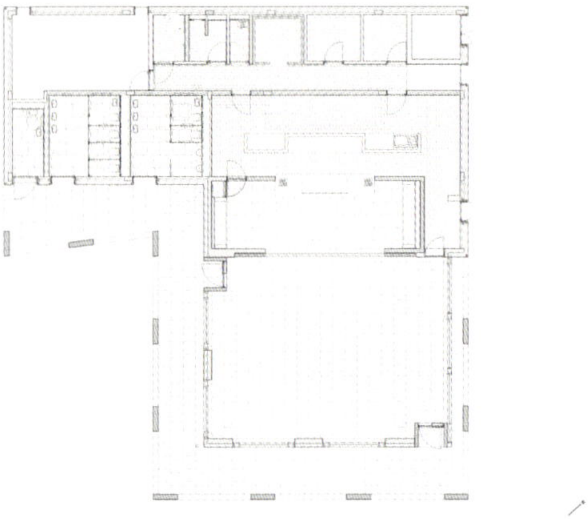

**Newport St. Gallery**

*London, United Kingdom, 2004–2015*

This private gallery in Vauxhall has involved the conversion of an extraordinary terrace of listed industrial buildings, that were formerly theatre carpentry and scenery painting workshops. The gallery forms the whole length of the street, with the three listed Victorian buildings flanked at either end by new buildings. The ground and upper floors within the five buildings are continuous, allowing them to be used flexibly in many combinations, to accommodate both large and small exhibitions. There are 3 large galleries on each of the two floors, stretching in a line from one end of the building to the other. The two gallery levels are connected by new spiral staircases and a large lift.

Along Newport Street and facing toward the railway, the unusual proportions of the Victorian workshops, with their groups of low level windows and high blank walls above, have been continued in the design of the new buildings. The new facades are made with a hard pale red brick that closely matches the surface of the listed buildings. The five buildings next to each other, all different but obviously related, make a sheer and impressive street elevation.

The plans include a restaurant and administrative offices for the gallery. The building will show exhibitions of the client's extensive collection of contemporary art, and will be open to the public for free.

Client: Science Ltd.
Photography: Hélène Binet.

*Opposite page* Building in context / *Above* Exterior view / *Below left* Facade detail / *Below right* Exterior view / *Following spread* Aerial view

NEWPORT STREET GALLERY

*Opposite page* Stair / *Above & Below* Exhibition space

## Europaallee Baufeld E

*Zurich, Switzerland, 2007–2013*

This project won first prize in the invited competition for a 30,000sq m mixed use building of commercial space and housing. The project is located on a key site within the masterplan for the redevelopment of former railway land on the south side of Zurich Hauptbahnhof by the SBB (Swiss National Railways). The project is one of several large new buildings to be constructed along the planned Europaallee, a street running through the center of the masterplan leading southwest from the main station.

The unusual mixed program for the site comprises retail space on the ground floor with offices and apartments above, and is an opportunity to make a truly metropolitan building at a prominent corner location within the masterplan. The building is arranged with five floors of commercial space on the lower levels, with the upper part emerging as two apartment towers 13 and 11 stories in height. The complex figure has something of the qualities of the classic urban buildings of Manhattan from the 1910s and 20s. Like the New York examples, this individual expressiveness is reconciled with the continuity that is required, in the massing of the lower floors and in the tectonic of the pre-cast concrete facades, to make a good piece of city.

In collaboration with Bosshard Vaquer Architects.
Client: SBB.
Photography: Hélène Binet (interiors) & Georg Aerni (exterior views).

*Opposite page below* Site plan / *Opposite page above* Exterior view / *Above* Entrance / *Below* Plans / *Following spread* Building in context

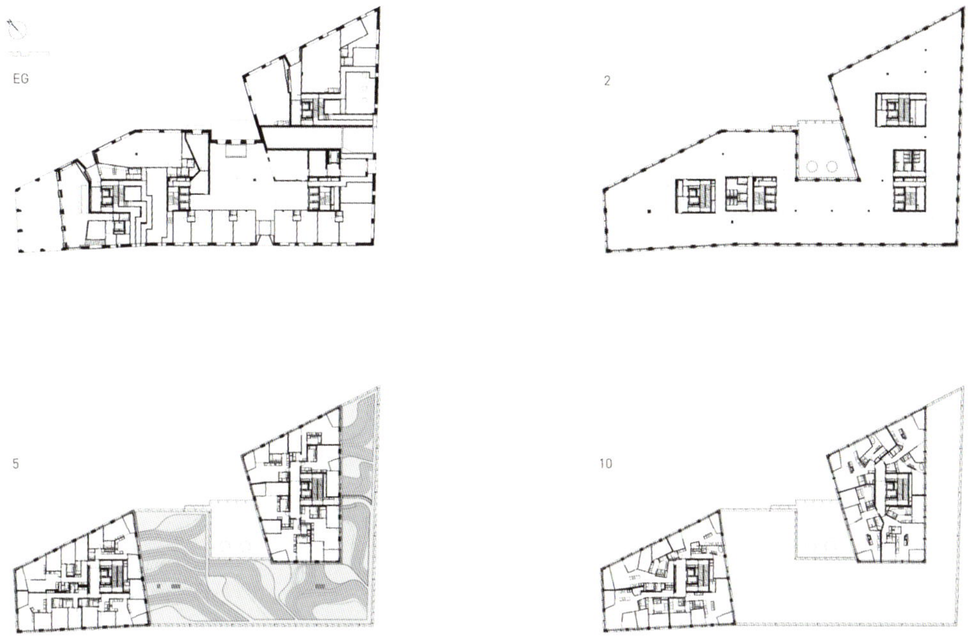

*Above* Entrance / *Below* Facade, Renderings / *Opposite page* Corner detail

*Opposite page below* Section / *Above* Interiors / *Below* Balcony

## Bremer Landesbank

*Bremen, Germany, 2011-2016*

What should a Bank look like today? How should it project its identity within the surrounding city? Amongst the structures gathered together at Bremen's historic temple district, from the Romanesque spire of the cathedral, to the merchant's houses along the edge of the flower market, the Bank should stand like a city elder, taking its place amongst the other important figures. With its close proximity to the mediaeval Town Hall and the Cathedral, the Bank should be a dignified and reserved figure, but above all it should have an open and honest face. The design invests a lot of care in the face of the new Bremer Landesbank, which looks at the Cathedral across the Domshof. A very large doorway marks the public entrance to the building, leading to a large banking hall on the corner of the square.

The facades of the Bremer Landesbank refer to a Northern European tradition of expressive brick construction, where dark, hard clinker bricks form piers, buttresses and ornamental friezes - dressing the building in a thick masonry skin. The elevations have a vertical Gothic character, simultaneously monolithic and delicate, referring to the Wesserenaisance of the Bremen Rathaus and the Stadtwaage, and generally to a Hanseatic tradition of quality and reserve. Within the vertical grain of the external wall, expressive brick doorways mark the entrances for the clients and the staff.

The identity of the bank is not only in its facades, but also in its public interiors and its internal layout. The new building has a large courtyard at its centre that gives a simple and generous image to its organization. All offices face out to the city or inwards to this courtyard. Unusually, this central space is not an atrium, but is open to the sky and has its floor at pavement level. The space acts as a forecourt, and is semi-public, forming an extended threshold to the office entrance. Internal arrangements are very flexible, allowing for the maximum number of individual offices on each floor, each with an opening window. The large staff restaurant and the private client reception rooms of the bank are located on the top floor. From the restaurant, the five hundred staff can enjoy the extraordinary views over the roof of the city.

Client: Bremer Landesbank.
Photography: Hélène Binet.

*Above* Facade / *Below* Plans

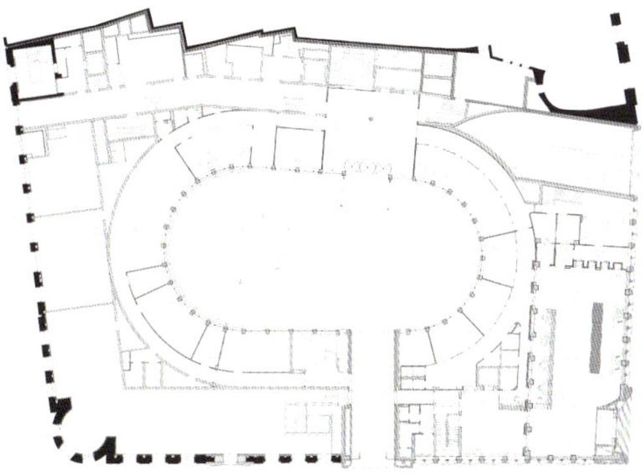

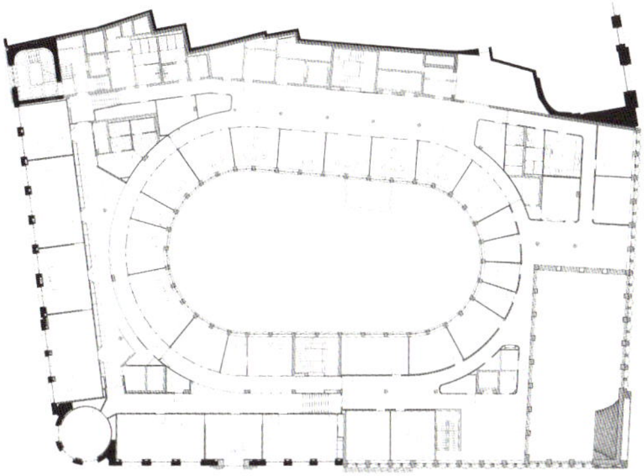

*Opposite page* Facade detail / *Above* Entrance detail / *Below* Elevation, Rendering

*Above* Interior / *Below left* Sections of door detail / *Below right* Section / *Opposite page* Central Yard

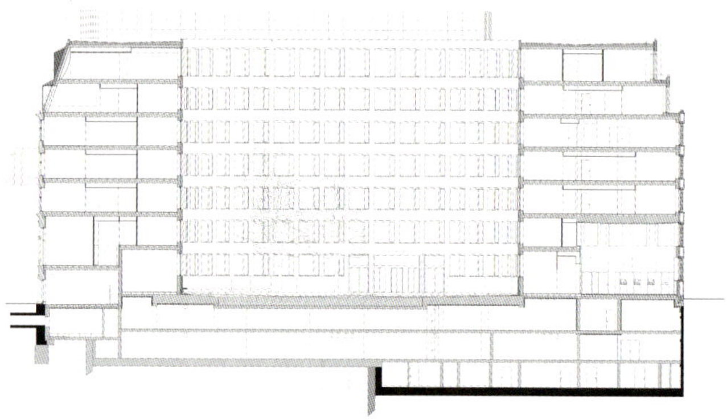

# 2A + P/A

Rome, Italy

**Sottsass's House**

*The House From A Drawing Of Ettore Sottsass*

*Research, 2012*

The project creates an exchange across time with the work of Ettore Sottsass. For us, Sottsass' mysterious yet highly expressive design was full of promise and open for development. Both the function and the context of the original project were unspecified. However, we do know that Sottsass made the drawing at his vacation home on the Italian island of Filicudi. Consequently, we interpreted the drawing as a house, located on an island overlooking the sea.

Design Team: Gianfranco Bombaci and Matteo Costanzo.
Photography: Antonio Ottomanelli.

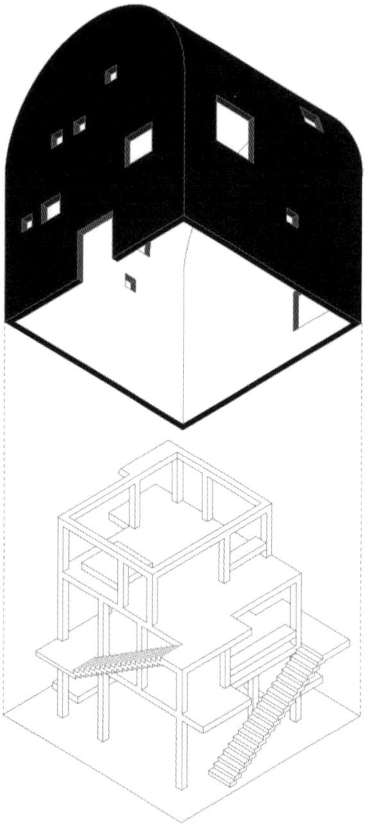

*Left* Axonometric / *Opposite page* Architettura monumentale, axonometric drawing by Ettore Sottsass, courtesy Gallery Antonia Jeannine

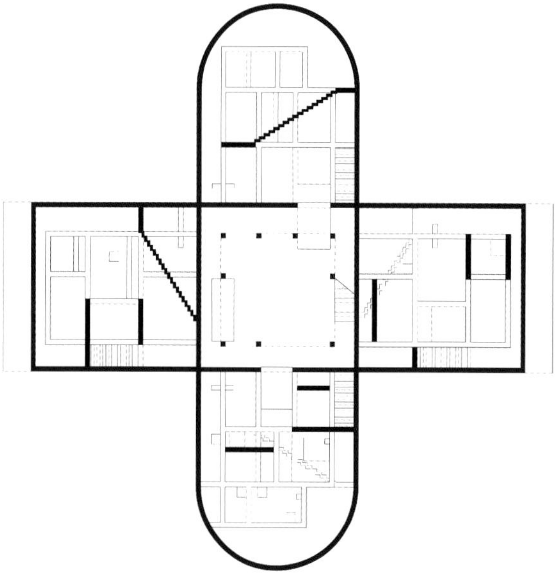

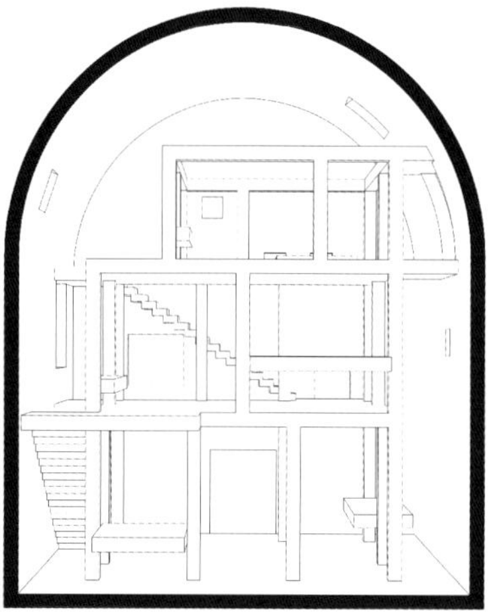

*Opposite page above* Composite Drawing / *Opposite page below* Section Perspective / *Above & Below* Diptych /*Following spread* Model in the landscape

*Opposite page above* Model in the landscape / *Opposite page below* Exterior, Collage / *Above* Interior, Collage

**Maria Grazia Cutuli School**

*Herat, Afghanistan, 2011*

Built in honor of Italian journalist Maria Grazia Cutuli, murdered in Afghanistan in 2001, this school represents an alternative approach to emergency school design for war-torn areas. Conceived as a small village, the complex is intended to resemble an unplanned juxtaposition of elements enclosed by a boundary wall. The project accommodates eight classrooms, various administrative offices, a double-height library, and a garden that acts as a 'green classroom'. Both external and internal spaces contribute to the shaping of the educational environment.

Built of reinforced concrete with brick cladding, the structures are painted rather than cladded for cost savings. The wall's range of blue tones is a 'lapis lazuli' pigment used in the production of local pottery, while window frames are in a contrasting red.

Design Team: Gianfranco Bombaci and Matteo Costanzo with Mario Cutuli, IaN+, ma0.
Client: Fondazione M. G. Cutuli.
Photography: Gianfranco Bombaci, Antonio Ottomanelli and Giovanna Silva.

*Opposite page* Floor plan / *Above* Courtyard view. Photograph by Antonio Ottomanelli / *Below* Exterior with school children. Photograph by Gianfranco Bombaci

*Opposite page & Above* Aerial views / *Below* Axonometric / *Following spread* Courtyard view. Photograph by Giovanna Silva

**Bamiyan Culture Center**

*Bamiyan, Afghanistan, 2015*

The Bamiyan Cultural Center should be a timeless building, a space able to interpret the desires and needs of a community. The primary ambition of the building's architecture is to be a place of collective knowledge, a place of cultural sharing that preserves and promotes the heritage of Afghanistan. The Bamiyan Cultural Center has been designed as an open building that, through its system of spaces, provides a direct connection with the natural landscape of the Bamiyan Valley.

Design team: 2A+P/A (Gianfranco Bombaci, Matteo Costanzo) with Tommaso Arcangioli Architetto.

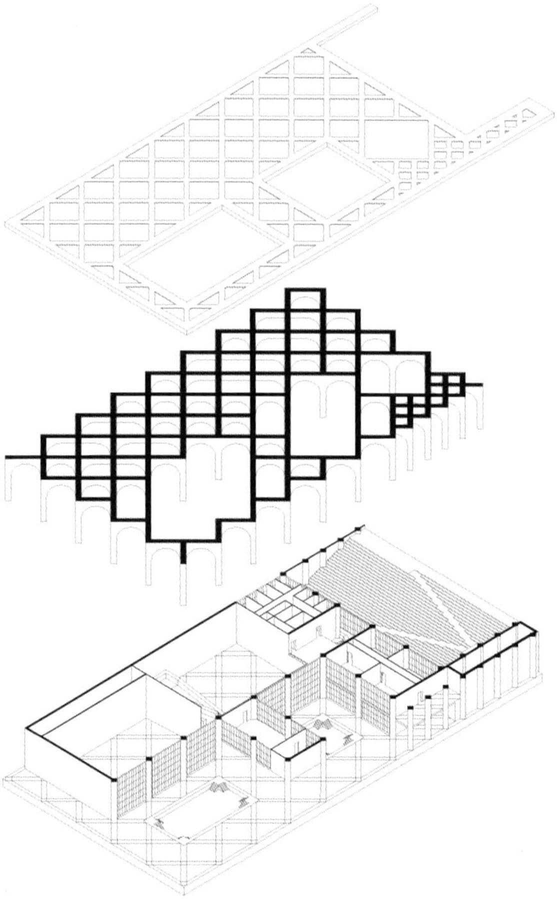

*Opposite page* Exploded Axonometric diagram / *Above* Courtyard, Collage / *Below* Entrance, Collage

*Above* Exterior corridor, Collage / *Below* Section Perspective / *Opposite page* Exhibition space, Collage

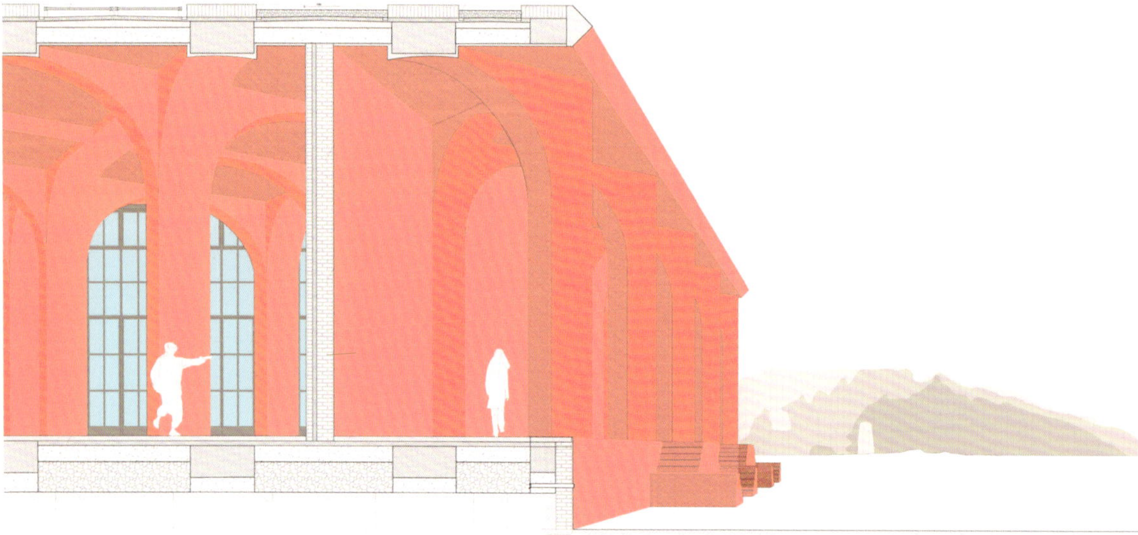

## Nine Square School

*Bellinzona, Switzerland, 2015*

The project involved the whole campus in Bellinzona, reconsidering the masterplan and improving the energy efficiency of the secondary school. The idea behind the new kindergarten is to break down the program by identifying the main elements: teaching units, functional areas of the kitchen and service, common spaces for canteen and for activities. All these elements have been incorporated within a fenced and protected area, and divided, through a system of covered and open corridors, in nine different gardens.

Design team: Gianfranco Bombaci and Matteo Costanzo.

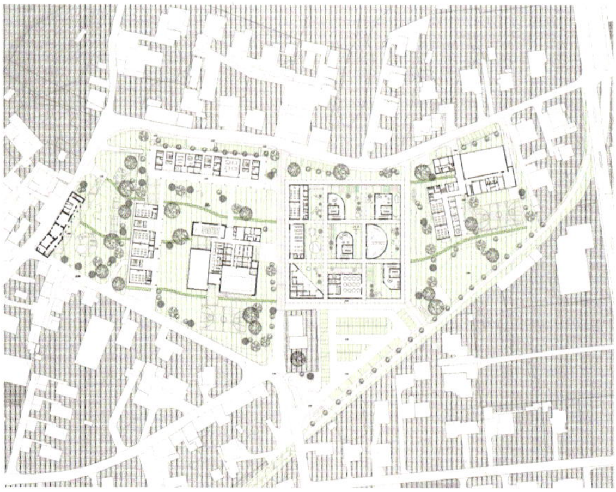

*Opposite page above* Garden, collage & exterior, Collage / *Opposite page below* Model & Site plan / *Above* Entrance, Collage / *Below* Axonometric

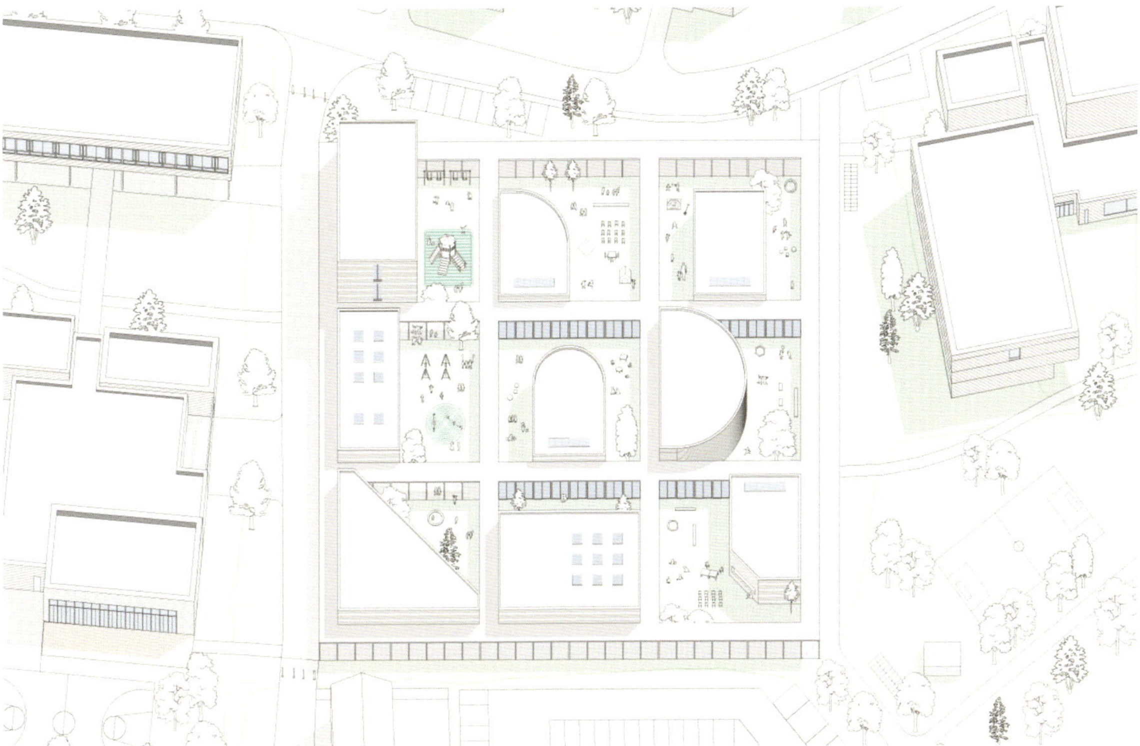

**Le Ciel Bleu**

*Thonex, Geneve, Switzerland, 2012*

The project organizes three buildings around an open court. An "L" shaped paved area defines a square, while the inner part of the court maintains its natural aspect and becomes a park with paths and leisure areas. One of the buildings is dedicated to housing for the elderly, and is organized by a gallery, which is not just a distribution space, but also a shared place for socializing. At each level the gallery is fully opened to the park. The groundfloor hosts the common facilities. The other two buildings are social housing units with commercial spaces at the groundfloor. The facades, opened to the inner courtyard, are characterized by a geometric grid that reflects the structural framework and defines a series of loggias for each apartment. Loggias work as solar greenhouses and extend the living rooms, creating wintergreens that everyone can customize.

Design team: Gianfranco Bombaci, Matteo Costanzo.

*Opposite page above* Model / *Opposite page below* Plans / *Above* Courtyard, Collage / *Below* Park view, Collage

## CÚRE & PENABAD

Miami, Florida, United States

**MAG Headquarters**

*Escuintla, Guatemala, 2015*

Can a building change the culture of a company? Can the design of the physical environment impact the way in which we communicate? These are a few of the questions that the project for the new MAG headquarters analyzed and attempted to address. Currently, the MAG Corporation is housed in a series of detached structures situated on a large tract of agricultural land in southern Guatemala. This configuration reinforces a separation of departments and limits the individual employee's ability to understand his or her role within the company. To reverse this condition, the new building is designed as a singular structure with a large open room, capable of accommodating 450 employees. The plan provides a variety of environments (both interior and exterior) for productive individual or collaborative work. Its overall form is inspired by both vernacular and industrial building

*Above* Building in the landscape / *Below* Model

typologies seen throughout the Guatemalan countryside.

Design Team: Adib Cúre, Carie Penabad, Carlos Berrios, Albert Rodriguez, Catherine O'Sullivan, David Chessrown, Nicolas Delgado Alcega, Michael Galea, Michael O'Neil, Victoria Pineros.
Client: Ingenio Magdalena.
Consultants: ARUP Engineers, Basulto and Associates.
Photography: Carlos Domenech.

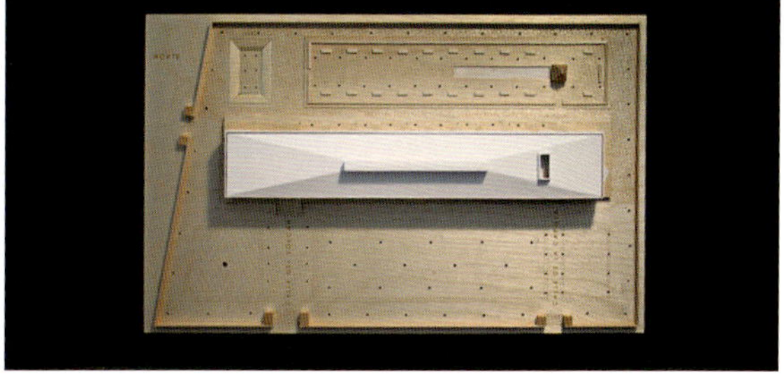

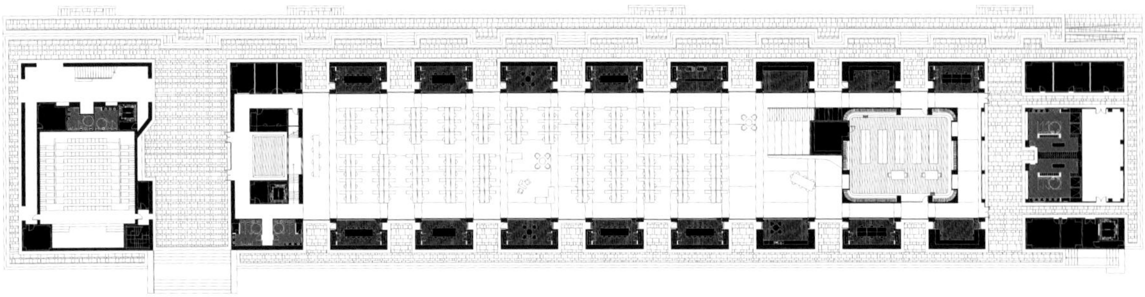

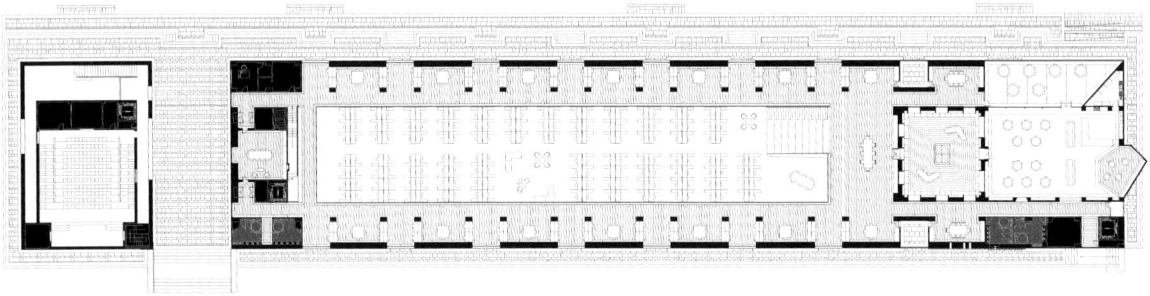

*Opposite page above* First floor and second floor plan / *Opposite page below* "The Eternal Present", drawing / *Above* Night view / *Below left* "Day of the Zafra", collage / *Below right* "Garden Chapel", Collage

*Above* Framed view of landscape from cafeteria / *Below left* Entry passage with company's first molino / *Below right* Covered passage with view of sugarcane fields and Agua Volcano / *Opposite page* Work room

*Above* View of work room from second floor/ *Below left* Longitudinal section / *Below right* Cross section / *Opposite page* Model

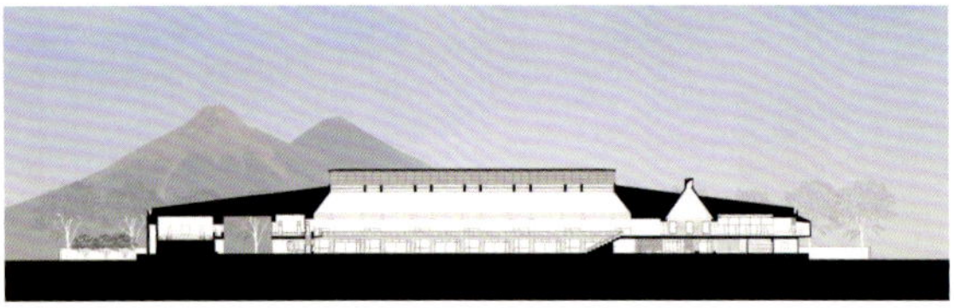

## Oak Plaza

*Miami, Florida, USA, 2007 (demolished, 2013)*

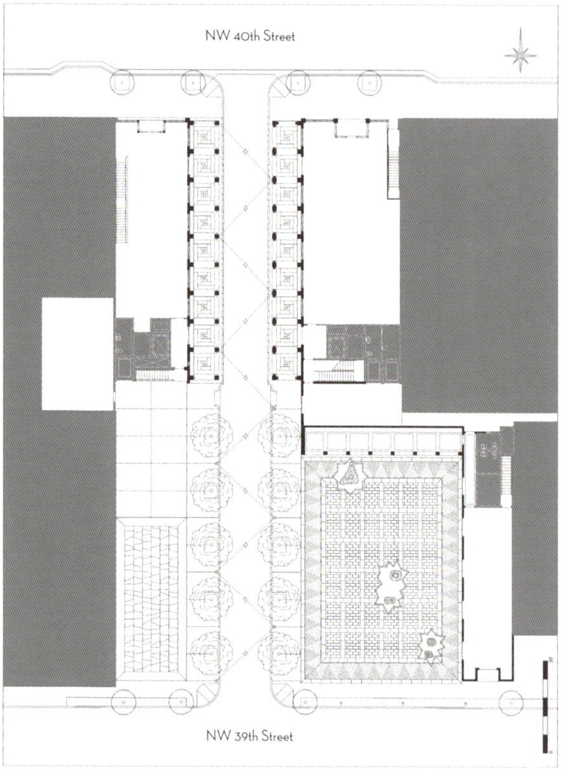


The district in which the infill project takes place is a unique, 18 block community located just north of downtown Miami. This neighborhood, long forgotten during the periods when suburban sprawl became the standard pattern of growth in the city, is now experiencing a dramatic urban renewal. While the district has already attracted leading retailers it has yet to contain the elements necessary to create a vibrant neighborhood. Currently, the district is absent of public spaces which can serve to provide a sense of identity and a place of congregation for the community.

The Oak Plaza project aspired to define a true center for the district by creating the first public space in the neighborhood. The design transformed an existing parking lot with a stand of mature white oaks, into a paved plaza of Caribbean limestone, lined by a thin retail building and an adjacent loggia. The walls of the building were clad in an undulating pattern of green and blue glass mosaic tiles that transformed the ordinary masonry surfaces into a vibrant urban mural. While small in scale, the project strove to define a coherent urban and architectural vision for the neighborhood in the belief that architecture is first and foremost a Civic Art.

Design Team: Adib Cúre, Carie Penabad, Carlos Berrios, Albert Rodriguez, Alvaro Briganti, Abraham Aluicio
Client: Dacra Development.
Photography: Steven Brooke and Corey Weimer (p. 125).
Masterplan with Khoury & Vogt Architects.

*Below* Location map /
*Above right* Site plan /*Opposite page* Loggia. Photograph by Steven Brooke

*Opposite page above* View of plaza from proposed street. Photograph by Corey Weimer / *Opposite page below* Entrance Mosaic detail / *Above* Mosaic detail

**MDO**

*Miami, Florida, USA, 2011*

The MDO building is situated along southwest 84th Street, one lot south of Tamiami Trial. Its immediate context is defined by a myriad of strip shopping malls and speculative office buildings set hundreds of feet from the main road to accommodate expansive surface parking lots. The result is a cacophony of structures that is emblematic of Miami's suburban landscape.

MDO reverses the typical urban patterns of the area by pressing the building close to the street and placing the surface parking lot along the rear of the property. Moreover, it sets itself in sharp contrast to its immediate neighbors by developing an architectural language of abstraction and restraint- where a few important elements, such as the recessed entry with its shop-front window, are set within large expanses of mute white walls that house nearly five thousand men's suits within.

The main double-volume retail space is the central focus of the building. Its thickened walls are lined with stacked rows of merchandise and its ceiling is composed of modified pre-fabricated double tees. The heightened volume is an unexpected spatial experience flooded with natural light and in direct opposition to the cavernous artificially-lit interiors, characteristic of the adjacent strip malls and office parks.

Design Team: Adib Cúre, Carie Penabad, Carlos Berrios, Albert Rodriguez, Alvaro Briganti, Johnson Montoya, Juan Quintana (contractor).
Client: Peter and Amy Nunez.
Photography: Steven Brooke and Catherine O'Sullivan.

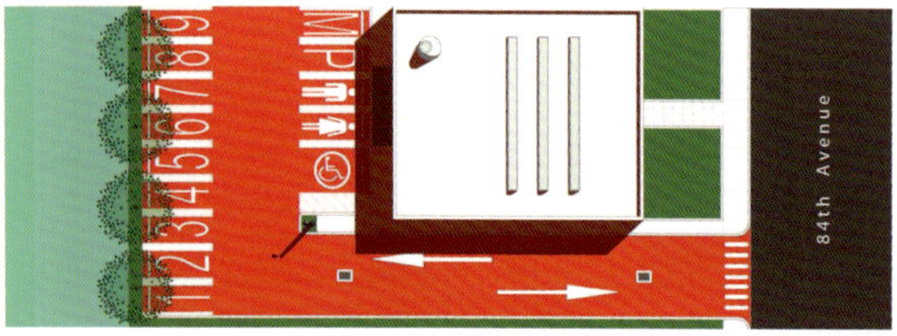

*Opposite page* Site plan / *Above & Below* East & West elevations. Photograph by Steven Brooke

IMDI

*Opposite page* Exterior view. Photograph by Steven Brooke / *Above* Elevation drawing, oil pastel on trace / *Below* Sketch, gauche on trace paper

*Below* Side elevation & First and second floor plan / *Bottom* Longitudinal section / *Opposite page* Circular window. Photograph by Catherine O'Sullivan / *Following spread* Night view from 8th street. Photograph by Catherine O'Sullivan

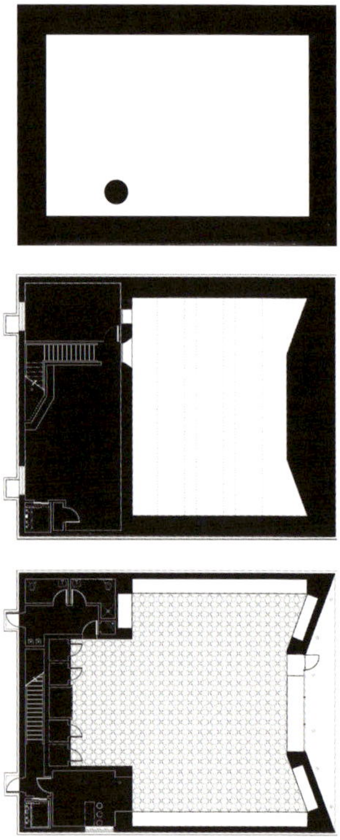

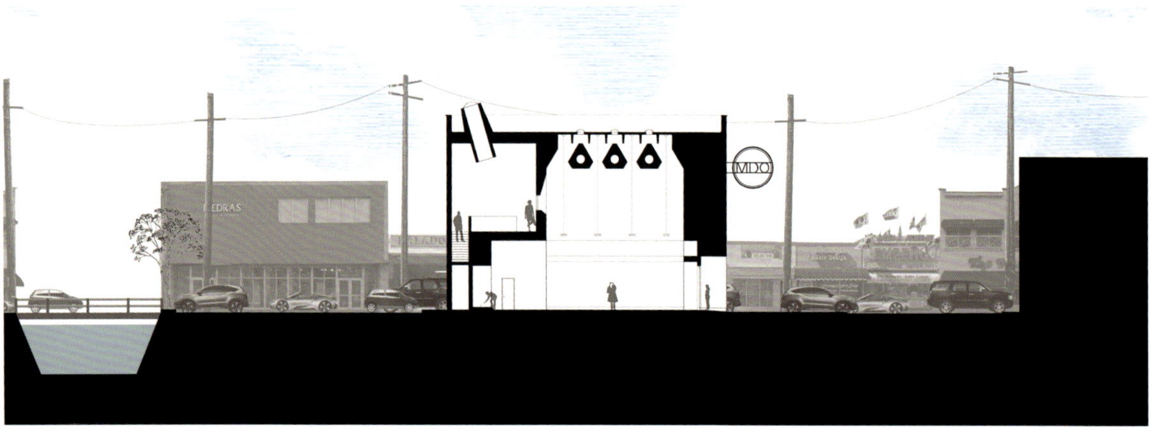

ATRY
PODIATRY
SW 8 ST
ITALIAN
STYLE
SUITS

MDC

# OFFICE OF ADRIAN PHIFFER

Toronto, Canada

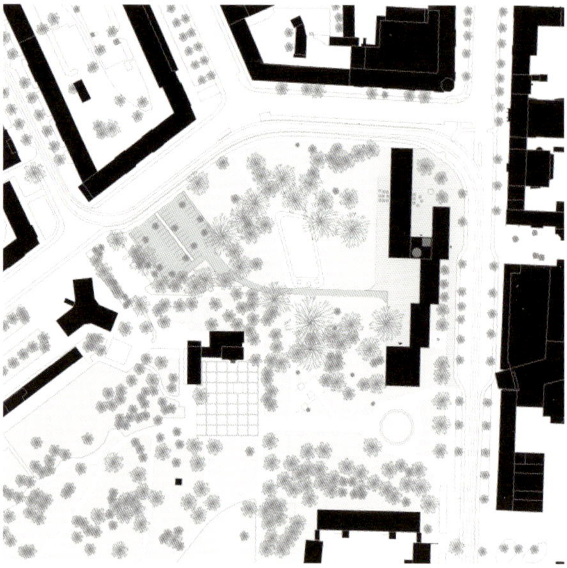

**Bauhaus Atlas**

*Bauhaus Dessau Museum Design Competition*
*Dessau, Germany, 2015*

An atlas is a collection of objects/images arranged according to a narrative. What is interesting about the concept of "atlas" is that everything, both objects and narrative itself, is alive; there is no dead element. An atlas is an open-ended composition.

The objects (architectural) we are arranging are obvious, almost to the point of being literal: the shifting volume of Meyer's Allgemeiner Deutscher Gewerkschaftsbund (1930); the uncompromised long volumes of Mies (1929), the bridge and tower like condition at Bauhaus Dessau (1926) by Gropius.

The narrative is two-fold. On the one hand, it follows the Bauhaus thinking of creating an efficient object, without losing sight of what one might call "good proportions" or "beauty". On the other hand, the narrative for our project creates a responsible act of urban continuity with the immediate site and the whole city of Dessau.

Bauhaus is not a terminated concept, but one that is very much alive and still relevant today. Our proposal is a Bauhaus Atlas.

Client: Foundation Bauhaus Dessau.
Credits: Dimitri Karopoulos, Adrian Phiffer, Goldie Schlaff.

*Opposite page below* Elevation, view from passage, Rendering / *Opposite page above* Site plan / *Above* Entrance, Rendering / *Below left* Interior, Rendering / *Below right* Axonometric, Rendering / *Following spread* View of entrance from street, Rendering

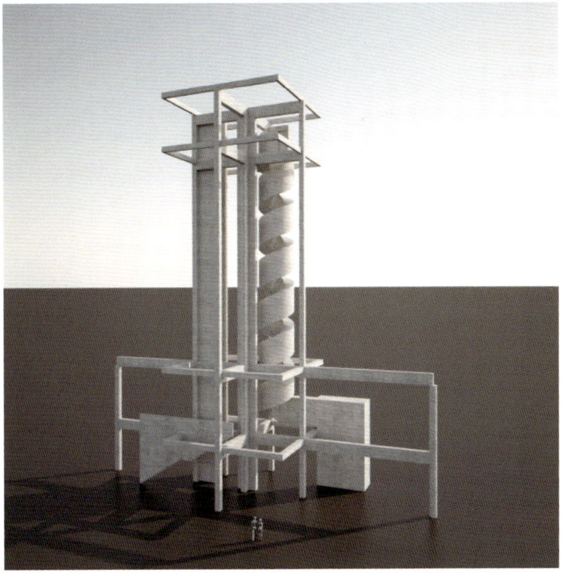

DESSAU

## Helsinki Guggenheim

*Helsinki, Finland, 2014*

Over the past few decades the Guggenheim Foundation has introduced a new way of bringing art into mass society by thinking of the private museum as a public event. The design of the Guggenheim museum in Helsinki offers an opportunity to further develop this approach by questioning the conventional idea of the museum building.

The project proposes to host the new Guggenheim Helsinki in a refurbished cargo ship, leaving the allocated site as an open-air museum linked to Tähtitorninvuoren Park. The cargo ship challenges the building's hegemony in exhibiting art. It questions authorship in the design and use of public space, moving away from useless oppositions such as iconic or political, global or local, container or content, fixed or moving.

Recent Guggenheim museums have explored questions regarding the hierarchy between exhibition spaces and artworks. The ship blurs the content-container friction and questions another current ideology: the "white box" as neutral and flat exhibition space. The ship interiors are not neutral. The unpredictable interaction among exhibition spaces, artworks, and places defines Guggenheim Helsinki's unique character.

Collaborators: Roberto Damiani, Tom Ngo, Adrian Phiffer.

Opposite page "Waiting for the bride", Rendering / Top A summer day in Helsinki & View of proposed Guggenheim Helsinki museum from Mainland, Rendering / Above Guggenheim Helskinki in Tallin, Rendering / Below Harbour presence & Guggenheim Helskinki in Copenhagen, Rendering / Following spread Aerial view, Rendering

*Opposite page above* Sol Lewit multi-floor installation, Rendering / *Opposite page below* Parkspace, Rendering / *Above* Temporary Exhibition Room, Rendering

**The Ends of the City**

*Europan 13 Competition, Second Place Prize*
*Nacka, Stockholm, Sweden, 2015*

Whilst many contemporary urban themes converge on the Nacka site: how to build the post-oil city, how to build the edge of the city, how to re-adapt industrial sites into domesticated urban areas, how to plan a highly adaptable city, and so on, our proposal brings to light an almost forgotten aspect of urban planning: the resilience of urban forms in time.

We prefer to start our project from the most basic condition of the site—the ground. Stripped of any built form, the site presents itself in a "naked" position revealing a complex collection of plateaus where different urban realities can be imagined. The proposed plan accepts the fragmented nature of the ground and takes it as a theme. Each plateau seems to dictate how it should be developed. This understanding of the site informs the basis for a design made up of solitary urban moments that vary in type.

The diversity of building types deployed on the site becomes a strategy in itself for addressing the requirements of adaptability for unpredictable futures. While determined by their relationship to the plateaus they occupy, the buildings vary considerably in scale. Conceived mainly for residential occupancy, their ground floors allow for multiple uses, while the overall dimensions are generic enough to permit re-adaptation from housing to labour or public functions.

Beyond the use of arcades, there is no fixed form or architectural vocabulary. These are subjective, depending on the project in question and allow for great individual freedom in the choice of materials and style. The matrix of open spaces is composed of well-established types: the plaza, the street, the courtyard, the backyard, the arcade, and the boardwalk. Above everything, our proposal emphasizes the collective and the public realm.

Collaborators: Dimitrios Karopoulos, Liusaidh Macdonald, Adrian Phiffer.

*Above* Interior perspective, Collage / *Below* Perspective, Collage

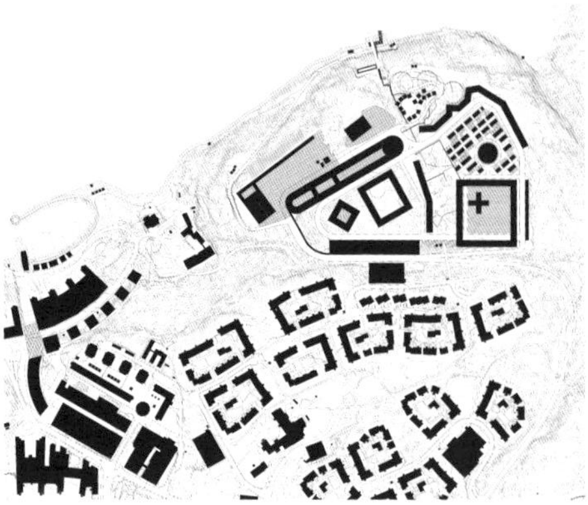

*Opposite page above* Site model & Site plan / *Opposite page below* View to Nacka from the water, model / *Below* View of market hall, model

*Opposite page* Yard, Collage / *Above* Boardwalk, Collage / *Below* Arcades, Collage

*Opposite page* Model / *Above & below* Detailed model

**Superflat, The Museum of the 20th Century and its urban integration**

*Competition*

*Berlin, Germany, 2015- 2016*

Faced with the presence of iconic and historically charged neighbors, the addition of a new architectural program for the Neue National Galerie is a project determined by its context. The design proposes to build a distinct architecture and landscape for the Neue National Galerie complex without overwhelming the established architectural and urban assemblage. The new exhibition architecture and plaza choreograph existing spaces and views while confidently joining the ensemble of architectural monuments initiated by Hans Scharoun and Mies van der Rohe. The new exhibition spaces define the edge of the Neue National Galerie Platz and strengthen the axis along Potsdamer Strasse. The Neue Nationalgalerie Platz and Complex, is viewed as the central gathering space for the adjacent cultural facilities, the Kulturforum more generally, and as a public platform for all Berliners.

The form of the new exhibition architecture is generated by the constraints of the site. A long, thin, vertical wedge addresses Potsdamer Strasse on its east façade while participating in generating a new public plaza along its western façade. Coordinating with the existing adjacent architecture, the addition creates a fourth facade for the central open space, redefining it as a collection of outdoor rooms- the Neue Nationalgalerie Platz.

The exhibition spaces are arranged as a vertical museum. Ensuring a minimal footprint and a strong central public plaza and park, the new building layers program vertically and horizontally into a slender wedge. Its presence as a vertical surface establishes an identity appropriate for such an ambitious work of architecture. The gallery's entry promenades define three outdoor rooms that together form the Neue NationalGalerie Platz. The plaza facing the existing Neue NationalGalerie , and the plaza that slopes down to the new secondary entrance, are resolved through stairs with long threads and short rises. The plaza facing the Philharmonie is a continuous ramp. Platforms are introduced into the sloped promenades for the exhibition of large sculptures. The ramps and terraces participate in the urban scenography of the site, each surface offering the backdrop for either the Philharmonie or the existing Neue Nationalgalerie.

Collaborators: Dimitrios Karopoulos, Liusaidh Macdonald, Adrian Phiffer, Trent Thompson.
Consultants: Landscape: Francesco Martire {large [medium] design office}.
Graphics: Mina Hanna, Sophie Tremblay.
Text: Kevin Murray.
Translation: Goldie Schlaff.

*Opposite page* Site model / *Above* Museum model / *Below left* Site plan / *Below right* View across Mies' Neue Galerie, model

*Above* Podium, Collage / *Below* Section / *Opposite page above* Museum framing Church, Collage / *Opposite page center* Frontal , Collage / *Opposite page below* Elevation

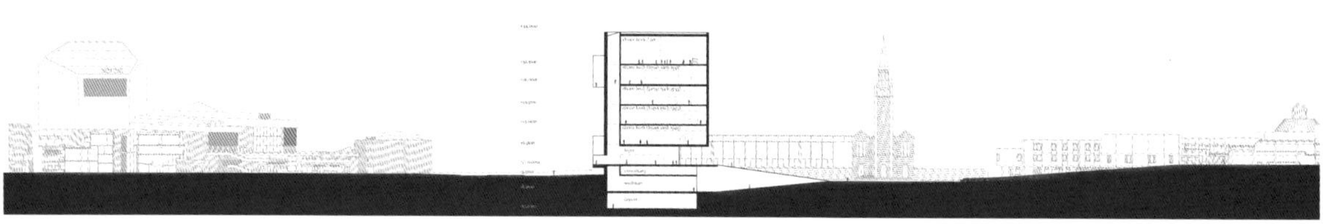

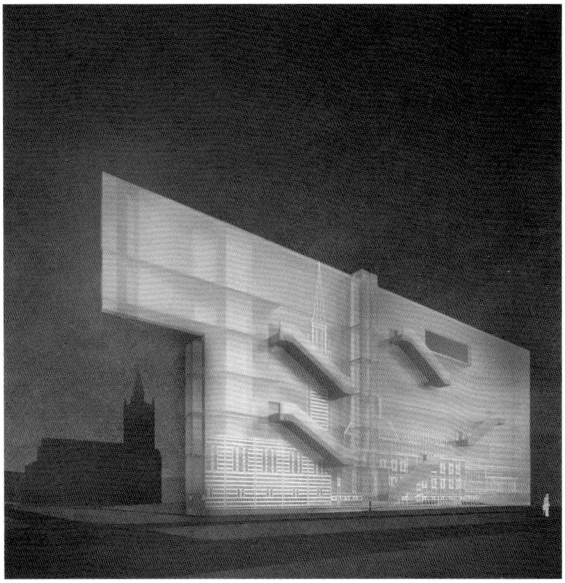

*Above left* Sharp Corner, Collage / *Above right* Perspective of proposed museum, Collage / *Below* Site plan / *Opposite page* Interior perspective, Collage

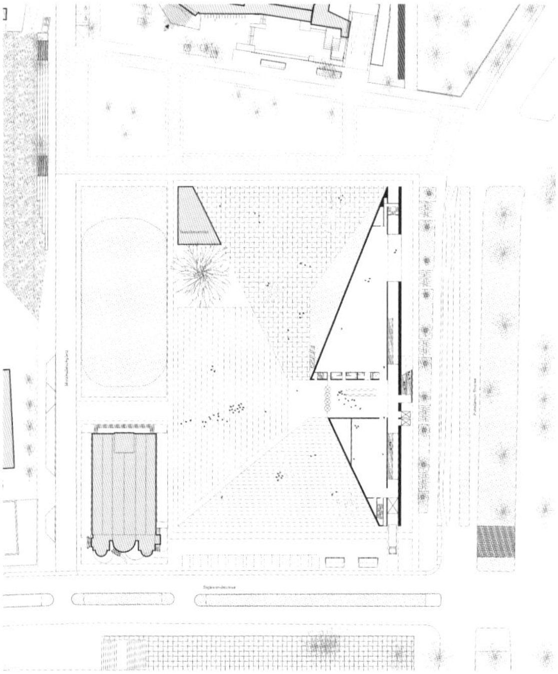

**The New Museum of Ethnography**

*Competition*

*Budapest, Hungary, 2014*

The New Museum of Ethnography takes shape from simple extrusions with manageable spans. This allows for the use of traditional building technologies without undermining flexibility and spatial quality.

The repetition of well-established types (tower, podium, courtyard, arcade) in a compact composition follows the concept of economies of scope rather than scale. The inherent efficiency of the proposal lies thus not only in its organization and accordance with functional guidelines, but especially in the variety of activities it can shelter in various spaces.

Collaborators: Roberto Damiani, Dimitri Karopoulos, Tom Ngo, Adrian Phiffer.
Client: Government of Hungary.

*Opposite page* Gallery, Rendering / *Above* Street Insert / *Below left* Plan / *Below right* Section / *Bottom left* Arcade, Rendering / *Bottom right* Elevation, Rendering / *Following spread* View from street, Rendering

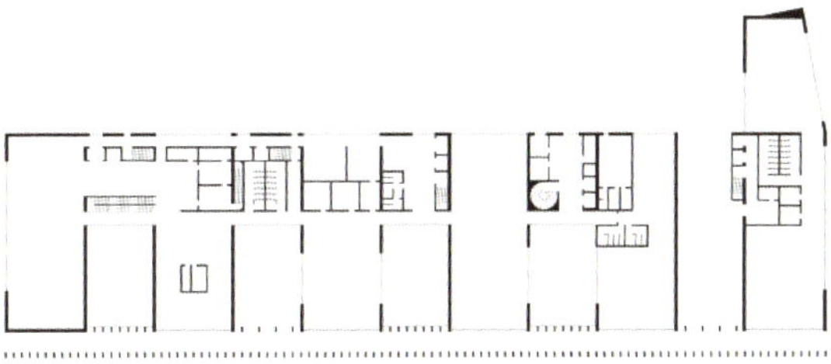

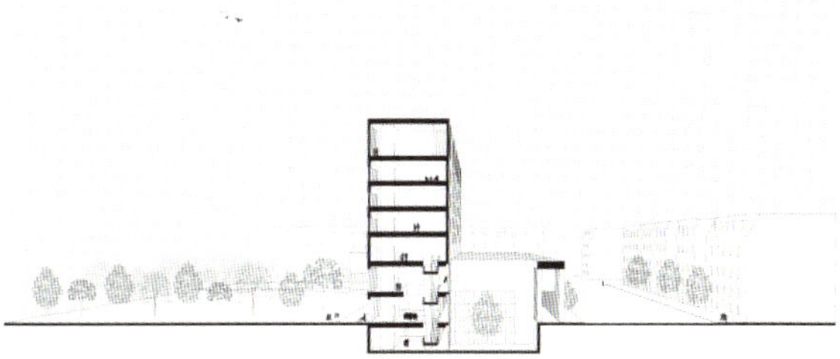

MUZEUM NE
MUZEUM NEP
MUZEUM N

MUZEUM NEPRAJZI
ZEUM NEPRAJ

## Urban Apparatus

*Open International Architectural Design Competition*
*Espoo, Finland, 2012*

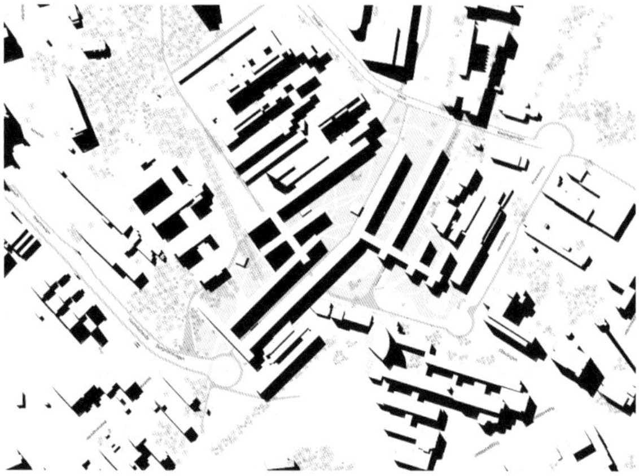

The proposal is as much a building for the future school of arts, architecture, and design, as it is an urban strategy to move people through the site. Mimicking Otaniemi's core formal composition, we have imagined thin, long buildings as simple extrusions of desired paths, that will conduct people through the entire site.

Collaborators: Adrian Phiffer, Shirin Rohani.
Client: Aalto University Properties Ltd.

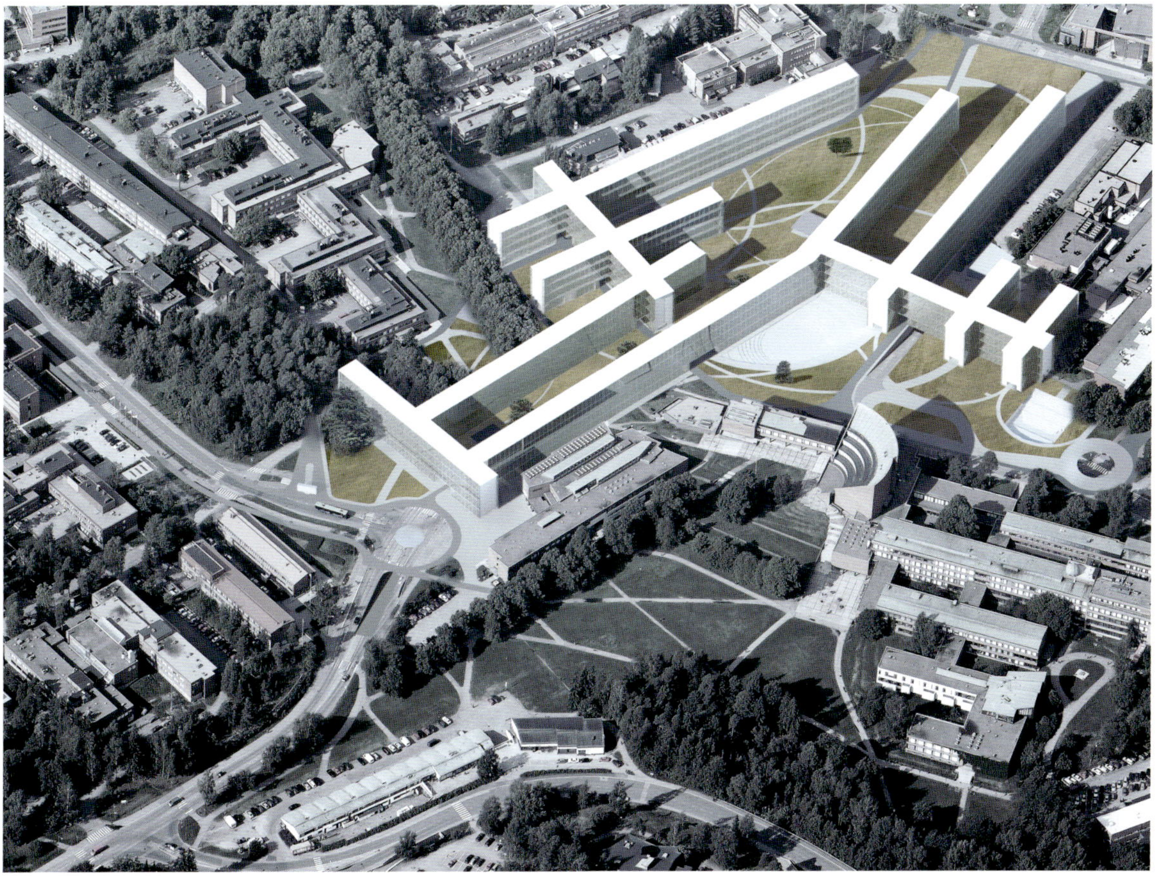

*Opposite page left* Elevation, Rendering / *Opposite page right* Site plan / *Above* Aerial view, Rendering / *Below* Entrance, Rendering

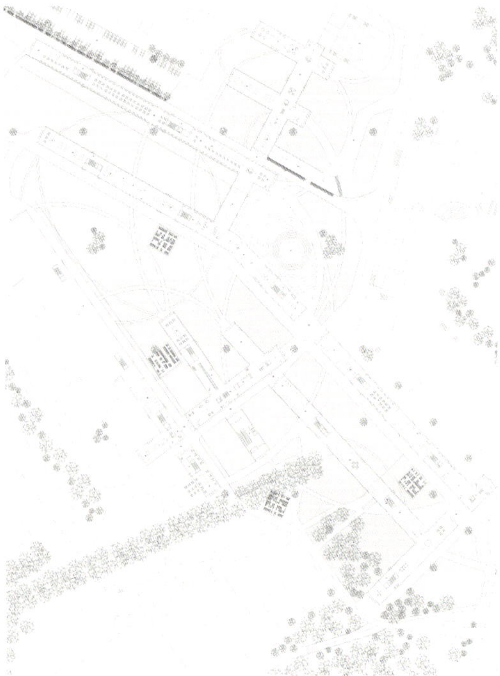

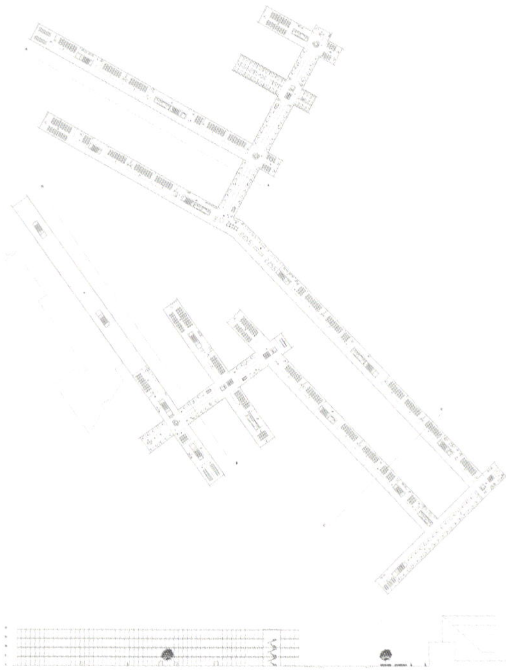

*Opposite page above* Interior, Rendering / *Opposite page below* Site plan & 2nd floor plan / *Above* Interior, Rendering / *Below* 3rd, 4th floor plans / *Following spread* Yard view from interior, Rendering

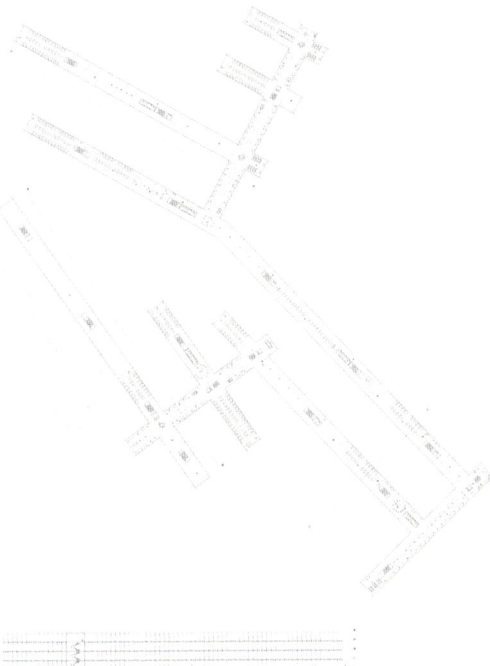

# SERGISON BATES ARCHITECTS

London, United Kingdom

**Welcome centre and offices**

*Pudong, Shanghai, China, 2016*

Located in the Pudong district of Shanghai, the new research campus for the Novartis Institutes for BioMedical Research forms an island settlement of laboratory facilities, office buildings and associated amenities surrounded by waterways, with a communal garden at its heart. The new 'Welcome center' is located at the entrance of the campus.

The building seeks to reconcile Chinese and Western traditions and root this hinterland site and its multi-national work force within the wider urban community. To this end, Sergison Bates engaged with numerous references: the proportions and tectonic order are inspired by buildings of the colonial period which are an important element of the city's morphology, while the building's materiality is rooted in indigenous construction techniques and local clay-based materials. The spatial concept for the interior was inspired by the organization of historical English country houses such as Hardwick Hall in Derbyshire.

The concept design for the interiors was carried out in collaboration with Studio Ilse, while the detailed design and fit-out of the interiors was completed by the client in collaboration with local consultants.

Photography: Kristien Daem.

*Opposite page left* Entrance / *Opposite page right* Site plan / *Above* Facade / *Below* Plans

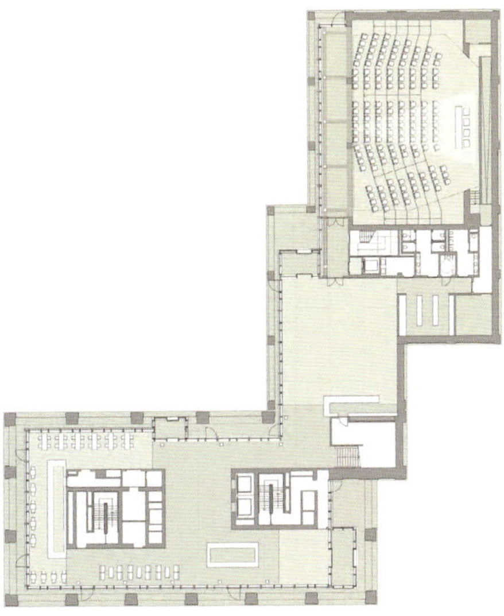

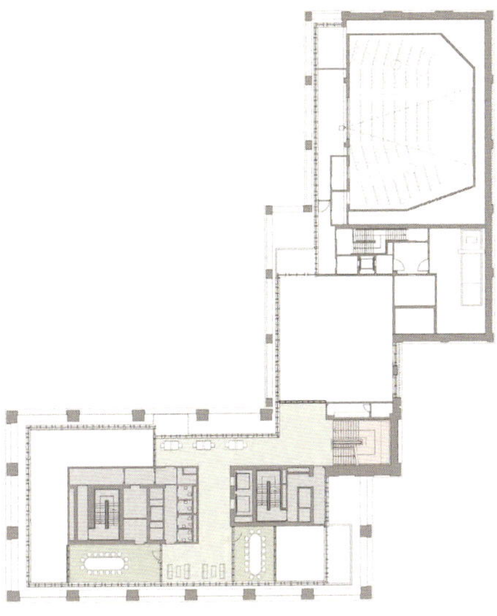

*Above* Entrance / *Below* Sections / *Opposite page above* Interiors / *Opposite page below* Section

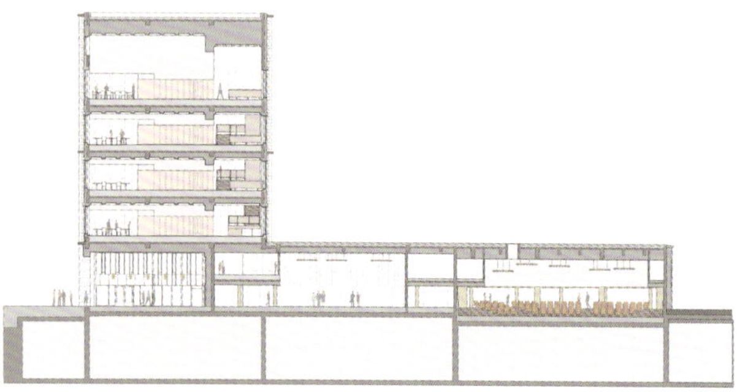

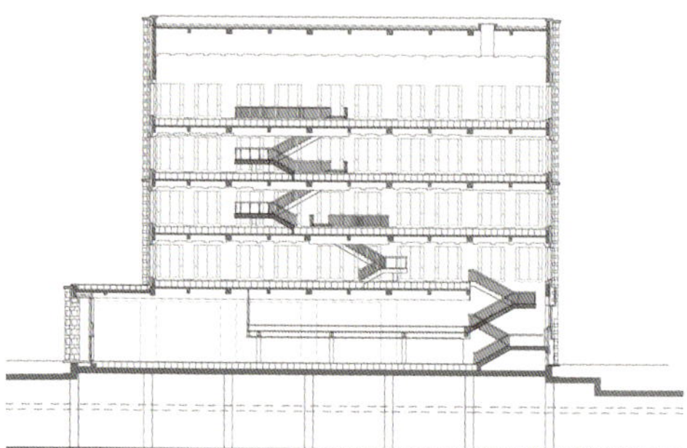

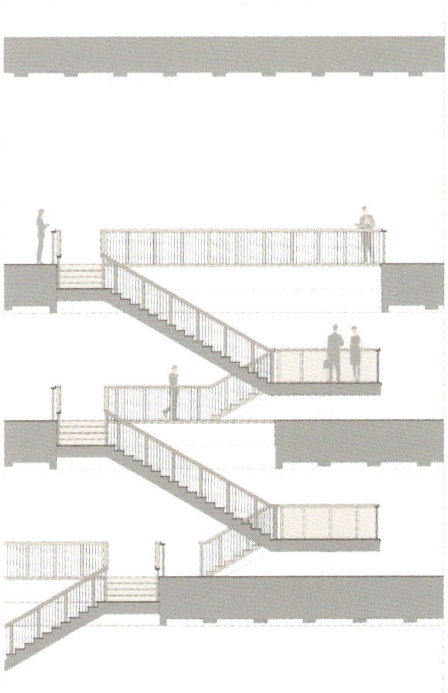

**City Library**

*Blankenberge, West Flanders, Belgium, 2011*

The project for the new city library in the Flemish seaside town of Blankenberge involved the refurbishment, re-organization and major extension of a former 19th century school building which has protected status as a local monument.

The brief required the creation of a variety of rooms, each dedicated to a specific kind of activity. The making of these different rooms harnesses and reinforces the memorable quality of the existing building. Tall, interconnected, book-lined rooms are quiet and comfortable, lighting is controlled and acoustics are soft. In the new building rooms have a different character: they are more spatially open, looser in their geometry, with generous views out to the cityscape.

The great variety of spaces is connected and organized by a new circulation arcade added at the rear of the building. New annexes at each end of the building connect to the arcade to form a continuous ribbon-like structure detailed and proportioned to match the civic character of the existing building. In this way, they mediate between the modest residential architecture of the street and the monumental presence and civic status of the existing building.

Photography: Kristien Daem and David Grandorge.

*Opposite page left* Interior. Photograph by Kristien Daem / *Opposite page above right* Street view of annex. Photograph by Kristien Daem / *Opposite page below right* Site plan / *Above* Rear Elevation. Photograph by Kristien Daem / *Below* Elevations

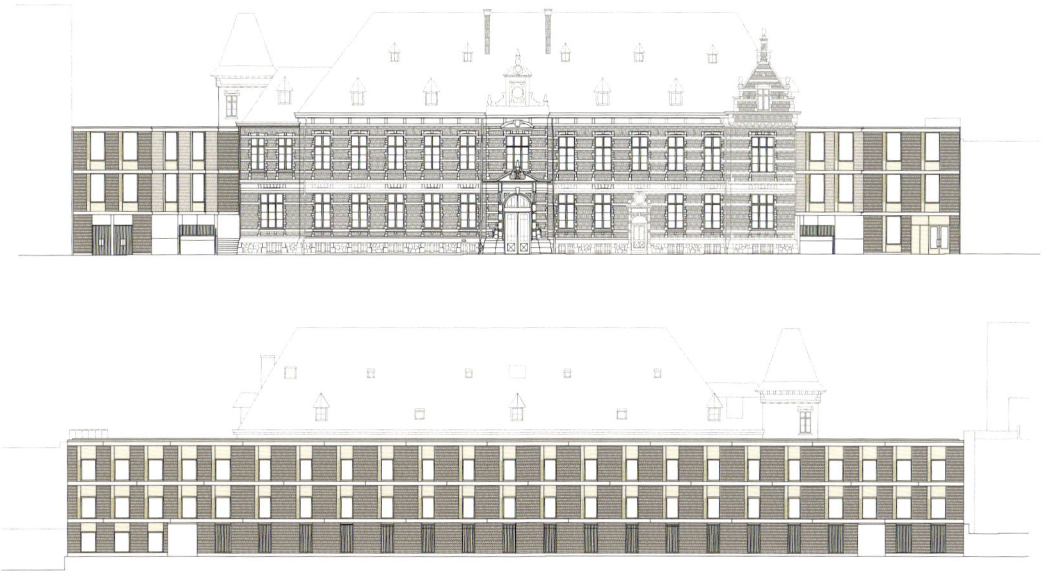

*Above* Exterior view. Photograph by Kristien Daem / *Below* Ground floor, 1st floor and 2nd floor plan / *Opposite page above* Enfilade of rooms and circulation arcade. Photographs by David Grandorge / *Opposite page below* Interiors. Photographs by Kristien Daem

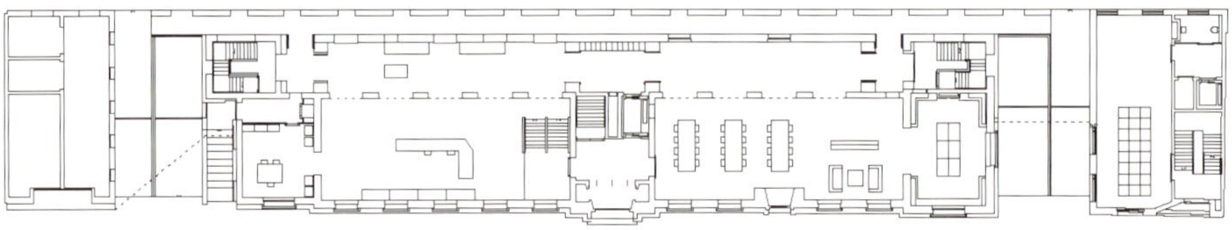

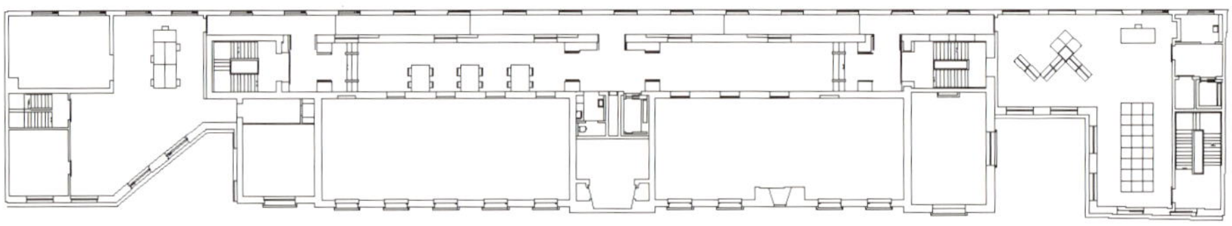

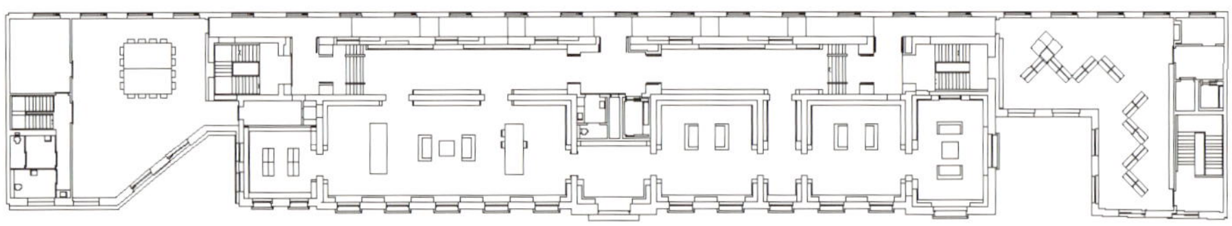

Romantiek

## Care Home

*Huise-Zingem, West Flanders, Belgium, 2011*

The project called for the design of a new 88-room care home set on landscaped grounds, in a rural village in Flanders. Three adjoining volumes are organized around two central courtyards, on three floors. Rooms are arranged in clusters around communal living rooms, with views out to the surrounding landscape and central garden.

The essential qualities of the residents' rooms—a view out to landscape, close proximity to a communal space, and a sense of being part of a large household—are complemented by furnishings, fittings and signage. Large amounts of controlled daylight and fresh air circulation ensure that the residents' experience is unlike that of a conventional "institutional" setting.

Photography: Kristien Daem and David Grandorge.

*Below* Exterior views. Photographs by David Grandorge / *Right* Site plan, Ground floor plan & Elevations / *Opposite page* Exterior view. Photograph by David Grandorge

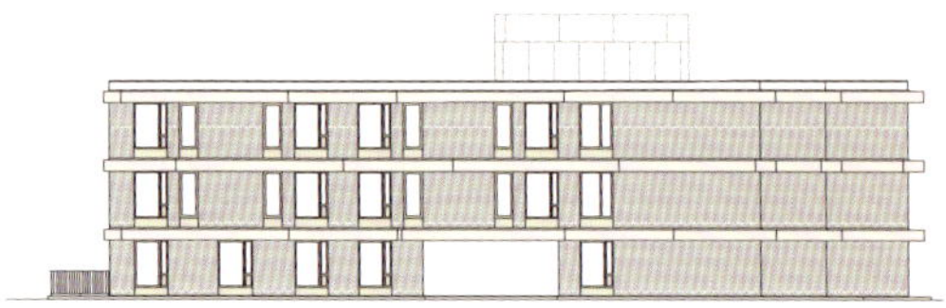

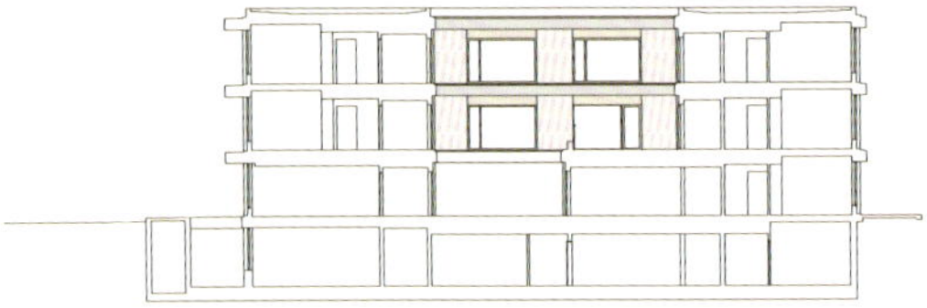

*Opposite page above* Terrace. Photograph by David Grandorge / *Opposite page center* Section / *Opposite page below* Exterior view. Photograph by David Grandorge / *Above* Facade. Photograph by David Grandorge / *Below left* Interior. Photograph by David Grandorge/ *Below right* Entrance. Photograph by Kristien Daem

# JOHNSTON MARKLEE

Los Angeles, California, United States

## Miami Design District

*Miami, Florida, USA, 2013*

The Miami Design District is a proposed development consisting of high-end retail spaces, galleries, offices, and restaurants, within a lush landscape of trees and outdoor sculpture in the postindustrial neighborhood of Buena Vista, Miami. The proposal includes the design of a façade which will inscribe Paradise Plaza, one of the primary anchors to a new pedestrian promenade that will run the length of the four-block development. The design aims to create a sense of urbanism in a moderate climate, highlighted by the complete integration of landscape, hardscape, sculpture, and water elements throughout the promenade and roof gardens on the majority of the new buildings. Founded on the concepts of the Rationalist movement in Italy, the design employs classical elements reinterpreted through the use of modern materials. The concave column grid that forms an arcade is constructed using a highly reflective metal which mirrors and multiplies the light and the trees of the plaza, creating a forest of imagery. The upper tier of the façade frames the rooftop landscape beyond, visually connecting the reflected forest between courtyard and sky.

*Bellow* Collage / *Opposite page* Facade model / *Following spread* Elevation, Collage

FENDI
CHANEL
GUCCI
LOEWE
GIVENCHY
PRADA

## Vault House

*Oxnard, California, USA, 2013*

Situated in a densely-developed beach site in Southern California, the Vault House transforms the shotgun, single view typology commonly found on narrow oceanfront residential lots. Instead of orienting only the main living spaces towards the single prime ocean view, the parallel orientation of the unidirectional vaulted rooms acts as a filter for light, view and ventilation that extends the unique coastal atmosphere from the Western beachfront façade through to the street at the eastern edge of the site.

The vaulted structure, extended beneath the living space, registers the changing levels of sand due to wind and surf, electing a traditionally unsightly zone of beach-front homes to become part of the overall spatial landscape of the house. In contrast, the garage to the east sits directly on the sand and is designed with walls that collapse under the pressure of wave surge. This results in an asymmetrical section, where, three floor levels—first floor, split level, second floor—are grouped around an open-air courtyard that serves as the main entrance to the house and a central outdoor room filtering light and air into the center of the home.

The extreme beach climate with pervasive winds and salty air demanded a simplified, weather resistant material palette. Limestone is used for all floors and as wainscots, both inside and outside, while an elastomeric, cementious membrane called "Grailcoat" wraps the exterior façade. The membrane eliminates the need for metal flashing and control joints, rendering the façade scaleless and forming an abstract backdrop for the play of light and shadow.

Photography: Jack Pierson (pp. 192-193), courtesy of Cheim & Read gallery and Eric Staudenmaier.

*Opposite page* Location map / *Above* Collage / *Below* Section diagrams

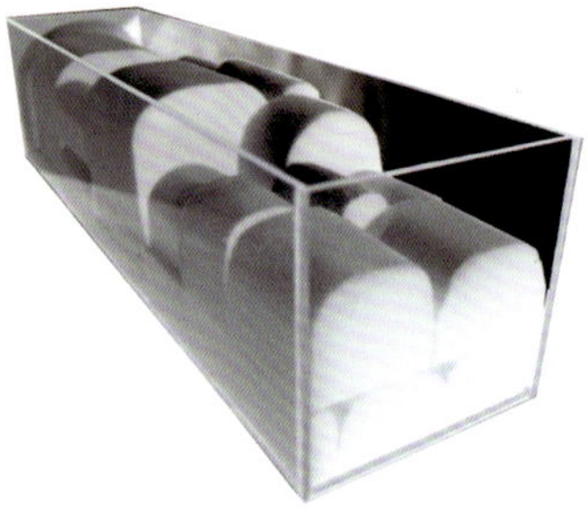

*Above* Exterior view. Photography by Eric Staudenmaier / *Opposite page below* Concept / *Below* Conceptual Model

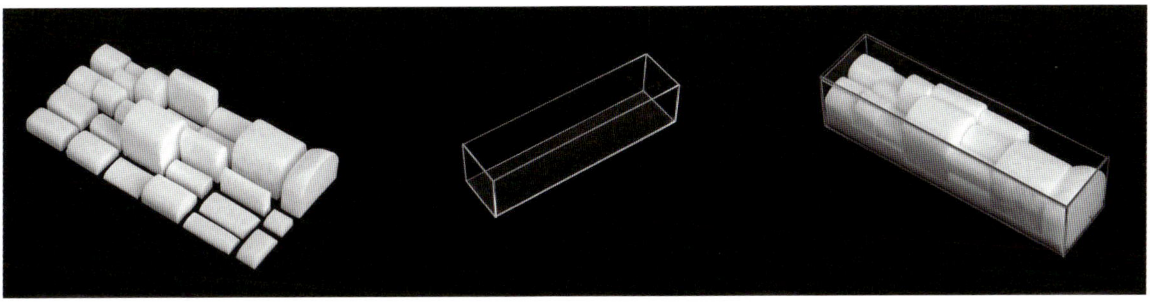

*Above* Model / *Below* Exploded Axonometric diagram / *Opposite page* Elevations, Sections and Plans

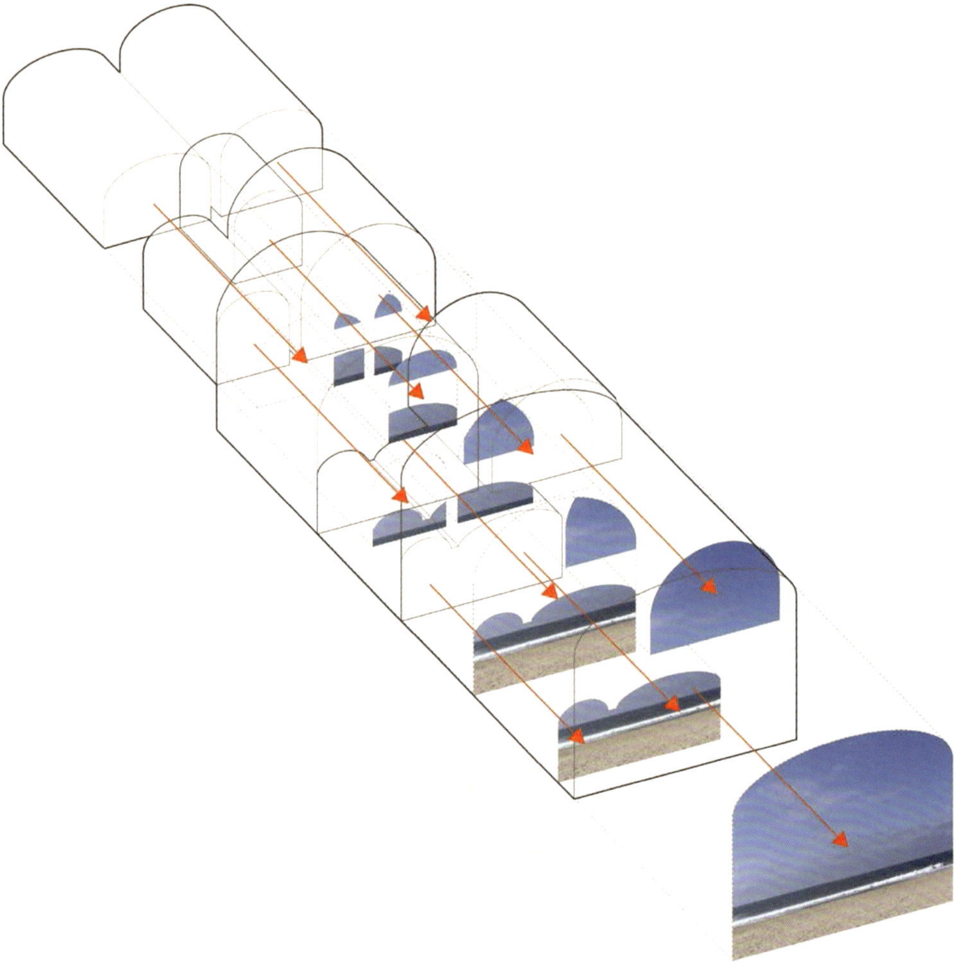

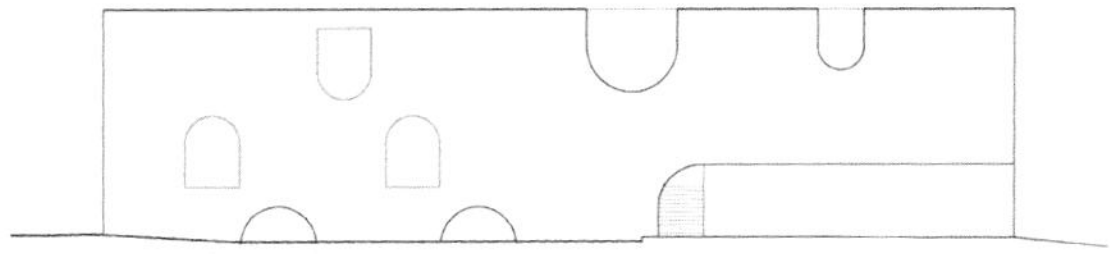

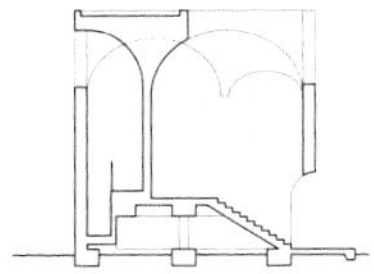

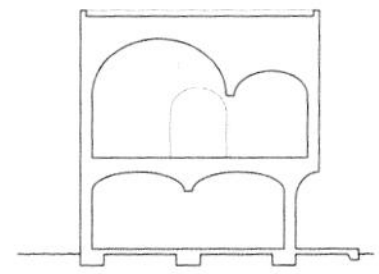

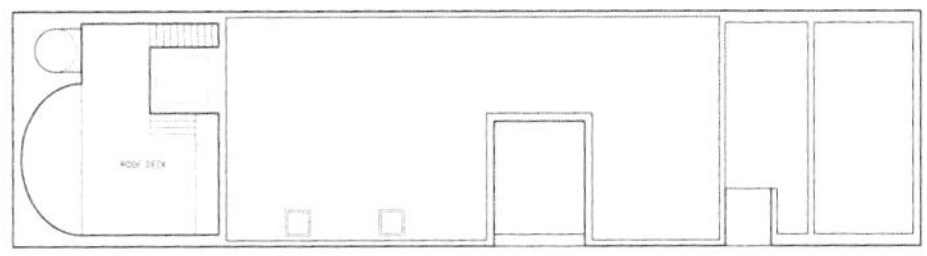
ROOF DECK

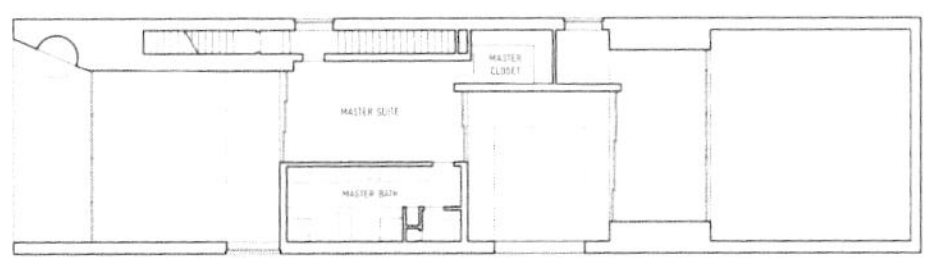
MASTER CLOSET
MASTER SUITE
MASTER BATH

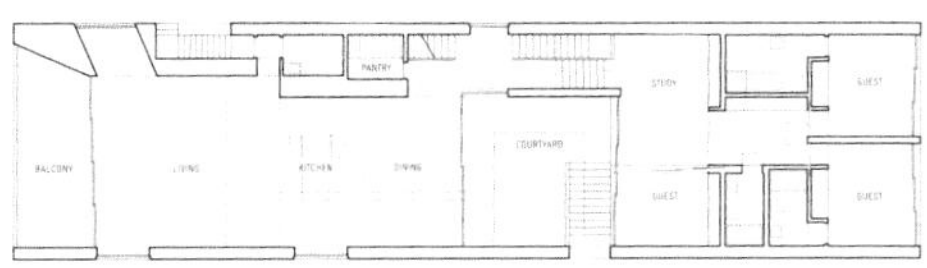
PANTRY
STUDY
GUEST
BALCONY
LIVING
KITCHEN
DINING
COURTYARD
GUEST
GUEST

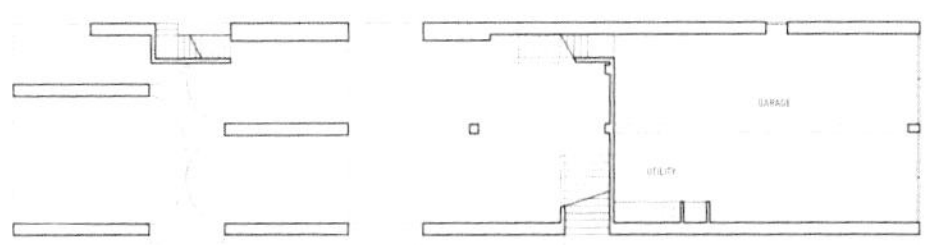
GARAGE
UTILITY

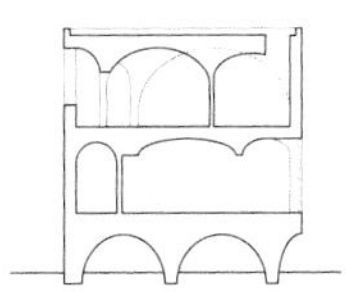

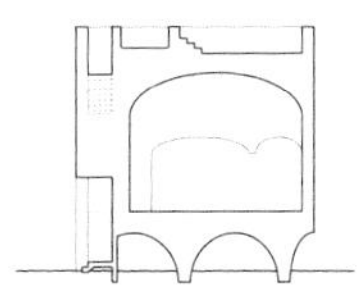

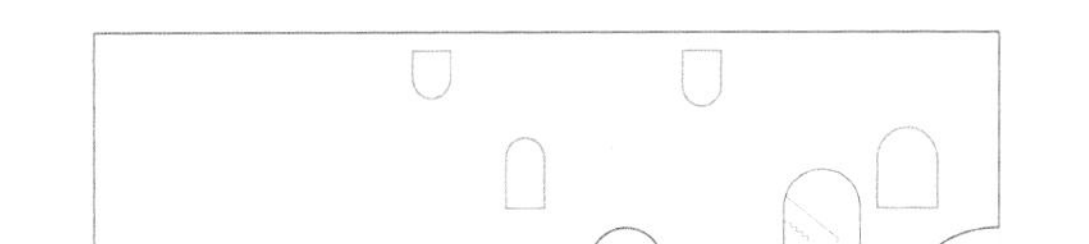

*Above* Exterior detail. Photography by Jack Pierson, courtesy of Cheim & Read gallery

*Above* Exterior detail. Photography by Jack Pierson, courtesy of Cheim & Read gallery

*Above & Opposite page* Interiors. Photography by Eric Staudenmaier

## Chile House

*Penco, Chile, 2011*

Situated at the edge of a forested hill in the center of Penco, Chile, the building appears as a monolithic bunker within the rough and uncultivated landscape overlooking the coast below. Surrounded by tall pine trees and untamed brush, the low-lying mass of uniform height emerges from the forest to the edge of the cliff capturing the expansive views of the city and ocean below.

Appearing as a singular mass from the exterior, the building —designed to house a community art center, the Chile House—is formed by two identical curved volumes hinged together at a single point. One volume, the entry court-yard, is oriented towards the sky, while the other volume, an interior hall, is oriented towards the horizon beyond. Visitors first enter a large elliptical courtyard, shaded by the canopy of trees above. Entry to the main building occurs at the hinge point, where the curve of the exterior courtyard walls meet the curved walls of the interior gallery. Visitors transition from the forest, to the intermediary skyward courtyard, to the polished stone walls of the interior hall that sweep outward to reveal views of the coastline, mirroring the atmospheric light-deep into the space. Thus the two spaces engage the disparity between the horizontality of the ground and the vertical presence of the sky.

The ancillary programs, including offices, storage, and bathrooms are located in the negative space between the two main volumes and the exterior façade, which unite the building into a singular mass. The uninterrupted elliptical volumes of the courtyard and gallery maintain a pure procession from the entry to the view.

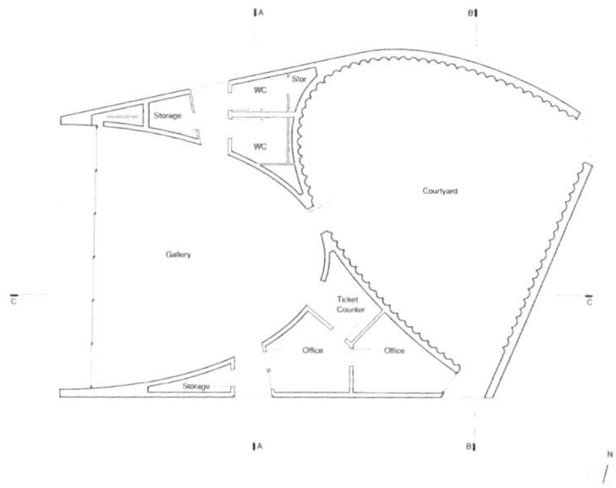


*Top left* Interior, Rendering / *Top right* Exterior, Rendering / *Above* Floor plan / *Below* Proposed building in the landscape

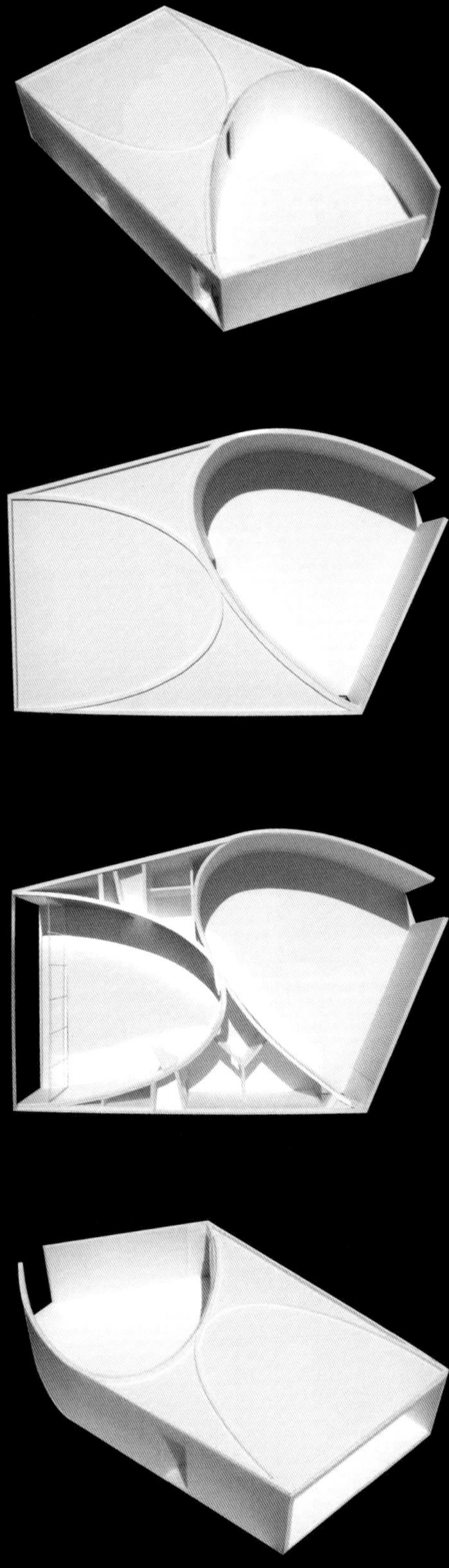

*Opposite page* Study models / *Below* Elevations (North, East, South, West) / *Bottom* Sections

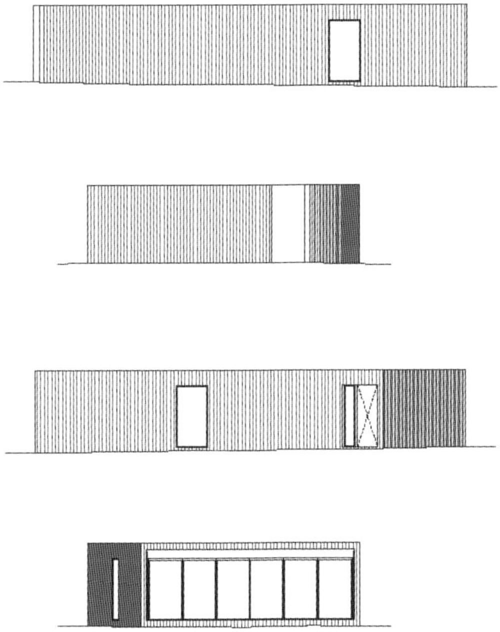

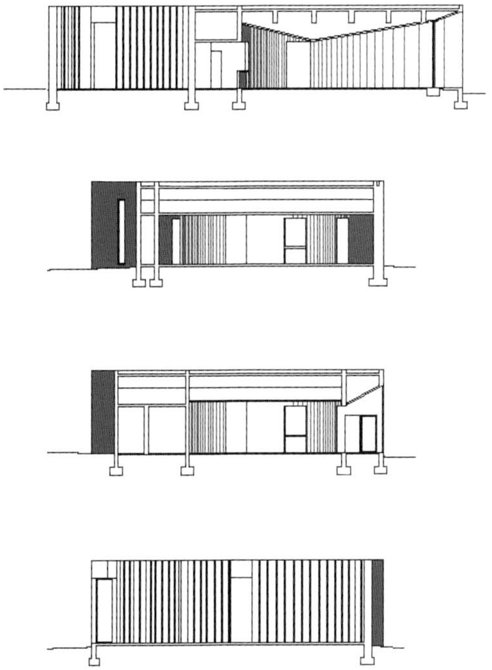

*This & Opposite page* Interiors

# KHOURY LEVIT FONG

Toronto, Canada

**Courtyard Mat: SEEH**

*Heraklion, Greece, 2012*

The three schools that form the SEEH (Kindergarten, Primary, and Secondary) create a single sheltering precinct backed into the rolling landscape of olive orchards to the south and north. The angular forms of the plan are shaped by the site, with the regular figure of a courtyard, pinched and inflected by the pressures of accommodation to site geometries. Together the schools form a mat of courtyards, somewhat mysterious from the outside, and by contrast rich and luminous within, and quite open with many windows onto the main courtyard to the north.

The one and two story courtyard-mat-building does many things. Culturally, it summons to mind what have become iconic images of the ruins of the palace of Knossos and the imagined reconstructions that accompany it. The ruins have their own appeal different from the buildings of which they are the remains. Buried rooms open up to the sky from below, walls are beneath our feet, floors have become roofs; it is an architecture embedded in the earth. The architecture here has turned into something mysterious, embedded in the ground, to be discovered. We think that we have captured something of this feeling in the arrangements of our proposal for the SEEH. The building follows the site boundary, it is an irregular shape, backing on most of its faces towards rising ground and at its southern tip digging in and buried up to the roof level. The roofs of the building are covered with suspended grape vines (above head-height) supported on posts and strung-wires and lending to the whole building the feeling of something unearthed and overgrown.

Also, in what remains of the Palace of Knossos, and what is seen in the many imaginative reconstructions of it, is an elemental architecture of walls and heavy trabeation. We have taken this idea of a stratified architecture of walls, columns, and beams and reimagined it in contemporary terms. A combination of steel-reinforced concrete columns, precast concrete beams and joists, and arched ceramic ceiling tiles create an open framework filled in with large glazed partitions creating an interior which has weight, but glowing with the light of multiple courtyards. The large amounts of glass not only transmit light but provide broad horizons of visibility across the many rooms of each school lending a very contemporary twist to closed and cellular qualities of the ancient architecture to which the project makes reference. The shallow vaulting in the ceilings running through all the schools creates a patterned spatial continuity throughout each building and draws to everyone's attention the relationship between individual rooms (classrooms, canteens, offices, et al) and the building as a whole and by analogy draws a relationship between the discrete events (of learning, of eating, of administrating) and the whole institutional community.

The pattern of the ceilings is similar to the grain of the vine plantings on the roofs and thus relates the spatial qualities of the building within to the landscape forms without.

The boundary walls that enclose the outermost perimeter of the building are made of stacked stone or pre-cast stone blocks that are laid up to make a rain screen around a glazed interior wall. The units are stacked in an elastic screen pattern taking advantage of the parametric controls over design and manufacture. The shifting degree of openness and closedness in the arrangements of this screen-wall are related to two factors, the desirability of view through the walls from within and the desirable amount of light penetration into the building. By virtue of making such a screen wall instead of more conventional windows the outer wall of the building can be adjusted with great flexibility to performative criteria but also create, through the uniformity of the screen-wall effect, the mystery and discovery that ensues from the shrouded nature of the world of the school within.

*Opposite page* Site plan / *Above* Aerial view / *Below* Entrance

*Above* Interior / *Below* Section / *Opposite page* Plans / *Opposite page below* Section

By contrast, the wall to the courtyard, also made of pre-cast elements, columnar in this case, is now much more widely spaced with an abundance of glass. The transparency of this large-courtyard wall creates a more immediate relationship between the school's interiors and the shared space of the large courtyard space.

There is a dramatic event that takes place every day in the lives of students, and it occurs every time they pass into the school thick with classrooms and courtyards. The matrix of passages, courtyards, and the many classrooms, lab rooms, cafeterias, offices, and spaces of assembly that are a deep and wide mat of spaces make of these schools something like the cloistered spaces of medieval campuses but here made fresh, light and airy—there is a sense of an entire world within, thick and deep, sheltered and glowing into which students enter every day for their studies. Within the matrix of courtyards is wide and deep, but not disorienting, due to the clear organization of the plans, the orienting effects of the courtyards and cross views through the building, and the regulated visibility of the outside world. It is a place replete with historical resonance and contemporary sensibility.

Khoury Levit Fong in partnership with Matar Rahmeh Studio.
Principals in Charge: R. el-Khoury and R. Levit.
Matar Rahmeh Principals: Hoda Matar and Talal Rahmeh.
Team: Faisal Bashir, Timmie Chan, Yie Ping, Farnoush Saman.

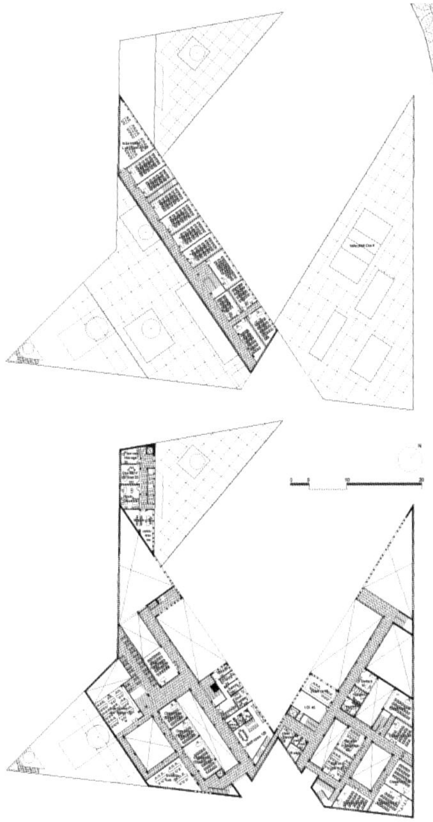

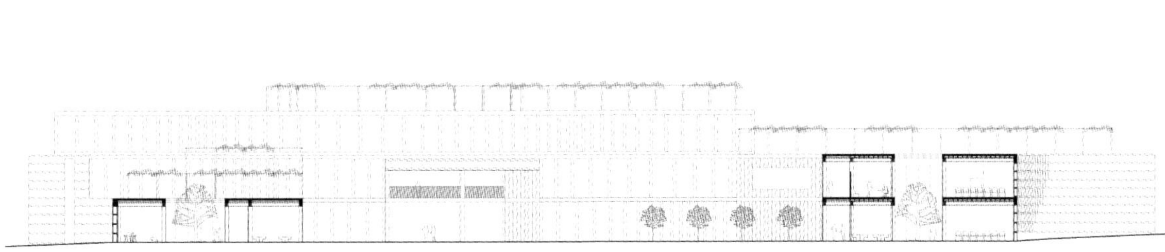

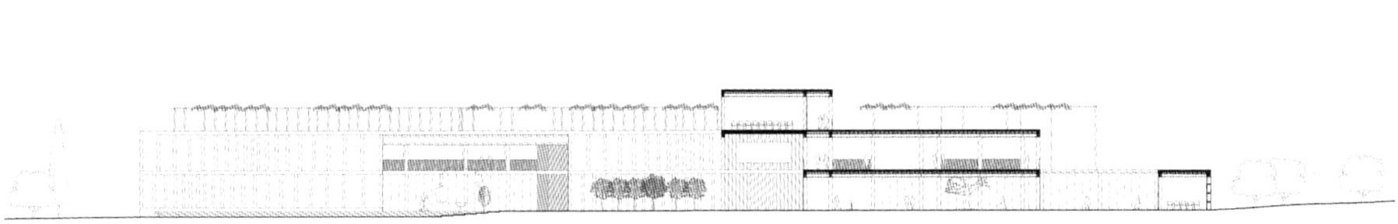

**Warp + Woof Museum of Underwater Antiquity**

*Piraeus, Greece, 2012*

The Museum of Underwater Antiquities is to be housed within a building that is itself an artifact of great cultural significance: The Cereals Stock House Building. The underlying structure, the silos themselves provide the warp and the woof that organizes the collection of underwater antiquities–bringing these antique artifacts into intimate contact with the archaeology of a more recent history—the now iconic remains of Port of Piraeus's 20th century industrial past in the form of the silos of The Cereals Stock house building.

How to convert the small cellular nature of the grain silos into spaces adequate to the museum? Taking a cue from the artistic inventions of Gordon Matta-Clark we have cut conic voids across the tightly packed chambers of the silos. These voids provide a rich means of dramatic movement through the museum. In each of the voids that have been cut, escalators have been placed to provide for a pattern of choreographed movement through the whole building including: the six specified exhibition themes, each of which occupies its own floor.

The excavation of the silos provides a number of advantages. Like the boulevards that cut through the diverse neighborhoods of city binding them to the larger scale of the city as a whole, these excavated passages in the building permit the visitor to the museum to recognize the unity of an institution to be housed in what began as the non-communicating chambers of silos. Under the original conditions each silo remained utterly segregated from the next. The excavation is a cross-cut, more violent than the methods of contemporary archaeological excavation, but related to the act of uncovering, digging in, as it were, into the literally stratified material of the historical record. Here, the beauty of the internal organization of the silos is made visible to the museum visitor, both from within the museum and from without through the act of cutting or, to put it more thematically, through excavation.

The cross-cut voids opening up the silos slice great glazed openings into the outer wall of The Cereals Stock Building. They create fantastic views of the port from within the museum and, from without, reveal the complex internal spectacle of people. They expose to view the silo forms themselves and offer an X-ray of sorts into the building of the new Museum of Underwater Antiquities.

Principals in charge: R. el-Khoury and R. Levit.
Design Team: Dimitra Papantonis, Faisal Bashir, Minghui Cui, Roya Mottahedeh, Yie Ping, Farnoush Saman.

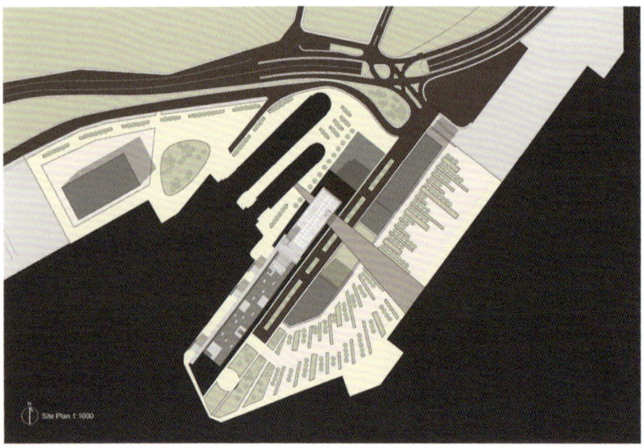

*Opposite page* Site plan / *Above* Aerial view / *Below* Concept diagram

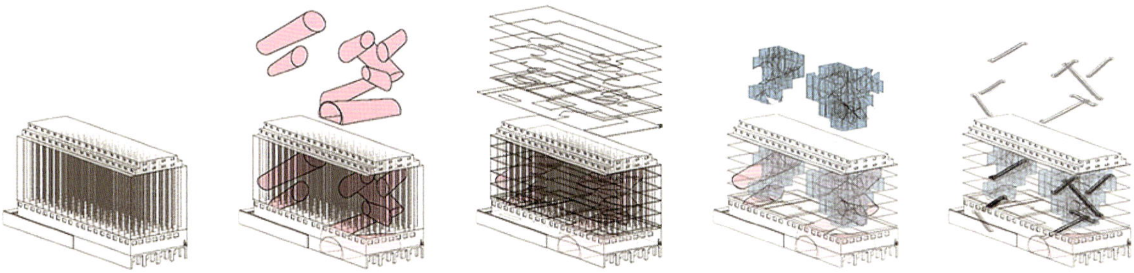

*Above* Crown / *Below* Longitudinal section / *Opposite page above* Exterior view / *Opposite page below* Ground Floor & Basement Plans

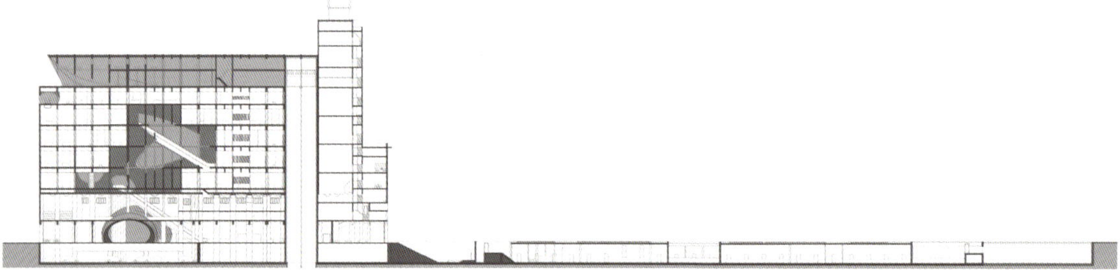

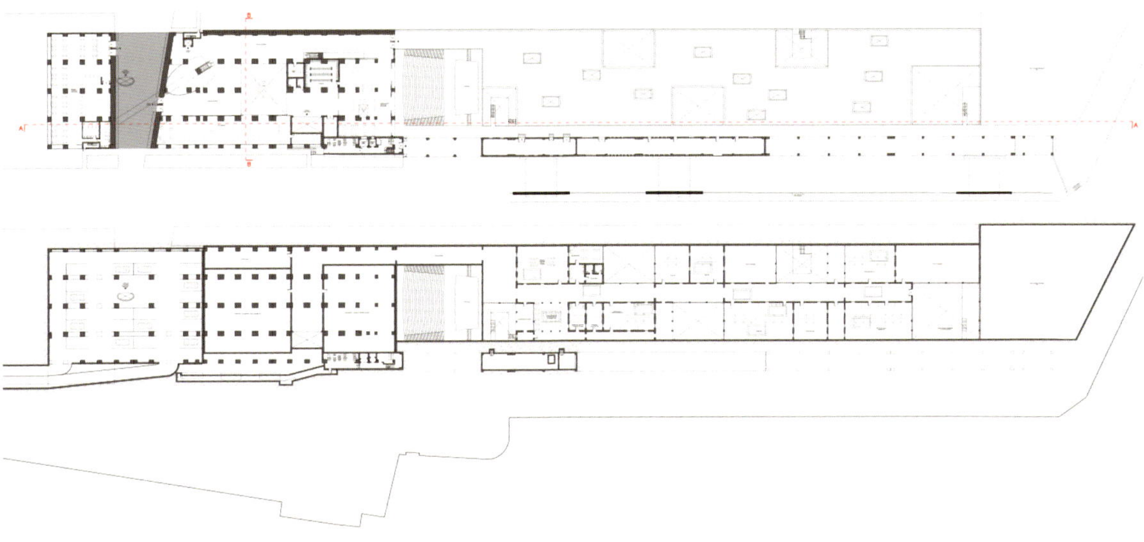

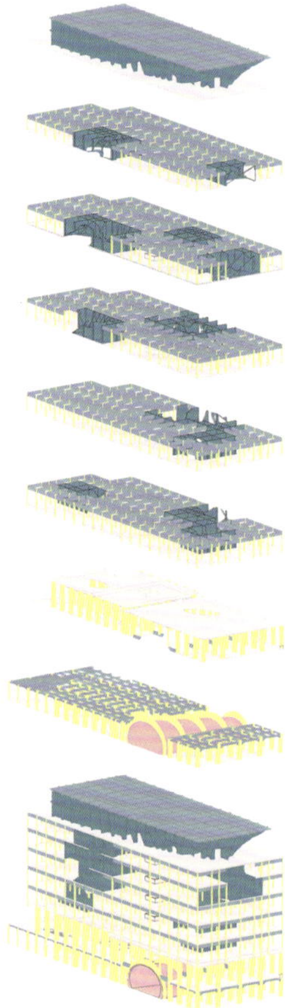

*Opposite page left* Construction, Renderings / *Opposite page right* Exploded axonometric / *Above* Exhibition space / *Below* Underground

# MACHADO SILVETTI

Boston, Massachusetts, United States

**The Ruth and Elmer Wellin Museum of Art**

*Hamilton College, Clinton, New York, USA, 2012*

Hamilton College challenged us to design a new type of museum, which would respond to and celebrate the institution's unique collection and teaching pedagogy. The museum was conceived as a teaching laboratory that would draw students and faculty from a wide range of disciplines. The Director envisioned a hands-on "cabinet of curiosities" that would challenge students to search for new meanings through the juxtaposition of disparate objects.

The Wellin Museum coupled with the presence of the Art history department as its neighbor, will create a new arts quad at Hamilton and help develop visual and pedestrian connections between the two sides of campus. The design brings museum visitors directly from campus paths and outdoor sculpture areas through a monumental two-story glass archive hall that showcases the College's unique collection. The building's plan and massing follows a clear tripartite diagram, with the "cabinet of curiosities" entry lobby and archives at the center flanked by a gallery wing to the West and a service wing to the East. To put the workings of the museum on display, holding and receiving areas, archive spaces, administrative offices and seminar rooms are all visible through the object-filled glass cases. The western wing of the museum houses a lecture hall, workshops, and a 6,200 s.f. exhibit gallery which can be reconfigured to support student curated shows.

The project is designed to meet the stringent temperature and humidity requirements of an archival museum. The museum draws its heating and cooling from a closed loop geothermal well field that has been placed beneath the sculpture terrace. Occupancy sensors, a high-performance building envelope and other energy efficient systems are used to meet the College's sustainability goals.

Principal in charge: Rodolfo Machado.
Consulting Principal: Jorge Silvetti.
Project Director: Edwin Goodell, AIA.
Project Manager: Evan Brinkman, AIA.
Project Team: Nathan Fash, Jeffry Burchard, James Setzler, Noel Murphy.
Photography: Anton Grassl.

Opposite page West elevation / *Above* North elevation / *Below left* First floor plan / *Below right* Second floor plan

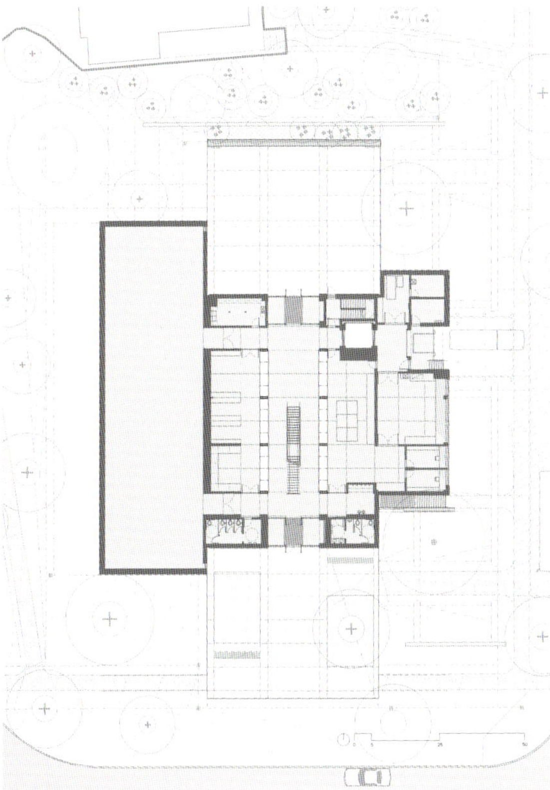

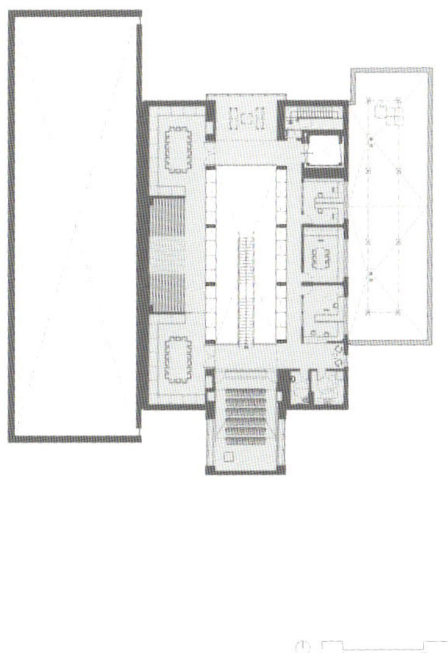

*Above* North-west perspective / *Below* Entrance, West view / *Opposite page left* Sections / *Opposite page right above* East Elevation detail / *Opposite page right below* West Elevation detail / *Opposite page right bottom* Interior

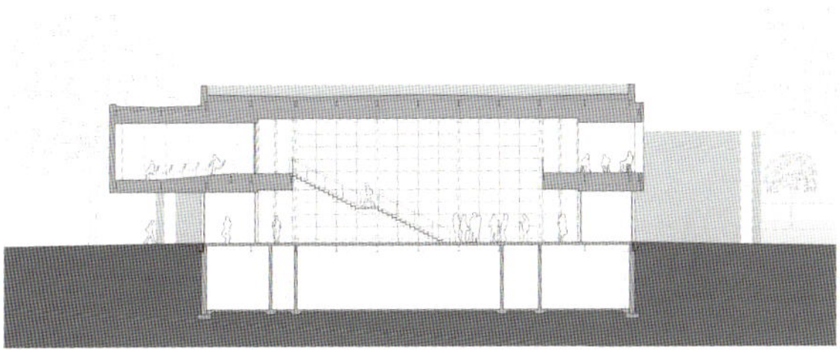

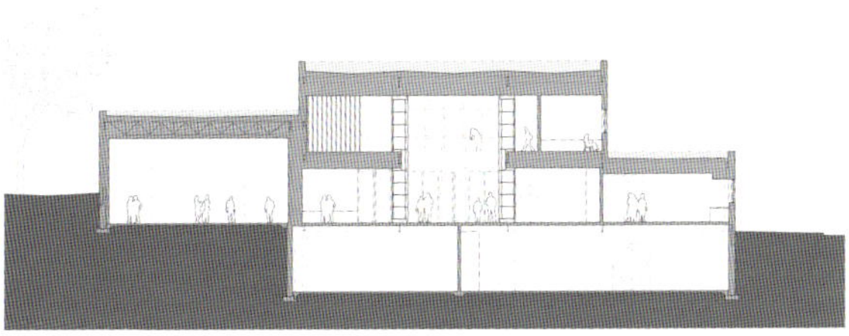

*Above* Eastwest view / *Below* South Elevation / *Opposite page* Interiors / *Following spread* Interior

## NADAAA

Boston, Massachusetts, United States

**New Hampshire Retreat**

*Bethlehem, New Hampshire, USA, 2013*

Situated north of the Presidential Range of the White Mountains, the New Hampshire House is a series of rooms—each operating as a frame capturing the surrounding panoramic views.

Programs of the house unfold as a linear sequence from private spa to master bedroom and bath. Designed as ample orthogonal volumes, the rooms of the house pivot around the elliptical plan; each rotation is calibrated for a specific view. The resulting voids of these rotations become shared exterior patios between adjacent rooms. The completed circuit of rooms encloses an interior courtyard. This private outdoor space—a highly controlled garden of crushed stone, pavers, and plantings—is a foil to the natural landscape just outside the envelope of the house.

Principals: Nader Tehrani, Katherine Faulkner, AIA.
Team: Ryan Murphy, Sergio Verrillo, Marta Guerra, Tim Wong, Tom Beresford, Lisa Lostritto, John Houser, Alda Black, Laura Williams, Wes Hiatt.

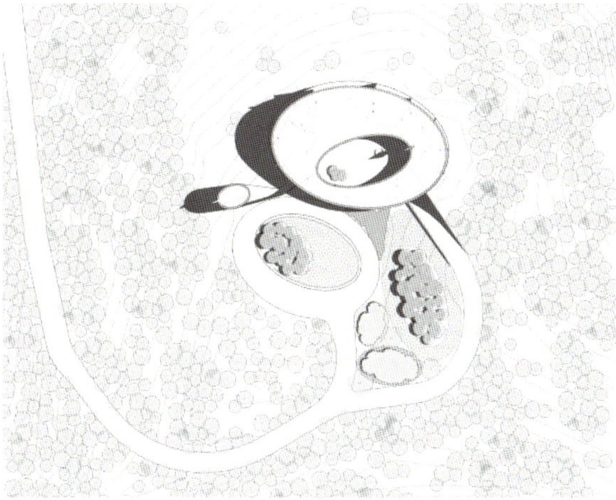

*Below* Aerial view, Rendering / *Above* Site plan

*Above* Exterior views / *Below* Exploded perspective / *Opposite page* Model

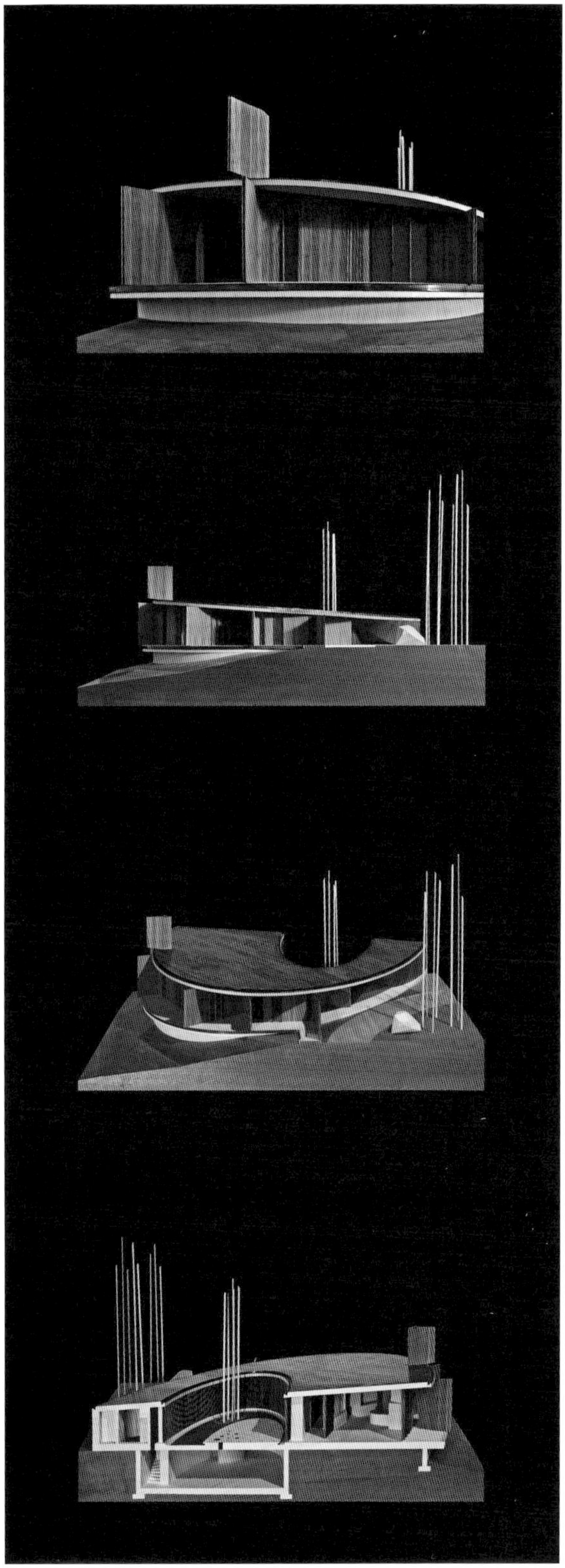

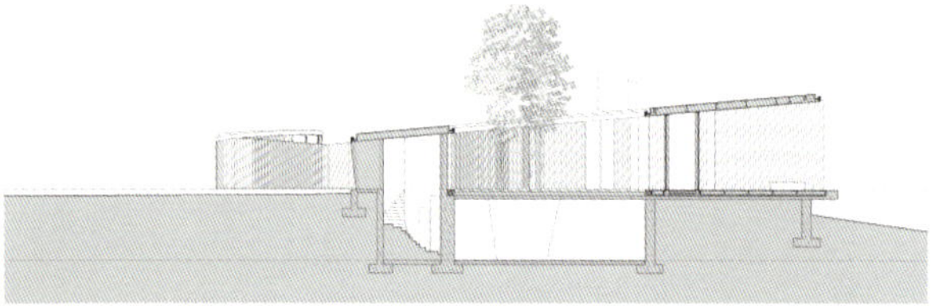

*Above* Section / *Below* Exterior view / *Opposite page above left* Elevation / *Opposite page above right* Entrance view

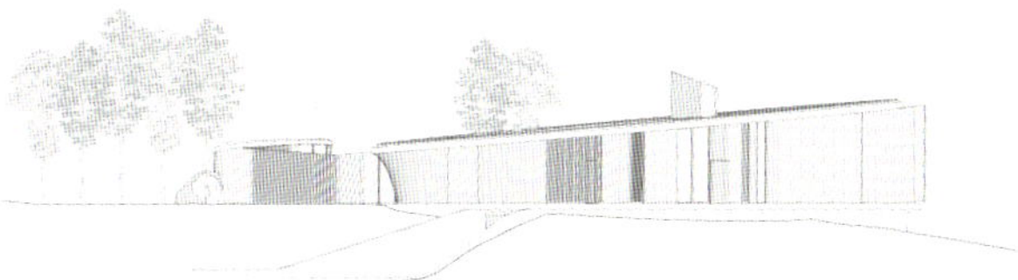

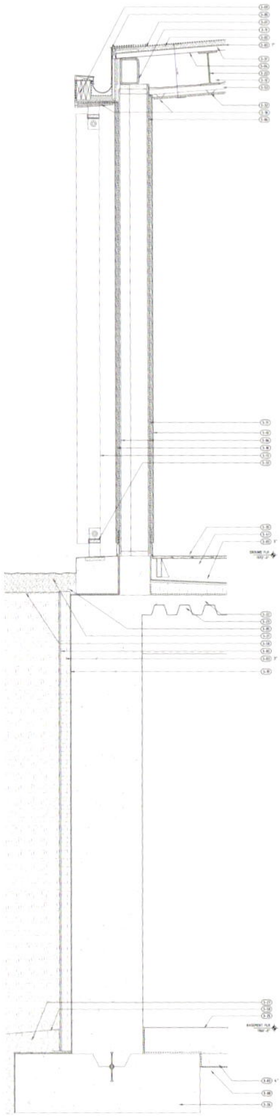

*Above* Wall detail / *Right* Section / *Opposite page* Exterior view

*Above* Exterior view / *Below* Plan / *Opposite page above* Wall Construction details / *Opposite page below* Section Perspective

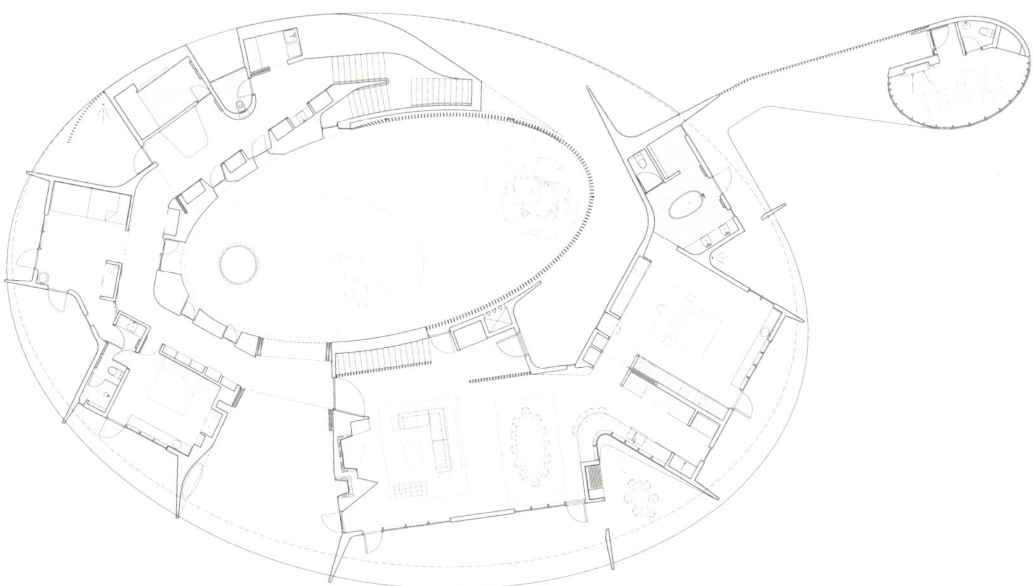

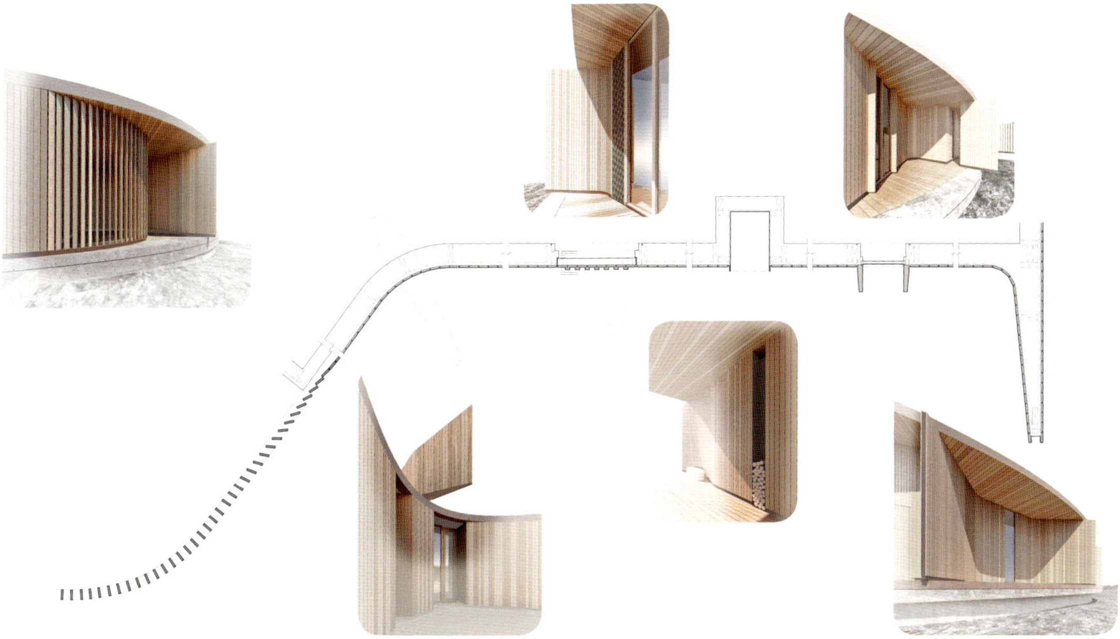

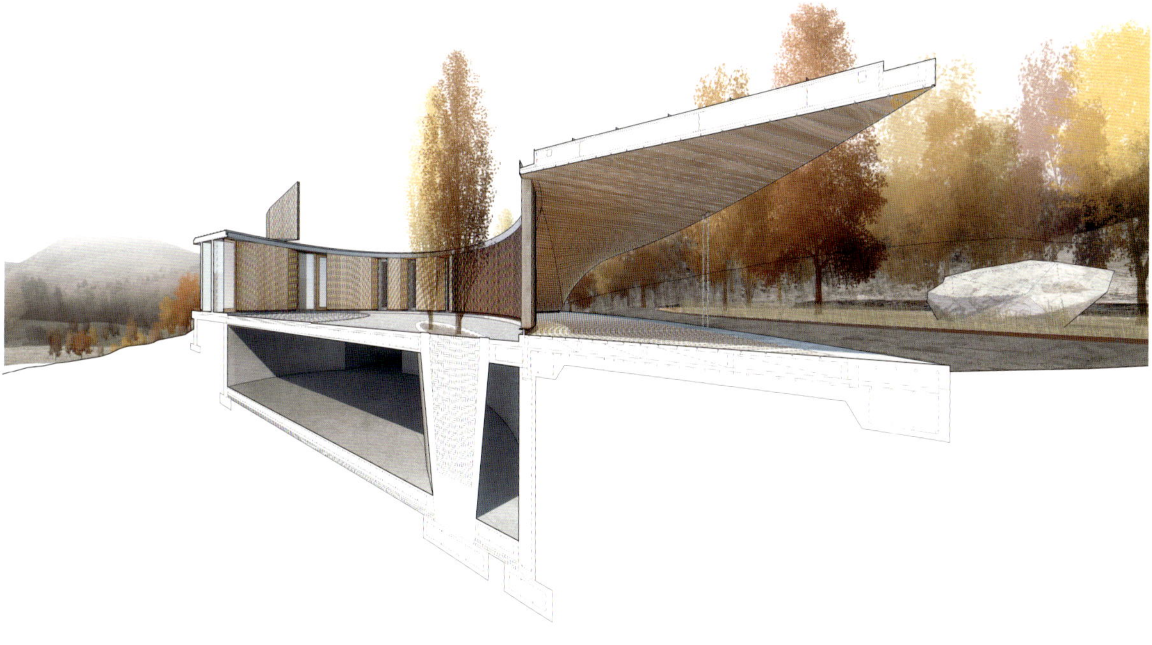

*Above* View of courtyard

**Ordos 20+10**

*Ordos City, Inner Mongolia, 2012*

This project is part of a larger group of tightly packed speculative office parks under construction in Ordos, China. These developments are all subject to zoning envelope regulations mandating multiple cubic volumes, without an immediate urban context. We developed three planning strategies to accommodate these parameters: first, we emphasized both pedestrian and vehicular approaches to the site as symmetrical thresholds; second, we developed a central public space that orients the assembly of cubic buildings; and third, we arranged the volumes to enable an innovative and flexible approach to real estate practices. These primary strategies produce a morphology of rotated buildings, linked together with a long interior promenade that enables both vertical and lateral layout customization for office tenants.

The basic logic of rotated and intersecting cubes is refined by strategically slicing the cubes corners. These operations share the same visual language, but their spatial effects vary widely, depending on where the cut is made. Some corner-cuts produce dramatic entrances, where others create archways, paths between buildings, sky-lit atria, or a dramatic mirrored level change. We selected a rough volcanic stone for the facade, which provides a counterpoint to the delicacy of openings revealed through corner slices. The array of stone panels produce a language of rhythmic openings that express a finely-grained cadence of work stations. The spandrel beams are concealed behind the logic of panelization, which produces an effect of "windows stacked on windows" similar to a masonry logic. The project's materiality and morphology combine to produce an abstract set of associations: volcanic geology, chunks of coal, the cuts of stone quarries. In spite of these readings, the project assembles itself with a rational logic of discrete spatial and typological organization that combines the mandates of real estate with aspirations for a shared public experience.

Principals in Charge: Nader Tehrani, Katie Faulkner, Hailim Suh.
Project Coordinators: Tom Beresford, Remon Alberts, Arthur Chang, Cyrus Dochow.
Project Team: Dan Gallagher, Tim Clark, Sarah Hirschman, Sina Mesdaghi, Li Huang, Andrew Manto, Jonathan Palazzolo, Tim Wong, Joanna Rafael, Caitlin Scott, Ryan Murphy.
Associate Architect: Himma Studio.
Local Architect, Structural Engineer, MEP Engineer: China Construction Design International (CCDI).

*Opposite page* Plan / *Above & Below* Exterior views, Renderings

*Opposite page above* Building in the landscape, Rendering / *Opposite page center* Interior, Rendering / *Opposite page below* Exterior view, Rendering / *Below left* Diagrams: Maximum Building Envelope, Plaza: Urbanized Exterior & Rotation: Urbanized Interior / *Below right* Exploded Axonometric Diagram / *Bottom left* Plans / *Bottom right* Sections

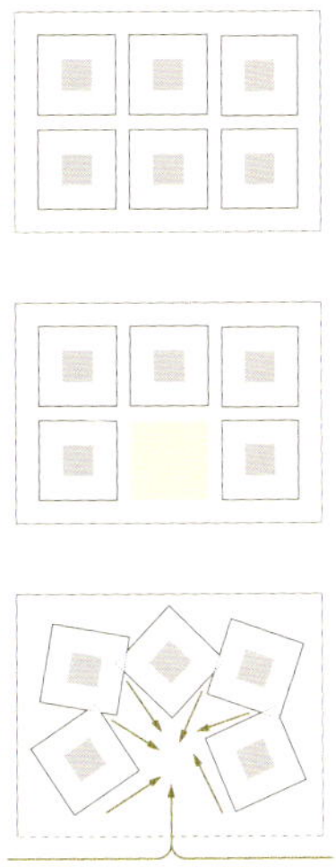

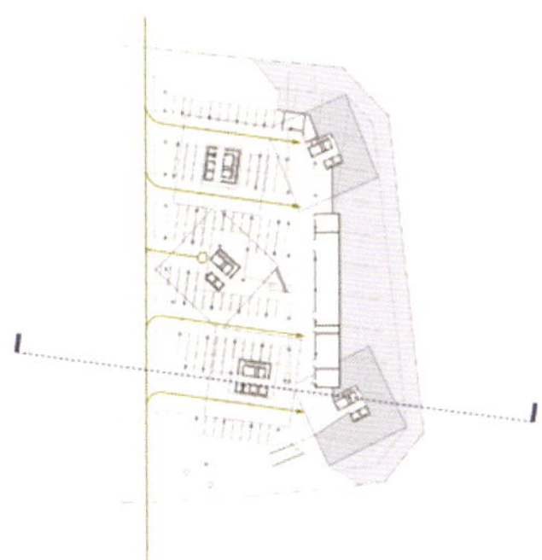

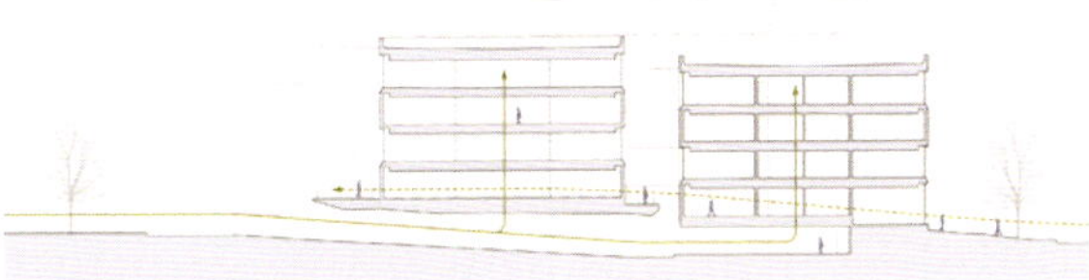

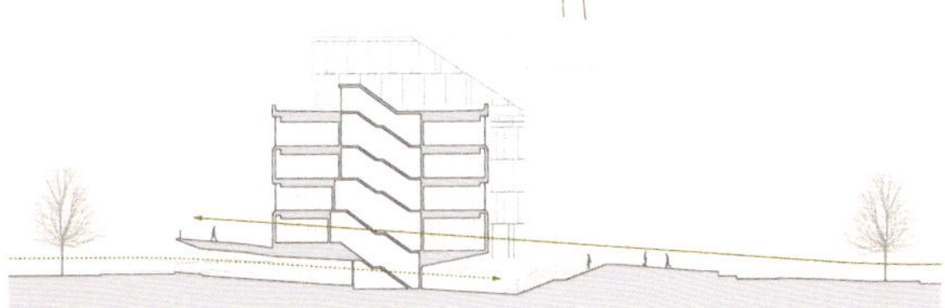

*Above* Wall detail, Rendering / *Below left* Cladding Elevation / *Below right* South & North Elevation / *Opposite page above left* Section / *Opposite page above right* Roof, Rendering / *Opposite page below left* Cladding Section / *Opposite page below right* Wall, Rendering

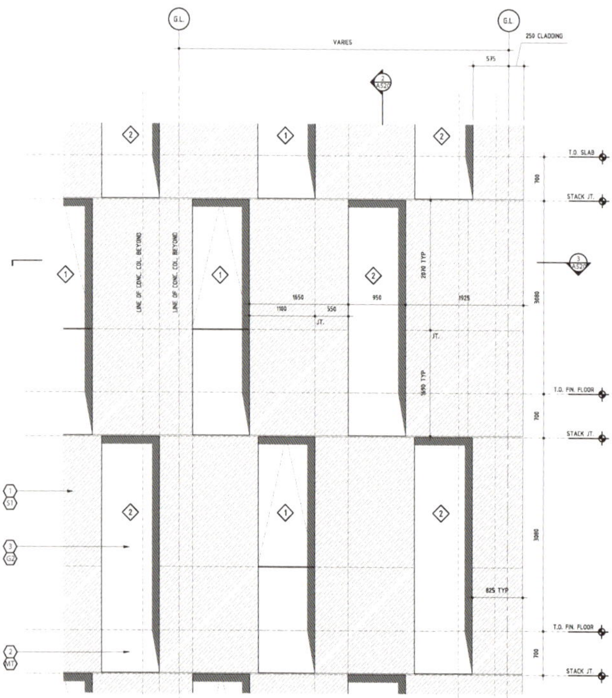


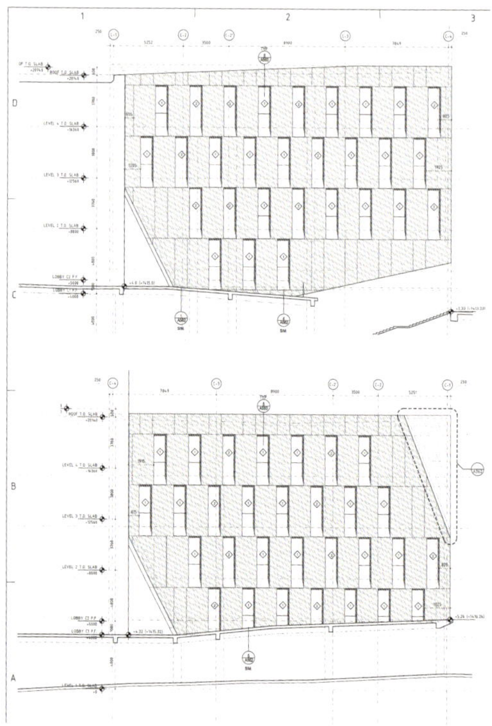

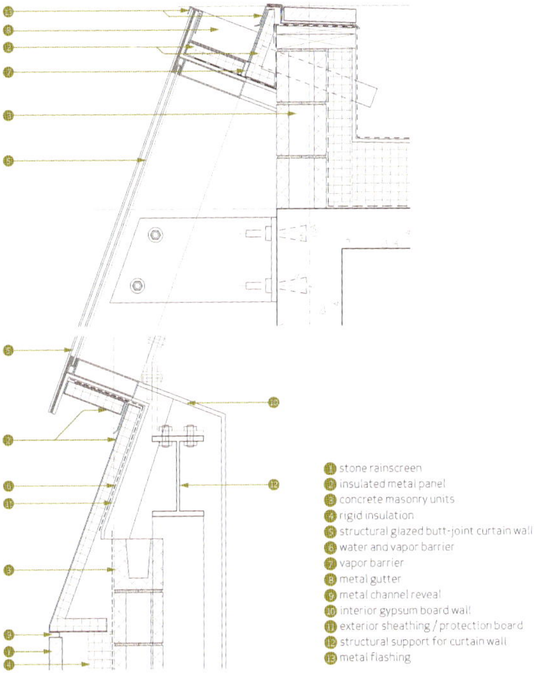
1 stone rainscreen
2 insulated metal panel
3 concrete masonry units
4 rigid insulation
5 structural glazed butt-joint curtain wall
6 water and vapor barrier
7 vapor barrier
8 metal gutter
9 metal channel reveal
10 interior gypsum board wall
11 exterior sheathing / protection board
12 structural support for curtain wall
13 metal flashing

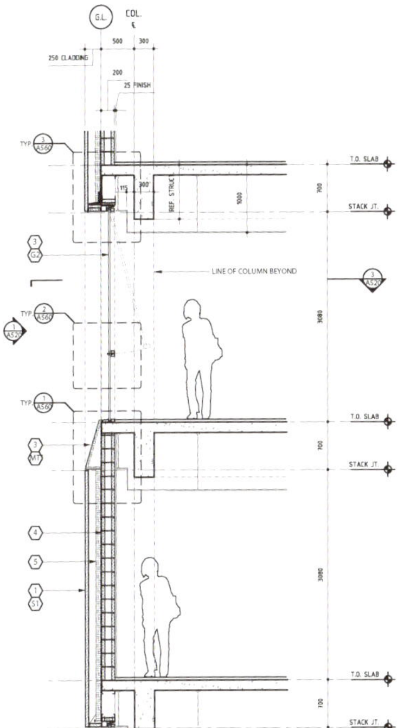
G.L.
COL.
250 CLADDING
25 FINISH
T.O. SLAB
STACK JT.
LINE OF COLUMN BEYOND

# OFFICE KERSTEN GEERS DAVID VAN SEVEREN

Brussels, Belgium

### OFFICE 90: Agricultural School

*Mechelsevest, Leuven, Belgium, 2014*

The agricultural school building is situated on the outskirts of Leuven, overlooking the city from its slightly elevated position in the landscape. The building consists of a linear block of five floors, housing the classrooms and facilities complemented by a horizontal volume—the sport hall—attached to it. The roof of the sport hall forms the play-ground with an equal volume. The playground lies before the classrooms, effectively working as the entrance to the school complex. This platform cuts through the classroom volume, marking the entrance to the school and providing a view to its agricultural fields. The main feature of the school is a parallel set of stairs and landings between playground and sports hall on the one hand and the classrooms on the other. This set of stairs makes the main façade of the building, executed in rough precast concrete, the mediator between all school activities. The school's façade is simply standard brick painted white. The entire volume of the school building turns away from the street to align with the orientation of the fields of the schoolyard. As a result, the building creates a set of secondary spaces that provide the bike storage and an entrance ramps to the main premises.

The volume of the school makes a distinct angle with the street and the neighboring buildings. Through its twisted position, it finishes the existing geometric layout of the fields behind, and at the same time, by opening up like a gate, allows for a view over the fields towards the city of Leuven, almost as a staged medieval city portrait.

Structural Engineer: Util Structuurstudies.
Building management: Bureau Bouwtechniek.
HVAC & MEP: Studiebureau R. Boydens.
Art integration: Richard Venlet.
Photography: Bas Princen.

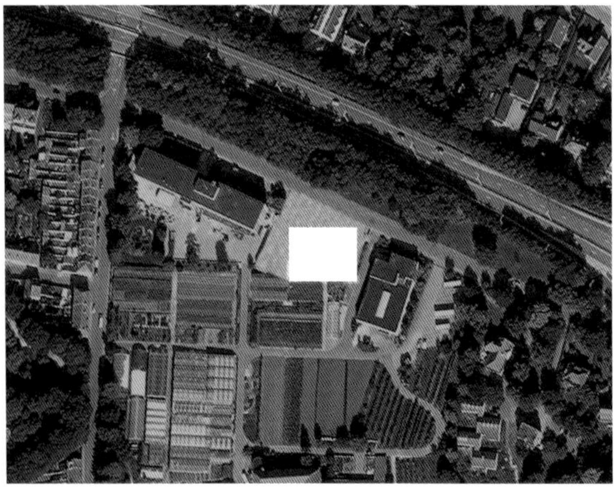

*Opposite page left* Location map / *Opposite page right* Site plan / *Above* View from surrounding landscape / *Below left* Corner detail with view of Leuven, Belgium in the distance / *Below right* Wall detail

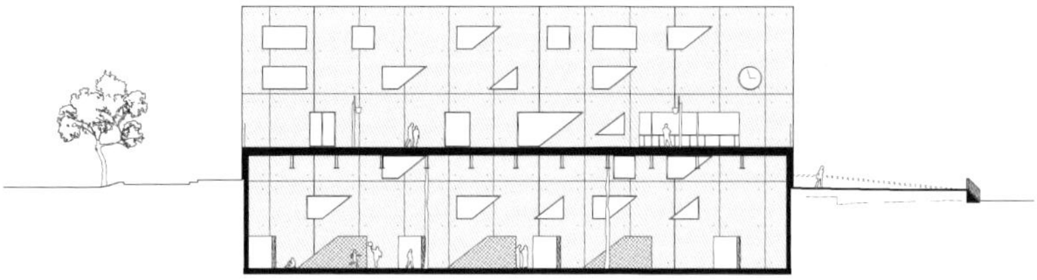

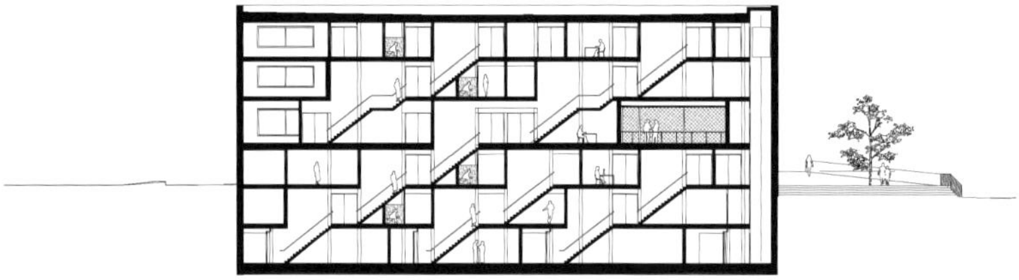

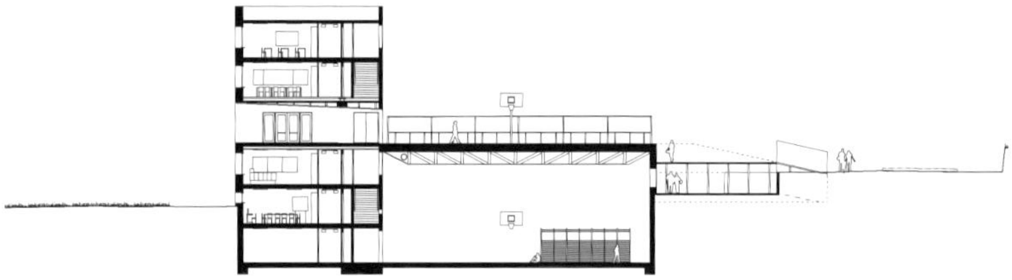

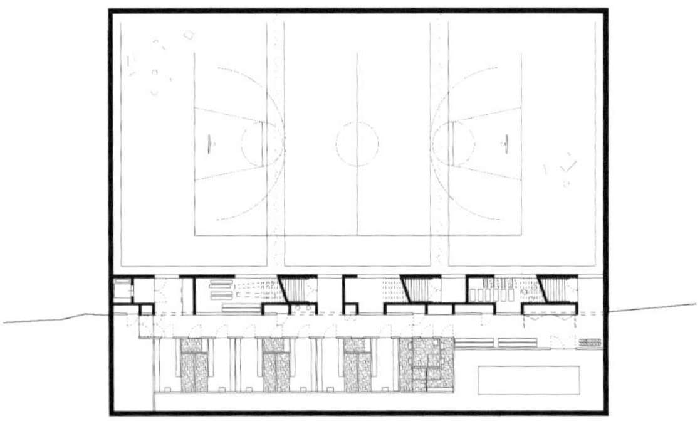

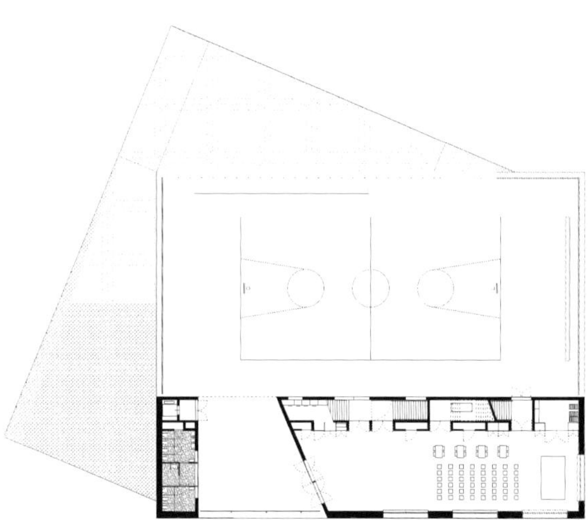

*Opposite page above* Sections / *Opposite page below* Floor plans / *Above* Mirrored entry / *Below* Collages / *Following spread* Elevation

**OFFICE 15: Border Crossing**

*International competition, 1st prize*
*Mexico/United States, 2005*

An oblong volume provides a border crossing for pedestrians between Mexico and the United States, and interrupts the endless demarcated boundary. A nine-meter high wall defines a no-man's-land between the two countries. Within the white walls a grid of palm trees imposes order on a large, shaded garden. Pavilions for passport control and administration are spread around here and there, becoming part of the garden. The oasis is a point of reference in the vast Tex-Mex landscape, hidden within the open landscape by its walls. In all its simplicity it raises questions about the desire for the promised land.

Collaborator: Wonne Ickx.

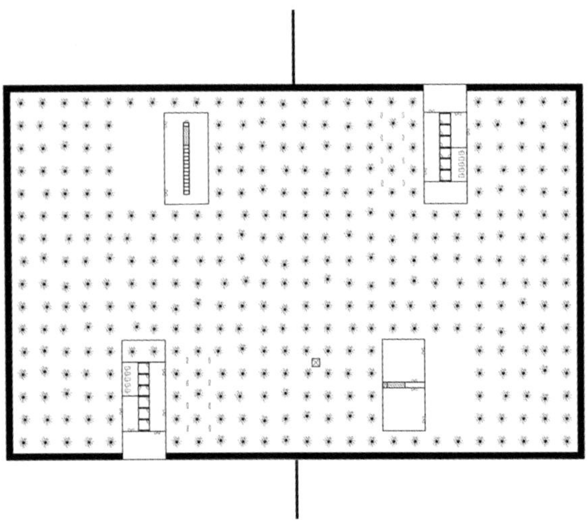

*Opposite page* Site plan / *Above* Entrance to garden, Collage / *Below* Aerial Rendering

**OFFICE 35: Cité de Refuge**

*Project for Architecture Biennial of Rotterdam,*
*Special Mention Award*
*Ceuta, Spain, 2007*

Cité de Réfuge is a project that was developed within the context of the 2007 Rotterdam Architecture Biennale, the theme of which was 'Power'. Ceuta is a Spanish enclave on Moroccan soil. The project gives a face to the politicized border crossing at Ceuta: a refugee city in the no man's land between two cities (Ceuta and Tangier), between two countries (Spain and Morocco), between two continents (Europe and Africa). This city is formed by a large square of 482 x 482 meters that is surrounded by a colonnaded structure, like a thick rampart. Within this wall all the infrastructural elements of a border crossing are to be found: offices, hotels, stores, etc. The walled plaza is left undisturbed, without a program. It is a market square and a reception space, like a quay. In this way, the Cité de Réfuge reflects the powerlessness to achieve solutions to the problems occurring on this border. At the same time the project investigates the city in its most radical, concise form: as a deliberate act, a political decision.

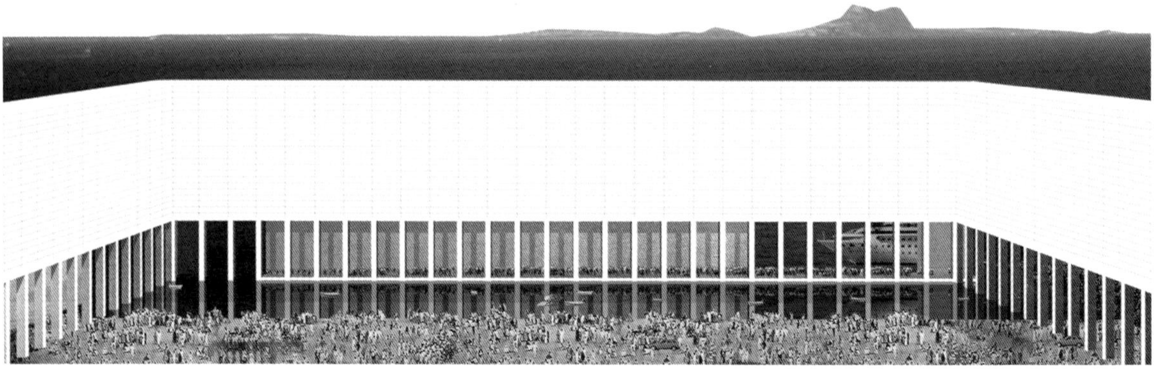

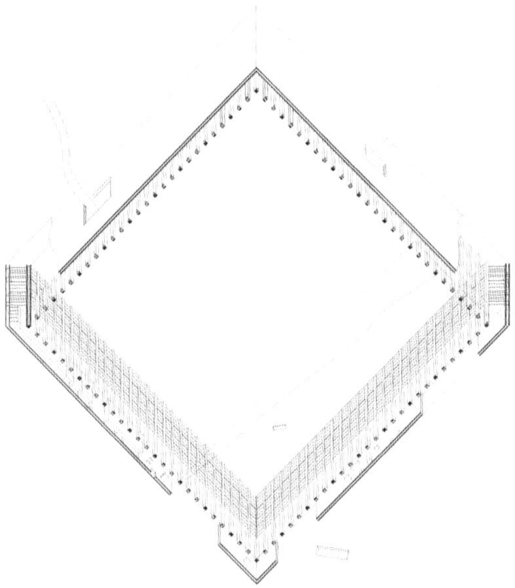

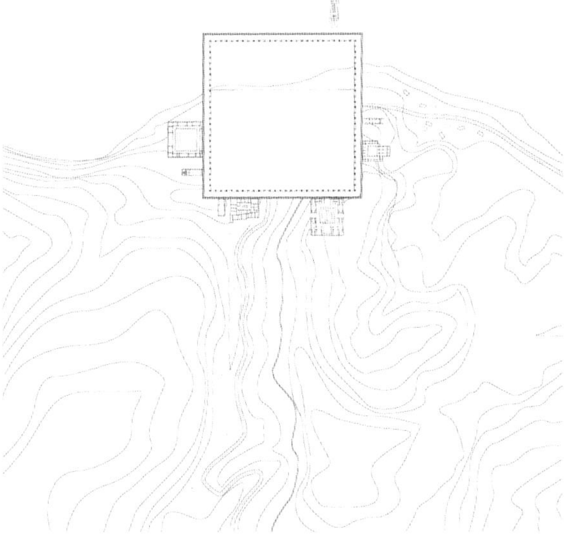

*Opposite page* Perspective view, Collage / *Above left* Axonometric drawing / *Above right* Site plan / *Below* Collage

**OFFICE 57: Central Park Turnhout**

*Masterplan for the ringroad, park, tunnel and dike.*
*Competition, 1st prize.*
*In collaboration with Technum Turnhout*
*Turnhout, Belgium, 2008*

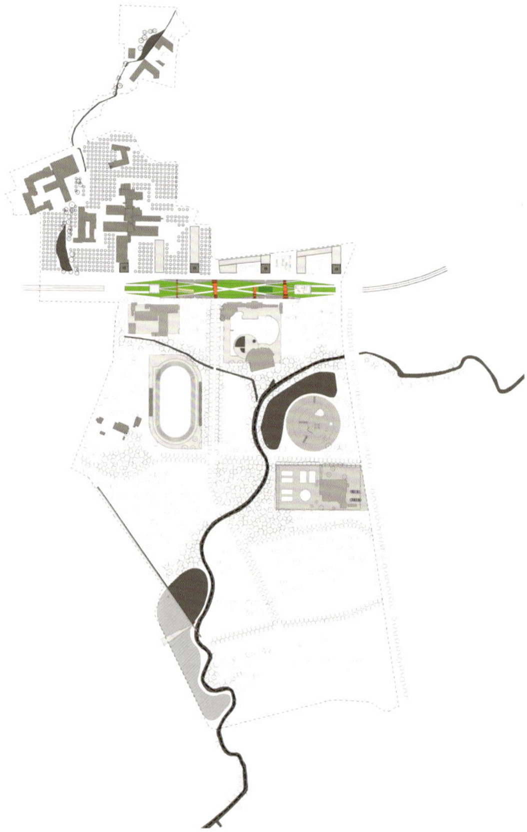

In the medium-sized city of Turnhout, part of the ring road will be tunneled, freeing an area between the center and the city park. The Master plan for this area comprises several interventions, reinstating the existing park as a 'Central Park' for Turnhout. The key element is a dike above the half-submerged tunnel. The dike formalizes a new urban edge and extends the park over the ring road towards the city. It is at the same time a barrier to and vantage point over the park.

In the park itself several scenic interventions enforce the existing structure. At the other side of the dike a row of four towers, evenly spaced, marks the southern limit of the city. The proportion of the towers allows for different programs including: living, offices, and the extension of the neighboring hospital. Between the towers low-rise buildings are developed around courtyards which open towards the park.

*Opposite page above* Site plan / *Opposite page below* Park & Towers, Collage / *Above* Building in landscape, Collage / *Below* Park & Towers, Collages

**OFFICE 51: 25 Rooms (Villa in Ordos)**

*Part of the 'Ordos 100'-project, selected by Herzog & de Meuron, curated by Ai Weiwei*

*Ordos, China, 2008*

The design for a 1,000-square-meter residence in the Mongolian desert is reduced to the design of just one component—a room, a rectangular space with four entrances and no prescribed function. The room receives its individual character only through its ceiling height and its relative position in the house. Twenty-four identical rooms are organized over three stories, on each floor an enfilade surrounds a central atrium that is protected from harsh winds and sand storms. The inner garden is the actual outdoor space of the house, to which all of the rooms are oriented. Two flights of stairs, which stand in the middle of the room like pieces of furniture, provide the connection between the stories.

Because the building is sunken into the ground, only the top story can be seen in the residential neighborhood, like the tip of an iceberg. As in traditional Mongolian settlements, the house forms a microclimate: its underground position profits from the relatively constant ground temperature, tempering the extreme temperatures of the Mongolian climate. The structural base of the project is a massive concrete base, which by its weight prevents the house from being pushed up by the water pressure. The concrete wall decreases in width towards the top. Inside, the walls between rooms are doubled, and the space in between is used to house the impressive array of ducts, vents, and other technical equipment required by a house of this comfort level. All rooms are equipped with double glass doors, allowing for each room to be closed off separately to maintain its singular logic.

The luxurious aspect of this residence is not in an extravagant form or use of materials, but in the abundance of spaces. The enigmatic twenty-fifth room on the roof is for the attendant: a lookout post on a thick wall.

*Opposite page left* Inner Garden, Collage / *Opposite page right* Section / *Above* Exterior view, Collage / *Below* Axonometric / *Bottom* Plans

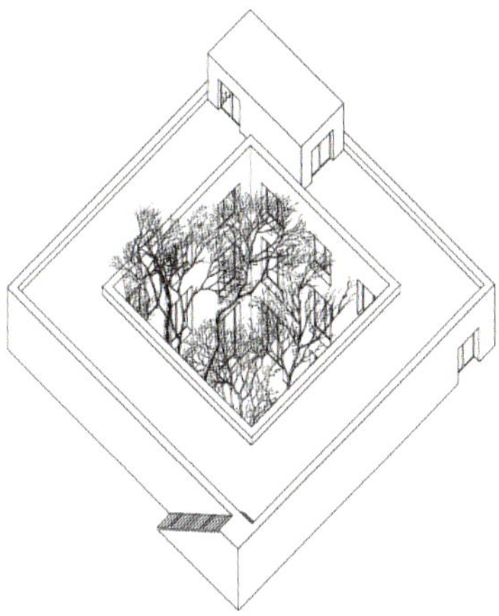

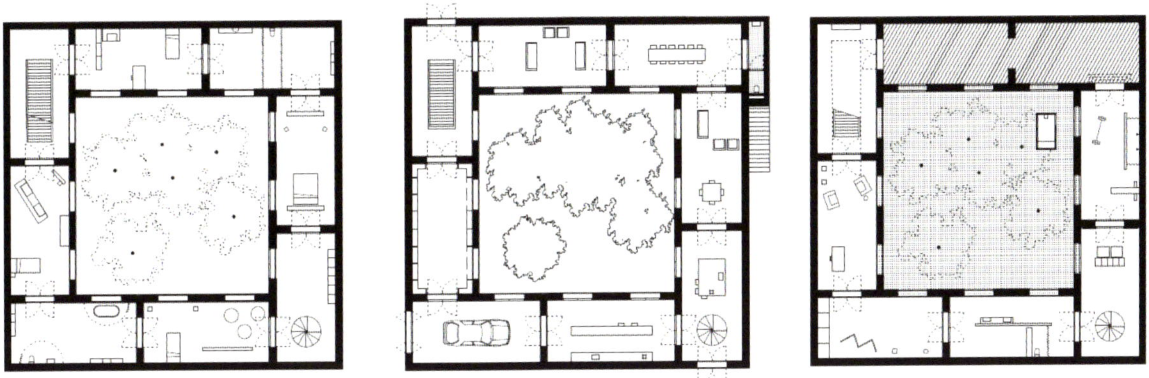

## OFFICE 73: Garden Residence

*Lommel, Belgium, 2009*

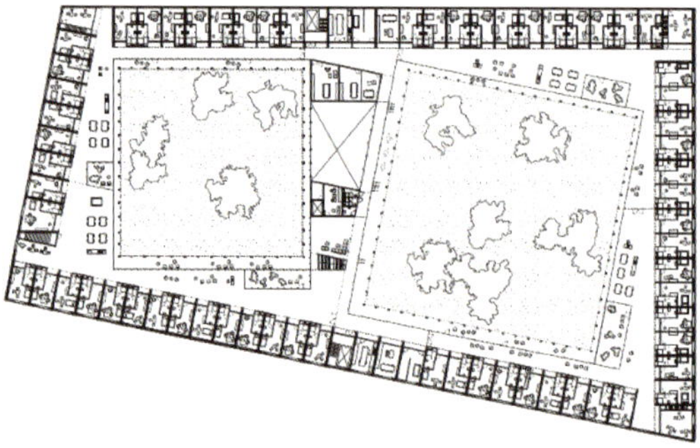

A care center is a big house with everything within hand's reach. It should be designed to provide its inhabitants with spatial and landscape stimulants, while keeping in mind their limited mobility.

Garden Residence, a care center with 120 rooms, is designed as an island, framing its surrounding landscape. It offers a set of different spatial qualities while maintaining its natural character. The apartments, organized in eight groups, are situated along the perimeter of the building, defining its prismatic shape. Two squares within the borders of the building create two inner gardens. The hallways between the flats, their shape defined by the regular square gardens and the irregular outer facade, double as communal spaces for the inhabitants, overlooking the gardens. The center of the complex, accessible via the gardens, forms the entrance and houses all administrative functions as well as a communal hall.

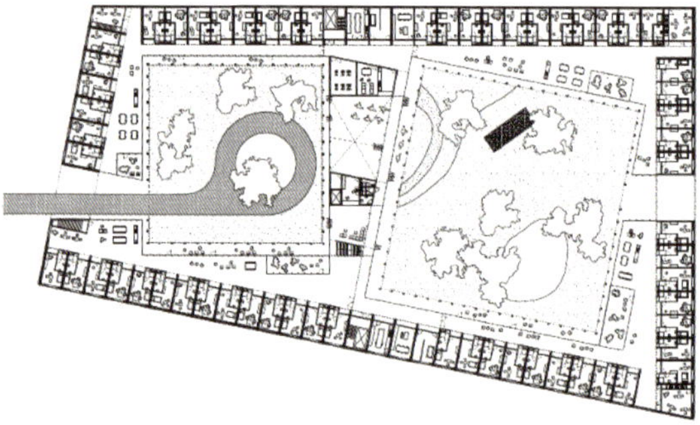

The organization of the complex is underlined by its structural concept and materiality. The perimeter of rooms is a solid concrete structure, which insures the necessary thermal mass and stability. The communal spaces are considered as 'garden rooms': light wooden additions in close contact with the gardens.

In collaboration with HHF Architects (CH).
Structural Engineer: Util Structuurstudies, Brussels.
Technical Engineer: Studiebureau R. Boydens, Brussels.

*Opposite page below* Exterior view, Collage / *Opposite page above* Plans / *Above & below left* Inner Garden, Collage / *Below right* Interior, Collage

**OFFICE 126: Centres for Traditional Music**

*Selected competition, 1st prize*

*Muharraq, Bahrain, 2012–2017*

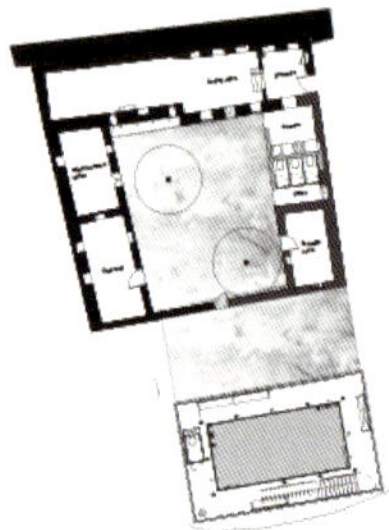

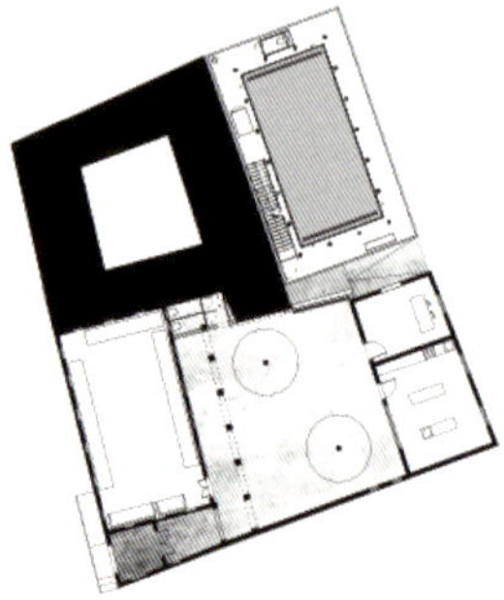

Dar Al Jinaa and Dar Al Riffa are part of a project of urban renewal in Bahrain. Each project consists of both the renovation of an existing Dar ('house'), and a new, added Majlis ('collective room'). The Majlis will be used as communal spaces for traditional music performances.

Both buildings consist of a simple structure of round concrete columns and platforms, Rectangular folding glass facades create interior spaces on the platforms. Stairs, sanitary boxes, and technical equipment form the 'furniture' which makes this simple structure functional. The entire building is covered by a painted steel mesh, providing cover from the harsh desert sun and transforming the buildings into enigmatic, 'veiled' objects.

*Opposite page above* Plans / *Opposite page center* Elevation / *Opposite page below* Exterior & Interior, Collages / *Above* Exterior, Collage / *Below* Section Perspective Collage

# PEZO VON ELLRICHSHAUSEN

Concepcion, Chile

**Meri House**

*Florida, Chile, 2014*

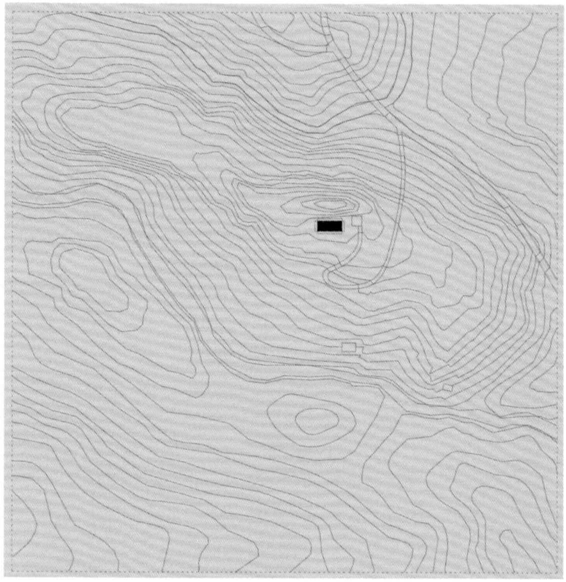

The Meri House was originally projected for permanent use. After important changes in the life of the family, the design was transformed into a smaller, temporary residence. Nevertheless, the goal was to maintain a luminous and relaxed presence atop the fictitious footprint of the original design. Utilizing the same existing artificial podium, the new house extends itself horizontally as an attempt to follow the flow of a sinuous river at the foot of the hill. The dominant position of this piece establishes a double front, articulated by a regular sequence of identical rooms.

Each side of the house has five rooms with a system of openings along the exterior walls that are indifferent to orientation or program and another system of apertures within the interior walls that is relative to the degree of privacy desired from one room to the other. Both sequences are structured by another system of ceiling apertures that forces perception diagonally across the depth of the plan. The center of the house is blurred by a series of tangential perforations that unify the rooms at every side. The perforated ceiling extends beyond the interior and renders each of the four sides in deep shade. The totality of the structure is impregnated pine. The exterior walls are clad with dyed rough pine boards and the interiors with softened and flat boards, with the same Petoruti painting inherited by the family.

The Austrian writer, Robert Musil said that everything that wants to closely approximate another has an elastic band tied to it, which tenses when extended.

If not, things could end up intersecting each other. It seems that at every movement and in every activity, there is an elastic that fortunately never lets us entirely do what we want.

Architects: Mauricio Pezo, Sofia von Ellrichshausen.
Collaborators: Diego Perez, Valentina Chandia, Simon Guery, Philpe Kempfer, Orlando Hartmann, Luisa Rocco.
Structural consultant: Luis Mendieta.
Builder: Ricardo Ballesta.
Building services: Luis Valenzuela, Daniel Garrido.
Client: Maria Rosa Gonzales, Alejandro Woloszyn.
Photography: Pezo von Ellrichshausen.

*Opposite page above* Site plan / *Opposite page center* Painting / *Above* Day view

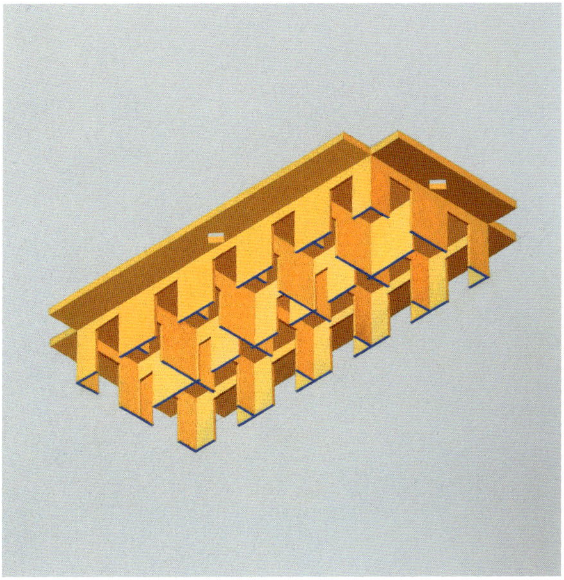

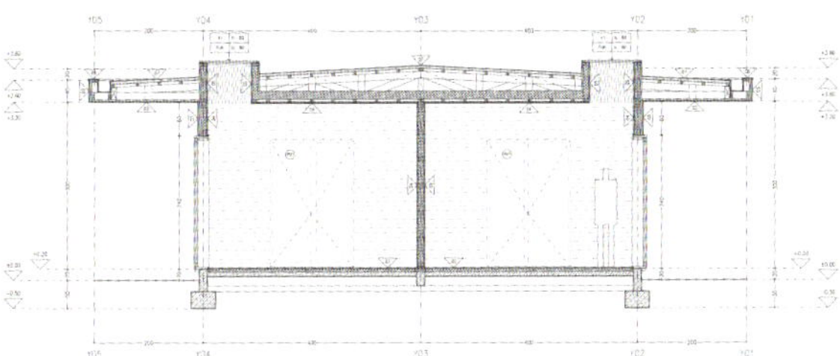

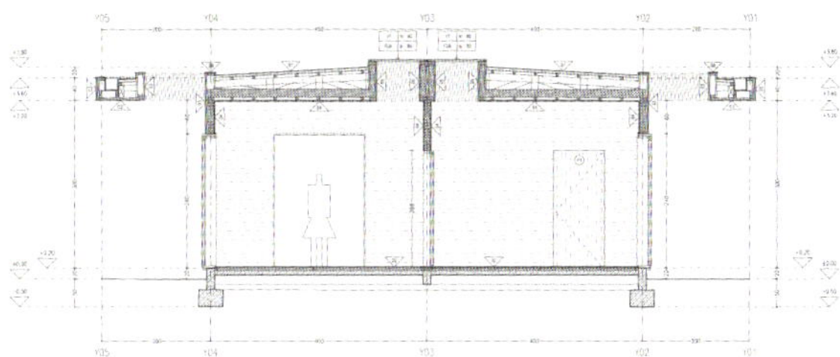

Opposite page Interior / Above left Painting / Above right Exterior detail / Center Sections / Below left View of kitchen / Below right Bathroom

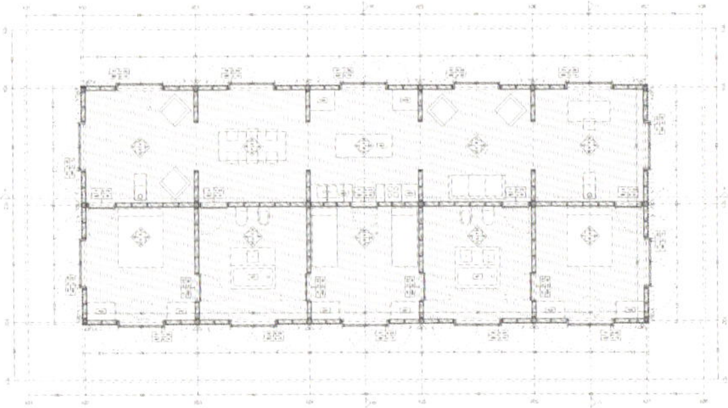

*Above* Night view / *Opposite page* Floor plan / *Below* Roof plan

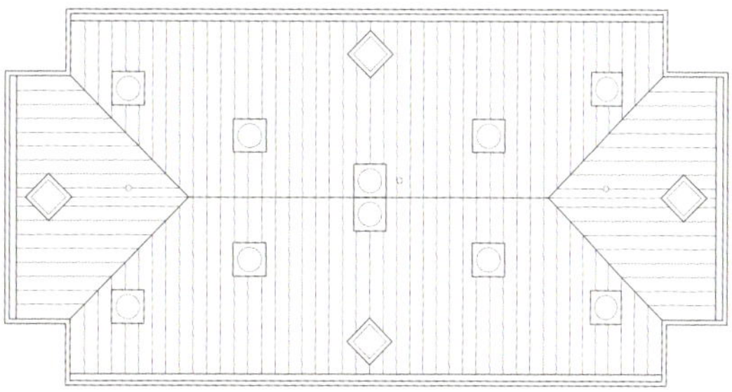

## Guna House

*Llacolen, San Pedro de la Paz, Chile, 2010- 2014*

Hemmed in between a steeply sloping hillside and a forest of eucalyptus trees, the narrow plot of land compels one to arrive through a garden, descending to the small bay of a lagoon. Overlooking the landscape, a monolithic prism of concrete attempts to articulate the contradictions of the topography. Its square top floor, measuring 20m on each side, balances on top of a compact bottom floor, measuring 8.5m on each side. The upper floor contains a central patio that is the same size as the bottom floor, therefore all the suspended rooms are exposed to the outside on four sides. This upper floor, a dogmatic piano nobile which compensates for the inconvenience of the diagonally set natural terrain, is based on a grid of four modules per side. Overhead apertures at the center of each enclosed space and the ends of the circulation paths, reinforce the vertical dimension of the layout, while also amplifying the shimmering of the lagoon.

The less formal, bottom floor of the house serves the more day-to-day functions of the domestic realm. Its square plan, divided into four equal quadrants, is cut back at the north corner—a subtraction that serves as a visual and functional short cut between the upper patio and the edge of the lagoon. As in Matila Ghyka's description of a landscape as a 'crystallization of a conflict of forces', the entire structure is a stony mass in apparent repose. The four walls of the patio act as Vierendeel girders resting in balance on the podium. Almost as if they were diffusing the stress, the concrete surfaces have the coarse texture of fine formwork boards with a diluted black patina.

Architects: Mauricio Pezo, Sofia von Ellrichshausen.
Collaborators: Diogo Porto, Joao Quintela, Lena Johansen, Cecilia Maderoz.
Builder: Pablo Vasquez; Structure: Luis Mendieta.
Client: Pablo Vasquez, Maria Paz Calderon.
Photography: Pezo von Ellrichshausen.

*Opposite page* Exterior view / *Above* House in the landscape / *Below left* Site plan / *Below right* Painting, Oil on canvas

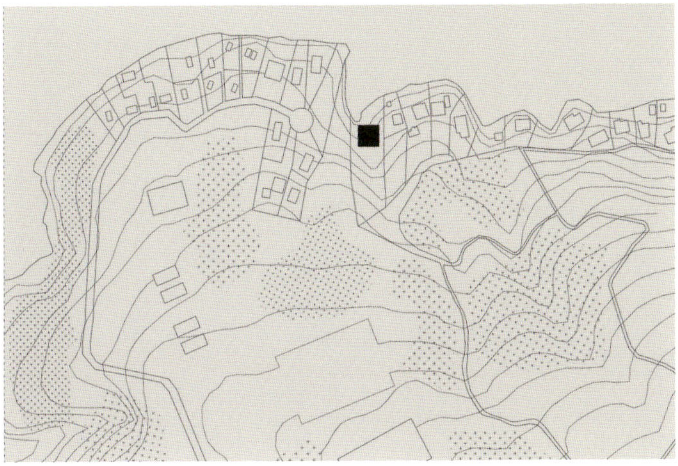

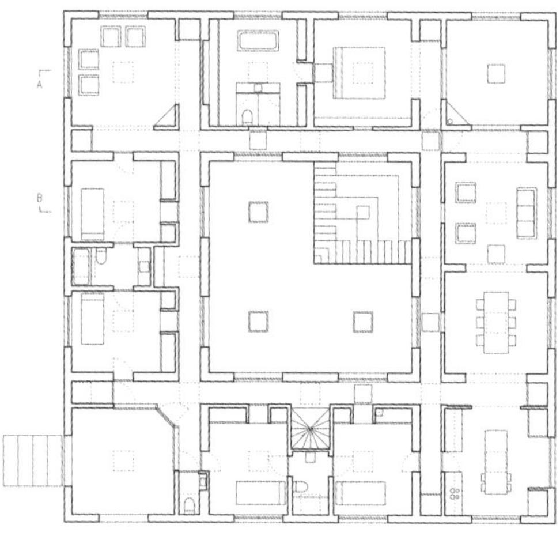

2F

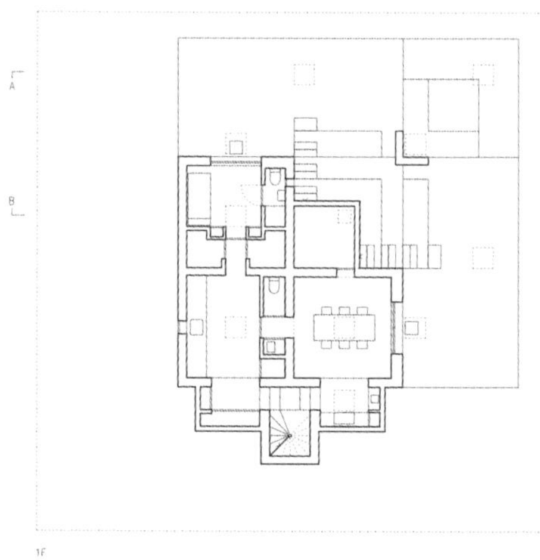

1F

*Opposite page above* Ceiling detail / *Opposite page below left* First floor plan / *Opposite page below right* Second floor plan / *Above* Covered entry with view to the landscape / *Below left* Roof plan / *Below right* Model

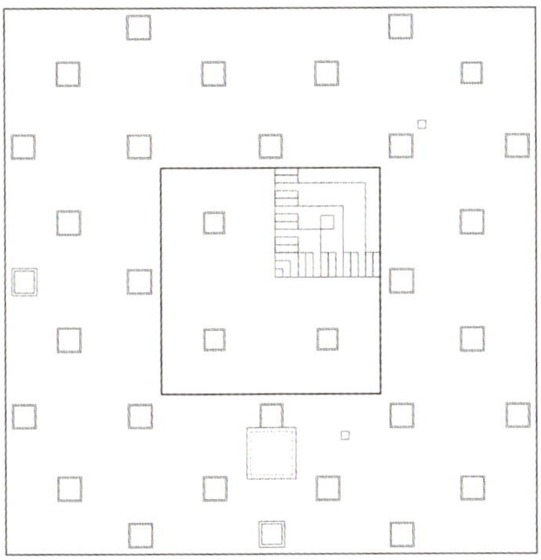

*Above* Elevated courtyard / *Opposite page top left* Stairs to elevated courtyard / *Opposite page top right* Second floor entrance / *Opposite page center* Interiors / *Opposite page below* Sections

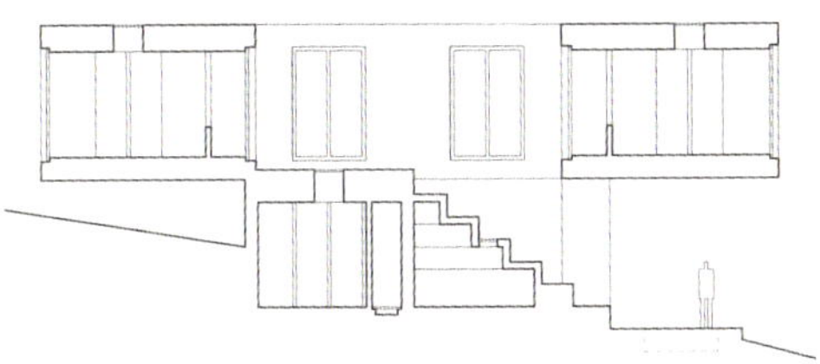
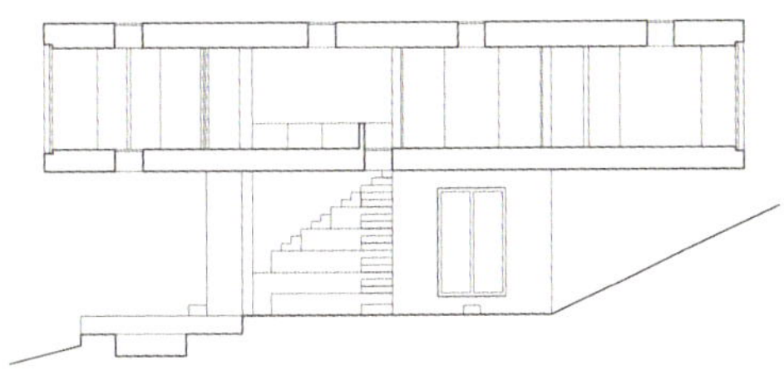

**Solo House**

*Cretas, Spain, 2009-2012*

The unique entity occupies a dominant position in a rural landscape of vineyards and olive groves, set against a general background of medieval villages and rocky outcrops. A bare horizontal volume is detached from the ground, suspended in an almost archaic time.

Transparent and monolithic, the building is balanced on top of a blind pedestal, in such a way that its outline is divided between an elevated portion visible from a distance and another that disappears behind the leaves of native plant species. The aerial realm of the platform indicates the cardinal points.

A panoramic perimeter ring is punctuated by a sequence of rooms with undefined functions. These crystalline, symmetrical living spaces are mutually independent and are linked by four open terraces at their corners. This portico is too narrow to contain a static living room and too deep for a balcony-cum-viewing platform. In this aerial realm, the only closed room (in the center) is not roofed; its four walls are perforated at their central point, while the floor is of water (the gentlest paving known to man), which reflects the sky.

After going along a sloping straight path, a bifurcated set of steps shapes the entrance; entering the house is like going into a twin tunnel that encircles the central swimming pool, with small openings at diagonals that allow glimpses of sky across the water. Under this access level a building services passageway goes around a room without use (and with scant overhead lighting).

The volume unity has something of the genetic sche-ma about it; its monumentally risky structure disappears into the outlines of its mass. It would seem that when Chilean theoretician Juan Borchers said that "architecture was physics incarnate", he was speaking not only of loads and tensions, but of life itself, which erases their effort.

Architects: Mauricio Pezo, Sofia von Ellrichshausen
Collaborators: Diogo Porto, Bernhard Maurer, Valeria Farfan, Eleonora Bassi, Ana Freeze.
Builder: Ferras Prats.
Client: Christian Bourdais, Solo Houses.
Photography: Pezo von Ellrichshausen and Cristobal Palma.

*Opposite page* Model / *Above & Below* House in the landscape

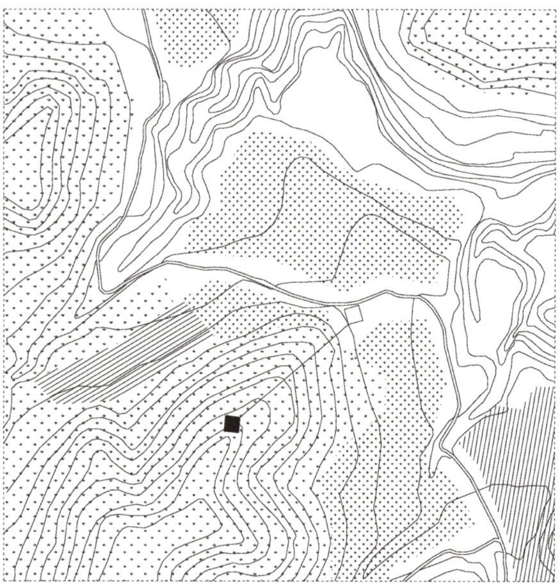

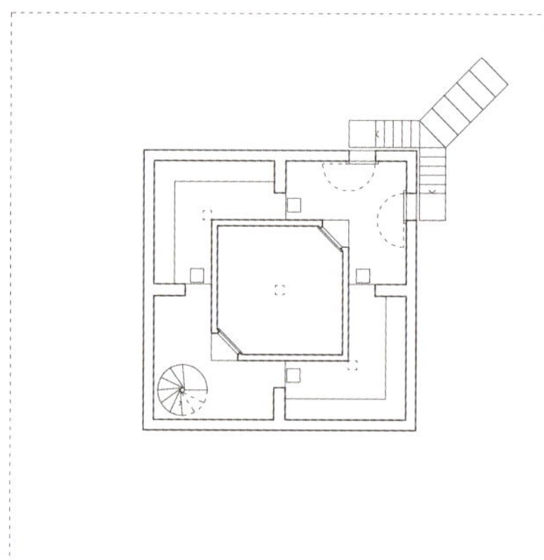

*Opposite page above* Elevation / *Opposite page below left* Site plan / *Opposite page below right* Second floor plan / *Above* Interior with view to the landscape / *Below left* Third floor plan / *Below right* Roof plan

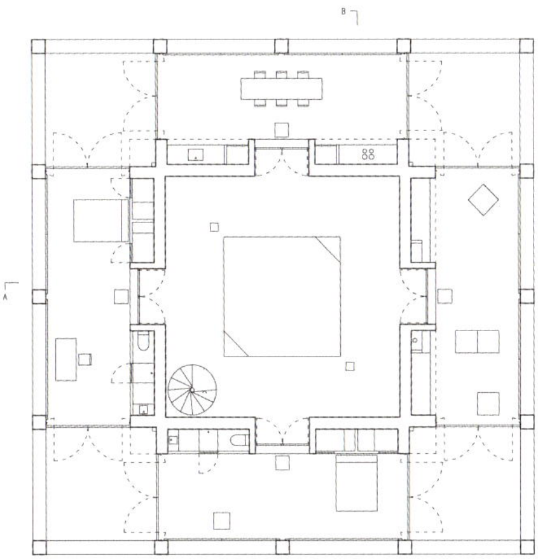

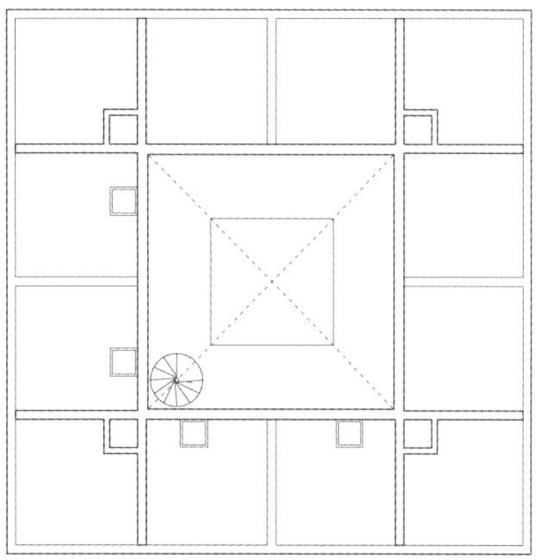

*Above* Swimming pool / *Opposite page above* Swimming pool corner detail / *Opposite page below* Axonometric painting

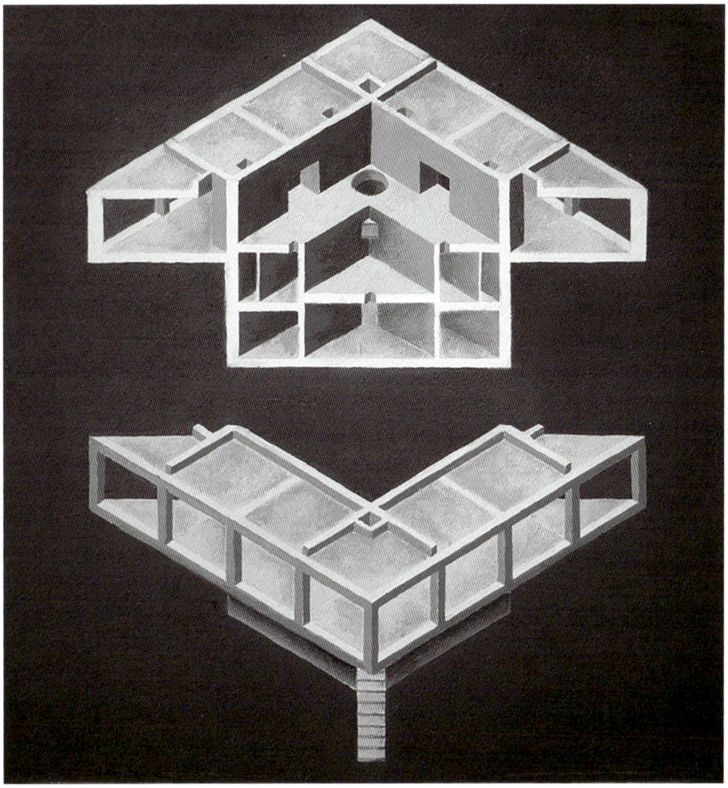

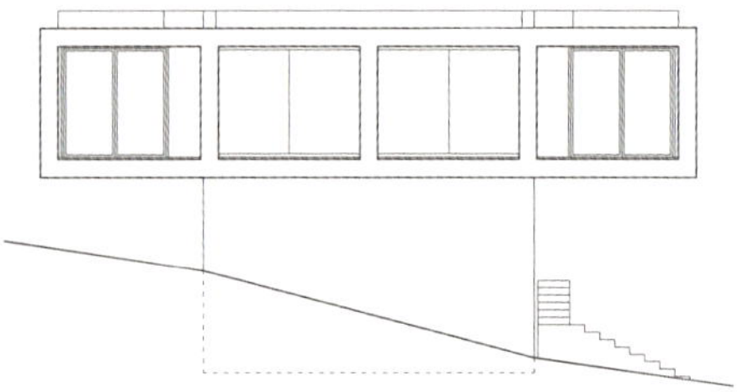

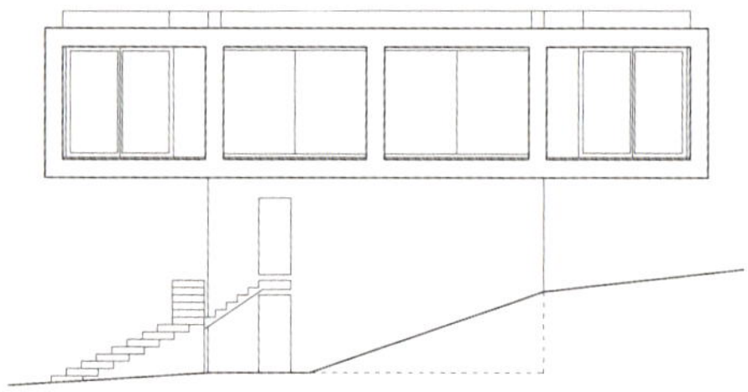

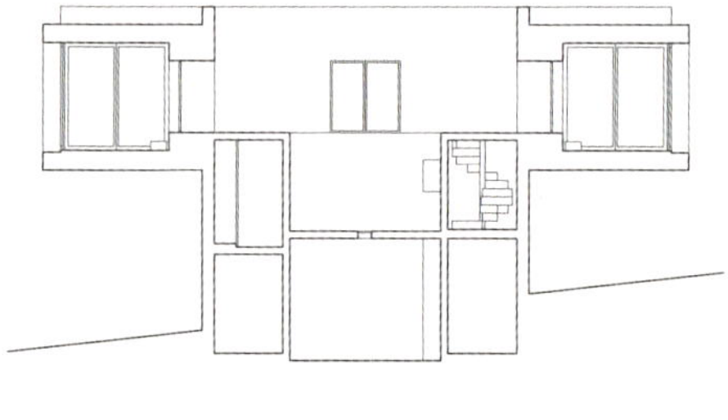

*Above & Opposite page above* Interiors with view to the landscape / *Opposite page center* Elevations / *Opposite page below* Sections / *Below* Axonometric

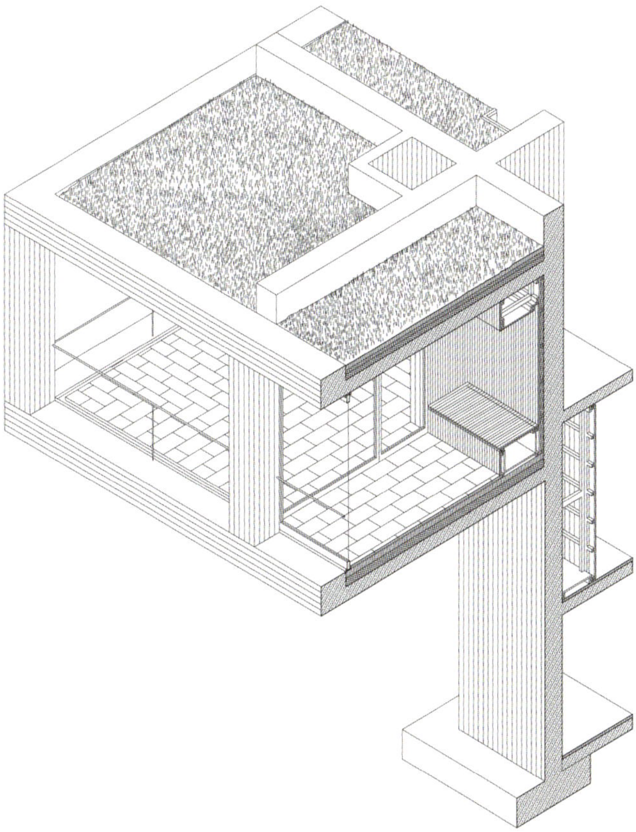

# R & R STUDIOS / ROBERTO BEHAR & ROSARIO MARQUARDT

Miami, Florida, United States

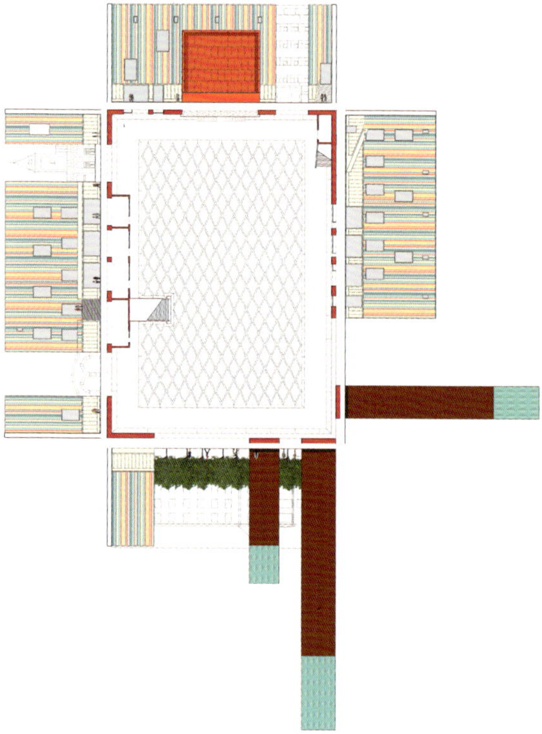

**Valby Square**

*Copenhagen, Denmark 2009*

Valby Square invents a new urban space, a kind of open castle for the people of Copenhagen that celebrates the city and illuminates the everyday life of Valby. The urban intervention performs simultaneously as landmark, square, and distinct urban ensemble. Each of these aspects of the project corresponds to three distinct scales; the metropolitan scale, the scale of the square, and the scale of specific conditions of the surroundings.

The square doubles as a public room, around which a diverse assemblage of architectures meet. The ensemble is composed of the public room, three towers that double as little skyscrapers, and a number of buildings of diverse types and scales—which assist the public room in meeting its surroundings. These three typological instances are woven into one another to become the center, or downtown, of New Valby. Together, they are symbol and gathering place, a beautiful and unique urban square, distinctive among Copenhagen's Plads, which contributes to the quality of life of the area.

Valby Square introduces an element of awe, dizzy, and adventure to the Valby urban landscape and, simultaneously, performs as a contemporary gateway to the city, a symbol of Valby's vibrant culture and a new and unique destination in the City of Copenhagen.

*Opposite page below* Oblique elevation / *Opposite page above* Composite drawing / *Above* Perspective, Rendering / *Below* Axonometric / *Following spread* Night, Rendering

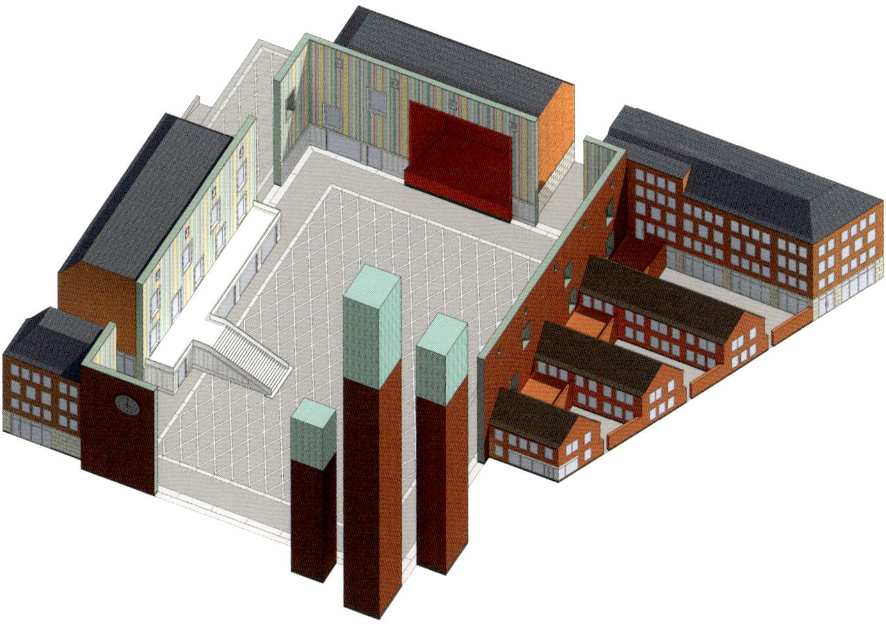

**Main Public Library**

*Rosario, Buenos Aires, Argentina*

The Main Public Library of Rosario, Argentina is proposed as a Palace of the People and place of encounters for the residents of the Southern District of the City of Rosario. The project is envisioned as an exceptionally public event woven together with the existing Municipal Center by Alvaro Siza and the fabric of the neighborhood into a complementary system of urban spaces varied in character and highly public in nature.

The transparency of the library invites participation and generates spontaneous encounters within. The open plan of the building invites the visitor to travel through the library and provides maximum flexibility and a variety of spaces to read, study and lounge individually or in groups.

The new Main Library of Rosario offers the book as the main subject and event throughout the building interior. The aerial views from the Library reading rooms democratize the experience of the city and the generous public terrace at the top culminates the spiral motion through the building with extraordinary views towards the magnificent Parana River and beyond.

The building carefully develops a series of public spaces around itself to perform simultaneously as public library, square, park, social terrace and open-air theater. The Library compact approach elevates the building upon the neighborhood to become a landmark in the area. At ground level the Library main entrance opens into a Public Square further defined by restaurants and cafes also serving the Public Park beyond. The auditorium located at ground level shares the stage towards the park and the amphitheater becoming an open air theater and further underlining the openness of the library to all.

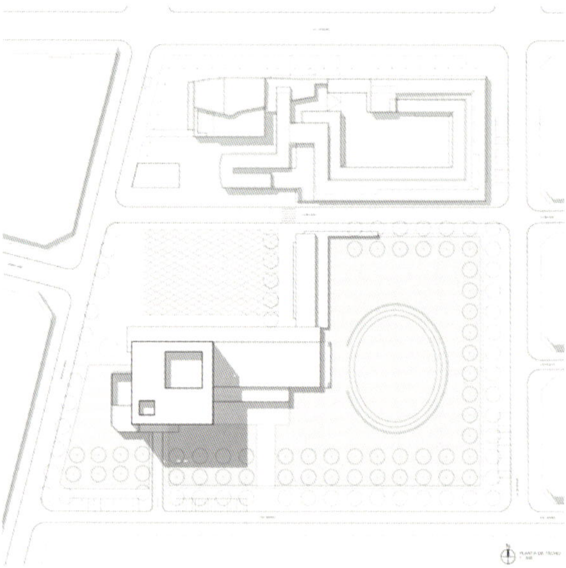

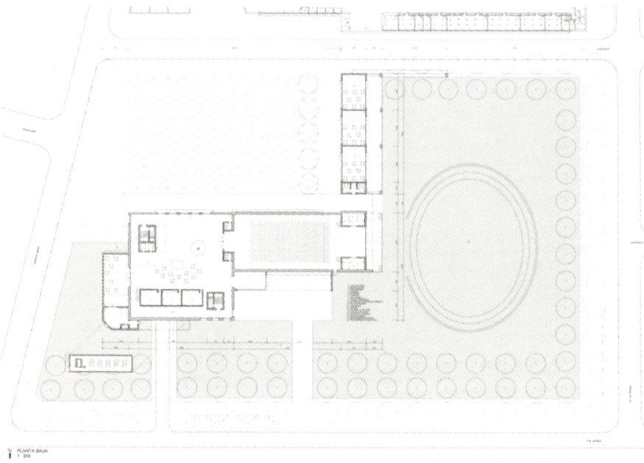

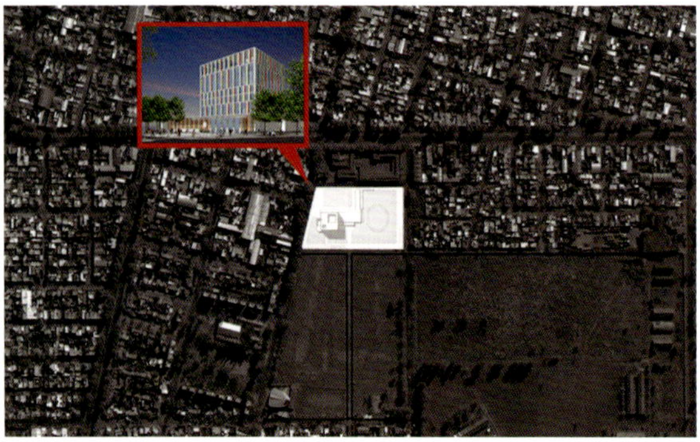

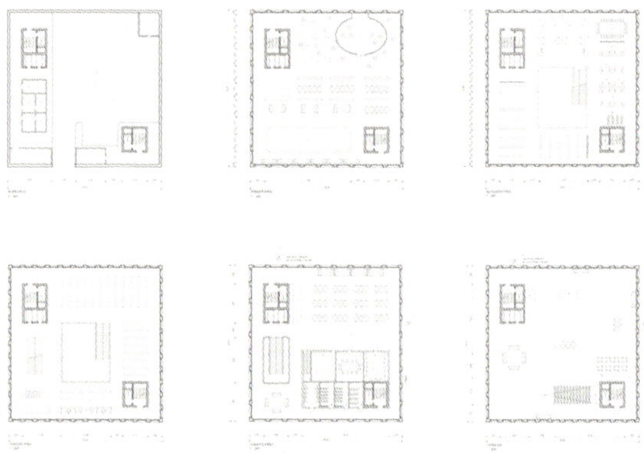

Opposite page left Location map / Opposite page above right Roof plan & 1st floor plan / Opposite page below right Plans / Above Perspective, Rendering / Below Elevation, Rendering

Entrance Perspective, render

# PRODUCTORA

Mexico City, Mexico

**House of Art and Culture**

*Competition*

*Beirut, Lebanon, 2009*

The urban concept envisages a clear geometric volume, which stands assertively on the plot. The façade of the building is conceptualized as a transparent theater curtain of columns: a rhythmic composition that turns the building into an expressive and recognizable element within the urban context. The juxtaposition of three perimeter layers of columns—of varying heights and separations between them—generates a filigree texture of lines, creating moving compositions of shadow and light along all façades during the course of the day. Towards the busy highway a denser composition of columns serves as an acoustical buffer. At moments, these in-between spaces widen out generously towards the city center, generating cool and shady terraces in response to the warm climate of Beirut.

Architectural Design: PRODUCTORA (Carlos Bedoya, Víctor Jaime, Wonne Ickx, Abel Perles).
Collaborators: David Ortega, Diego Escamilla, Gerardo Ramírez, Carlos Salas, Iván Villegas.
Project type: open international competition for cultural infrastructure.
Location: Beirut, Lebanon.
Organization: Lebanese Ministry of Culture.

*Opposite page* Model & Location map / *Above & below* Model

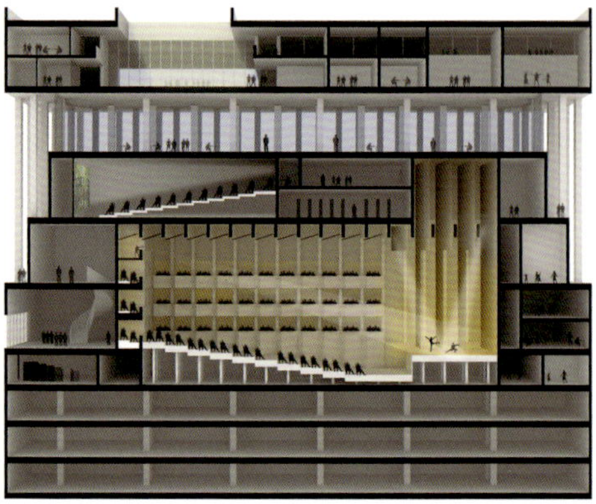

*Above* Section Perspectives / *Below* Section Diagrams / *Opposite page* Models

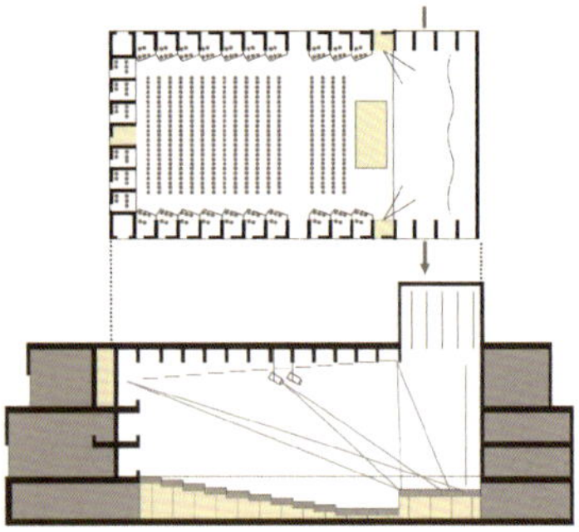

**OPERA / THEATRE / DANCE**

Main stage with direct connections to side and back stages / Stage formed by backdrop, wing curtains and borders along portals / Direction, light and sound control from upper balconies in rear end of the hall / Balconies closest to stage as 'houses' for light / Orchestra pit on lower level in front of stage (if required)

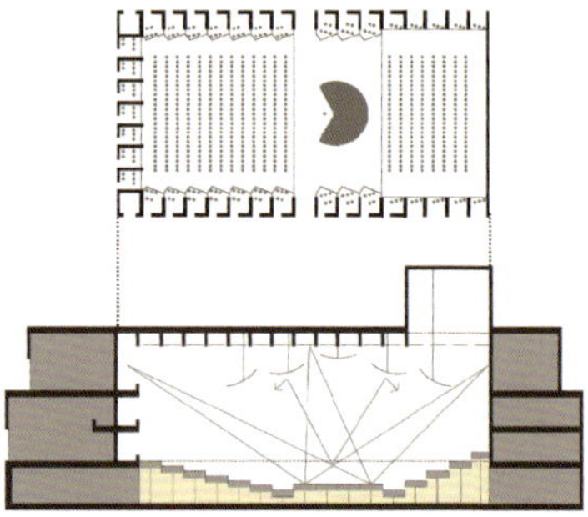

**CLASSIC CONCERT**

Semi-central position of philharmonic orchestra / Audience at both sides of stage and on all balconies / Convex acoustic panels suspended from technical ceiling for sound reflection / Direct access to stage for performers and director from -1 level

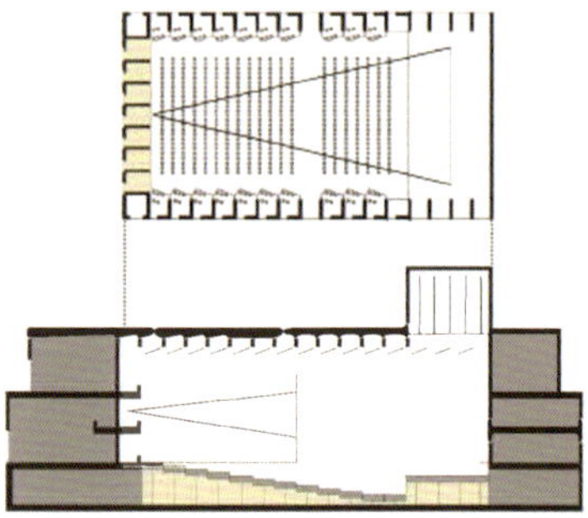

**CONGRESS**

Grades descending from 0 level to -1 level / Translation boots in balconies at rear end of the hall / Projection screen hanging from fly gallery / Control cabin in rear end balconies / Direct connection to dressing rooms off stage

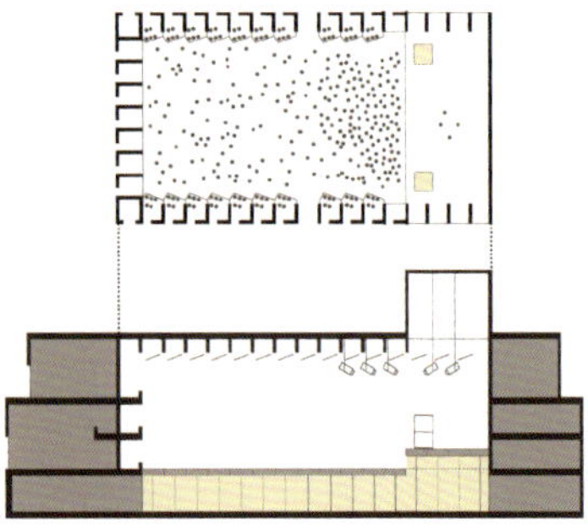

**ROCK / POP**

Floor leveled at +0 level for crowd / VIP places in balconies / Towers of speakers on both sides of stage / Light trusses from fly galleries, balconies and technical ceiling

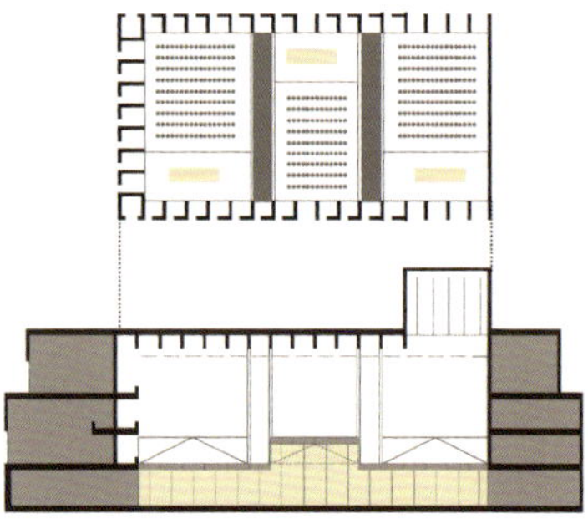

**THEATER / FILM FESTIVAL**

Double temporary acoustic walls (40db performance each) dividing the main space into different areas / Floors with grades in transversal sense / Entrances and projection from opposite loggias / Sound absorbing panels from technical ceiling

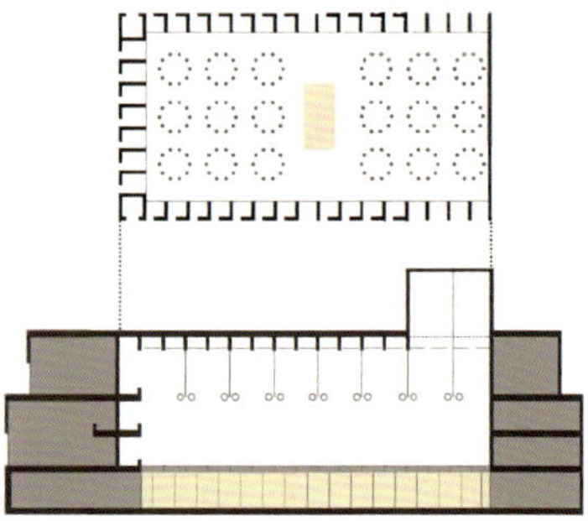

**SPECIAL EVENTS**

Floor leveled at +0 level / Large round tables for banquet / Chandeliers suspended from ceilings / Central bar or food area in direct connection with service facilities and loading dock at -1 level / Other configurations: catwalk, exhibition hall, culture fair,

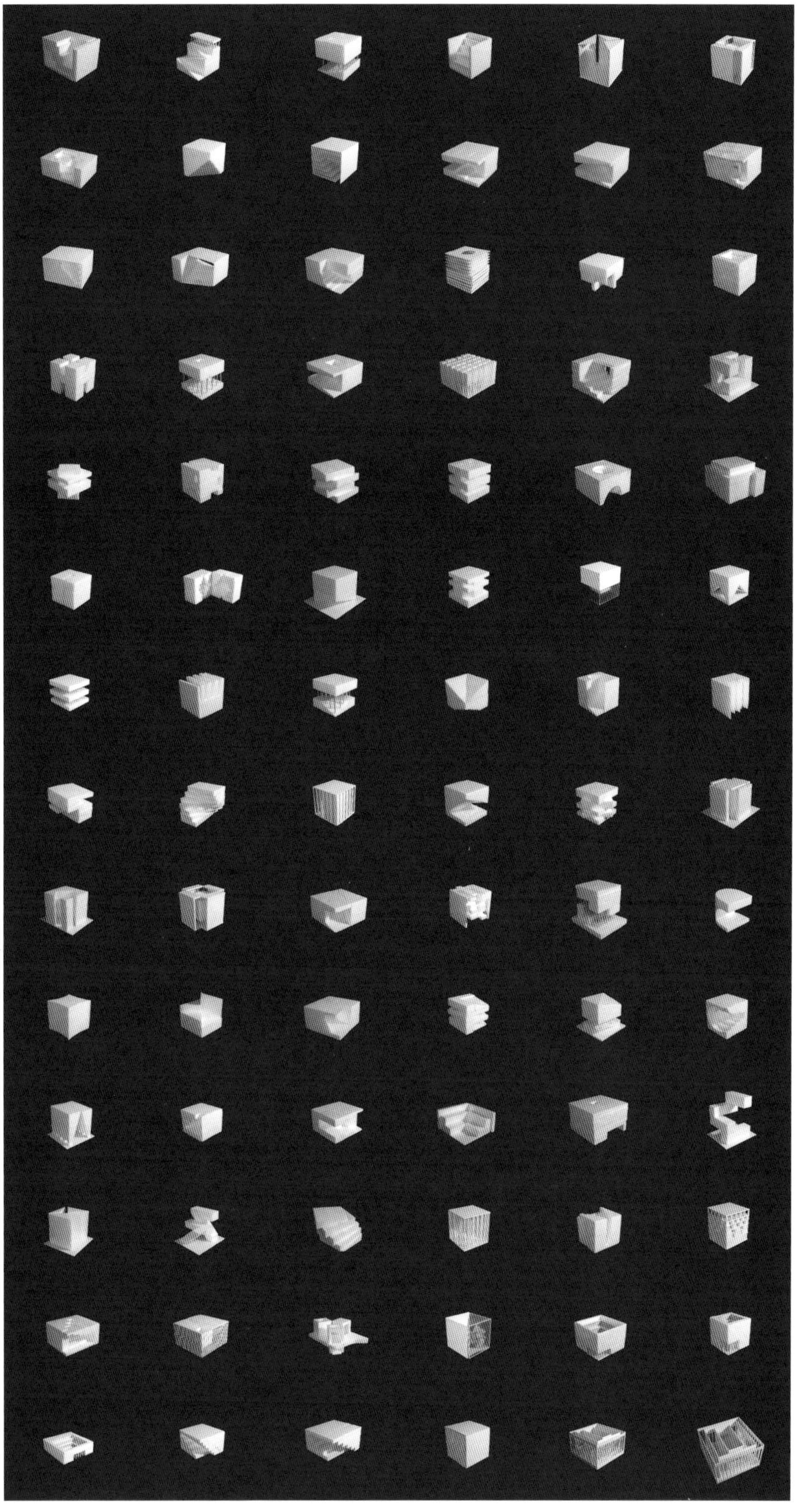

*Above* Elevation, Rendering / *Opposite page* Double loggia, Rendering

Project in context, Rendering

**Pavilion for the Culture Fair 2014**

*Mexico City, Mexico, 2014*

The Pavilion that represents Mexico City at the Culture Fair 2014, addresses the migrations that have influenced the development of Mexico City. The architectonic expression of these migrations is represented through a large boardwalk that brings visitors up to a balcony overlooking the main square (Zocalo) and that comes down again to stage a symbolical arrival to the center of the city.

This game of straight and curved ramps, balconies and walkways, wraps around an equilateral triangle that houses a multi-use space with a graphic exhibition curated by Alberto Odériz. As a reference to the ships that brought the first migrants to Mexico, the whole pavilion is made out of wood. In order to reduce overall costs, all wooden elements were sold and re-used for formwork construction when the fair was over and the pavilion was dismantled.

In close collaboration with our structural engineers (Veronica Correa of KALTIA) and our contractor (Fermin Espinoza – FACTOR EFICIENCIA) we designed this almost 25 feet high structure, so that smaller elements could be pre-fabricated off site and then assembled on the public square in seven working days.

The column-less interior space (an equilateral triangle with 50 ft. long sides) is covered by a large roof composed of smaller triangular segments that transfer the vertical forces down to the structural facades. These load bearing facades are designed with different rhythms of diagonal bracing, open and closed surfaces, and vertical elements all come together in a very lively textured expression. The resulting play in depth of the wooden members recalls a crafty texture as if it were a woven basket.

The surrounding circulation—with its straight upward ramp at the beginning, an elevated boardwalk in the middle and a circular spiral downwards to the plaza, wraps around the triangular volume, leaving one side open to organize the main access to the interior space. Under the elevated boardwalk a space is provided for an information counter that informs visitors about the fair. Regarding the visitor's experience of the pavilion, we had to take two very different functions into account. First, we wanted to create a smaller and more intimate space where people could dwell for a longer while, have a one-on-one relation to the exhibition, enjoy lectures, host cocktail parties or music events etc. The interior of the triangle is therefore open on just one side, to control access and occupancy. It is covered with stained and white panels to allow projections on its interior surfaces at night.

On the other hand, we had to accommodate the enormous amount of people that visit the Culture Fair (in 2014 the fair received more than 2 million visitors). Since we wanted to create an architectural proposal that could be enjoyed by large masses without having to wait in long lines under the hot Mexican sun, we designed a fast-track route that could allow you to experience the pavilion in a different way. A long architectural promenade would take you up to an elevated boardwalk from where visitors could enjoy a different perspective of the cultural fair, the square, the cathedral, and the presidential palace, as well as taking a peek into the triangular exhibition and event space from above.

The formal and volumetric definition of the pavilion is thus a literal translation of these two different routes, experiences, and time frames. The circulation narrates a story about migration and allows both an intimate as well as a quick experience for visitors.

Architecture: PRODUCTORA (Carlos Bedoya, Víctor Jaime, Wonne Ickx, Abel Perles).
Collaborators: Diego Escamilla, Lucrecia Sodo, Gerardo Aguilar.
Contractor: Factor Eficiencia (Fermín Espinoza).
Structural Engineering: KALTIA.
Museography: Alberto Odériz.
An initiative of the 'Coordinación de Asuntos Internacionales GDF' (Tatiana Alcázar) for the Culture Fair 2014 – CDMX.
Support by MASISA and PIRWI.
Photography: Luis Gallardo – LGM Studio.

*Top* Pavilion on the Zocalo, view towards Presidential Palace / *Center* Ground Floor & Level 1 plans / *Bottom* Northwest, South & Northeast Elevations

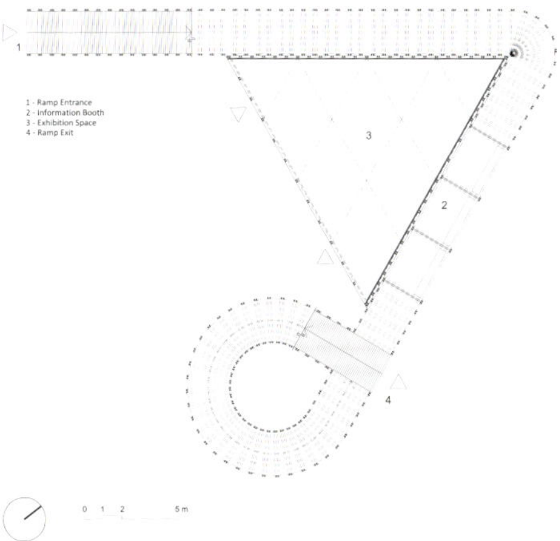


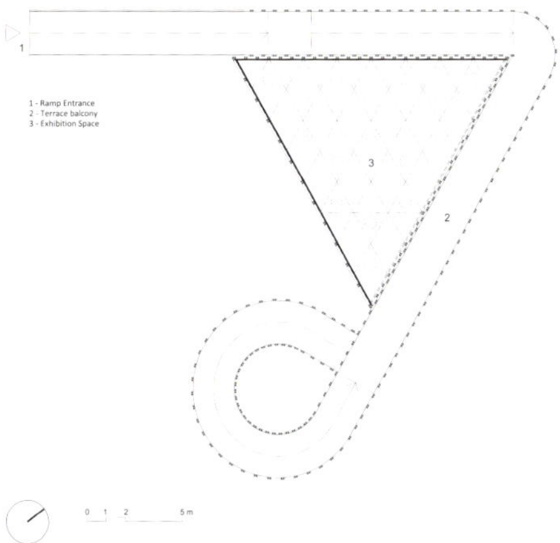


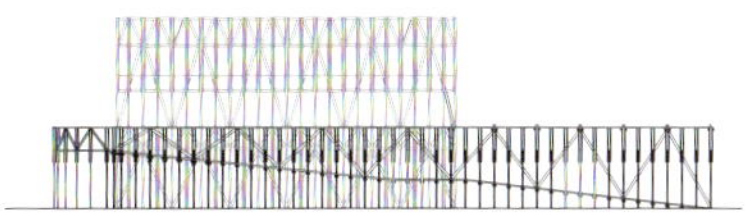

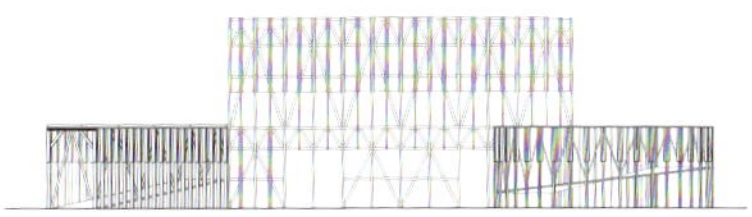

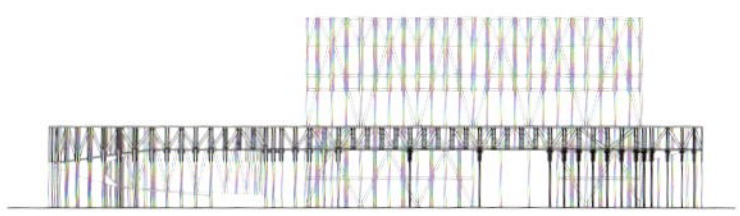

*Above* Pavilion on the Zocalo, view towards Cathedral / *Below* Site plan / *Opposite page left* Structural drawing of facades (KALTIA) / *Opposite page top right* Pavilion Under Construction / *Opposite page right* Northeast, Northwest, North views

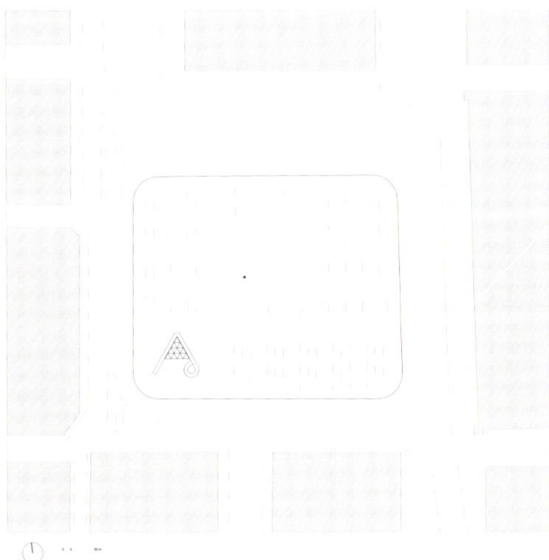

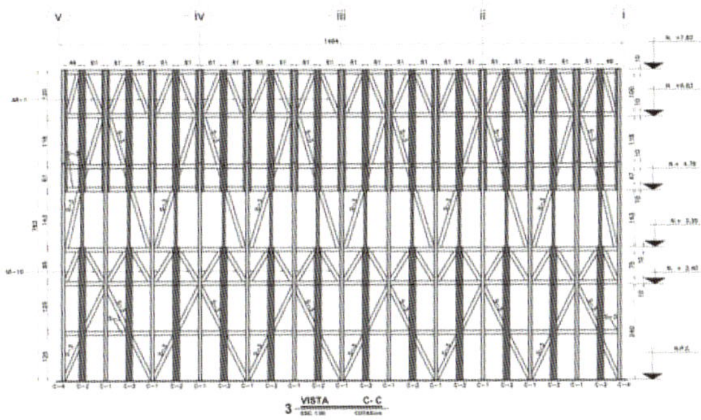
v
iv
iii
ii
i
3 VISTA C-C

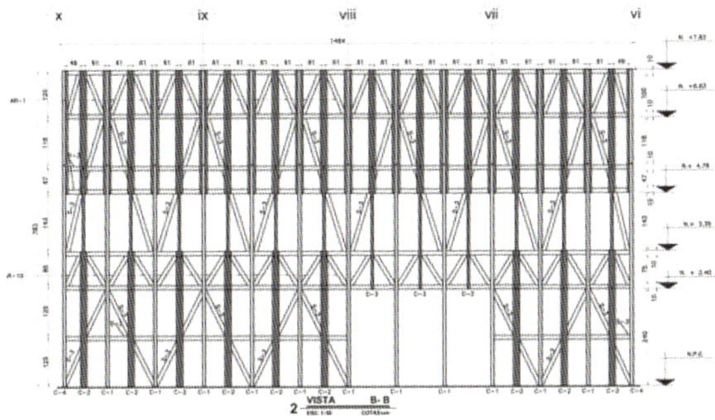
x
ix
viii
vii
vi
2 VISTA B-B

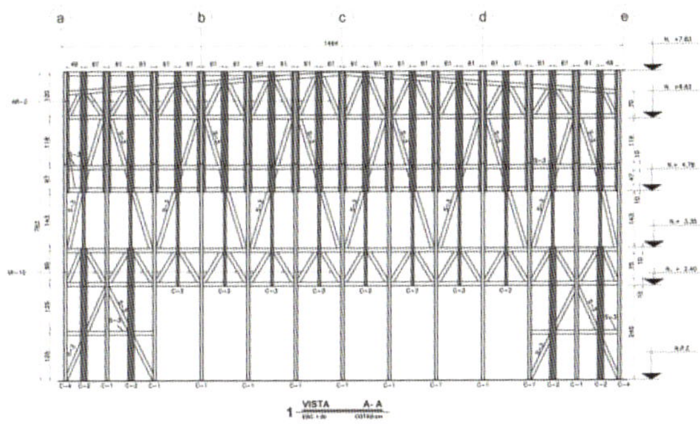
a
b
c
d
e
1 VISTA A-A

CULTURAS AMIGAS 2014

*Opposite page above* Night view / *Opposite page below* Ramp Entrance detail / *Above & Below* Exit Ramp

*Opposite page above* Ceiling detail / *Opposite page below & Above* Exhibition space, corner detail / *Below left* Exhibition space / *Below right* Night view

## Central Library

*Helsinki, Finland, 2012*

Contemporary, yet classic in its proportions and materialization, the new Helsinki library is envisioned as a bold and expressive volume that interacts directly with the urban surroundings through a series of L-shaped exterior terraces and canopies. These spaces are materialized as elegant facades of full and perforated brass plates, glass, yellow glazed bricks, copper colored ceramics, and endemic vegetation. The cross like form of the building acts as a powerful landmark in the park: an expressive elevation that can be seen as a distinctive visual icon from across the Töölönlahti Bay.

The central interior atrium allows the building to work efficiently in energetic terms with its large saw tooth roof, and establishes a proactive interrelation between all parts of the program. The visual relationships between different programmatic elements across the central hall and the combination of horizontal and vertical spatial experiences creates a dynamic composition for an animated and active public hall of culture.

Architectural Design: PRODUCTORA (Carlos Bedoya, Victor Jaime, Wonne Ickx, Abel Perles).
Collaborators: Andres Rivadeneyra, Guillermina Ceci, Alejandra de la Mora, Antonio Espinoza, Diego Escamilla, Eduardo Borges, Ivan Villegas, Uriel Piña.
HVAC & Building Energy: BioE (Alejandro Lirusso, Hector Juarez, Ariel Anuhar De La Cruz)
Structural Engineering: PBS-Ingenieros (Rodolfo Salmon).
Location: Helsinki, Finland.
Type: Public Library.
Organization: City Of Helsinki.

Central Hall / View from the park / Canopy towards the station / View of the canopy towards the park, with patio towards exhibition areas

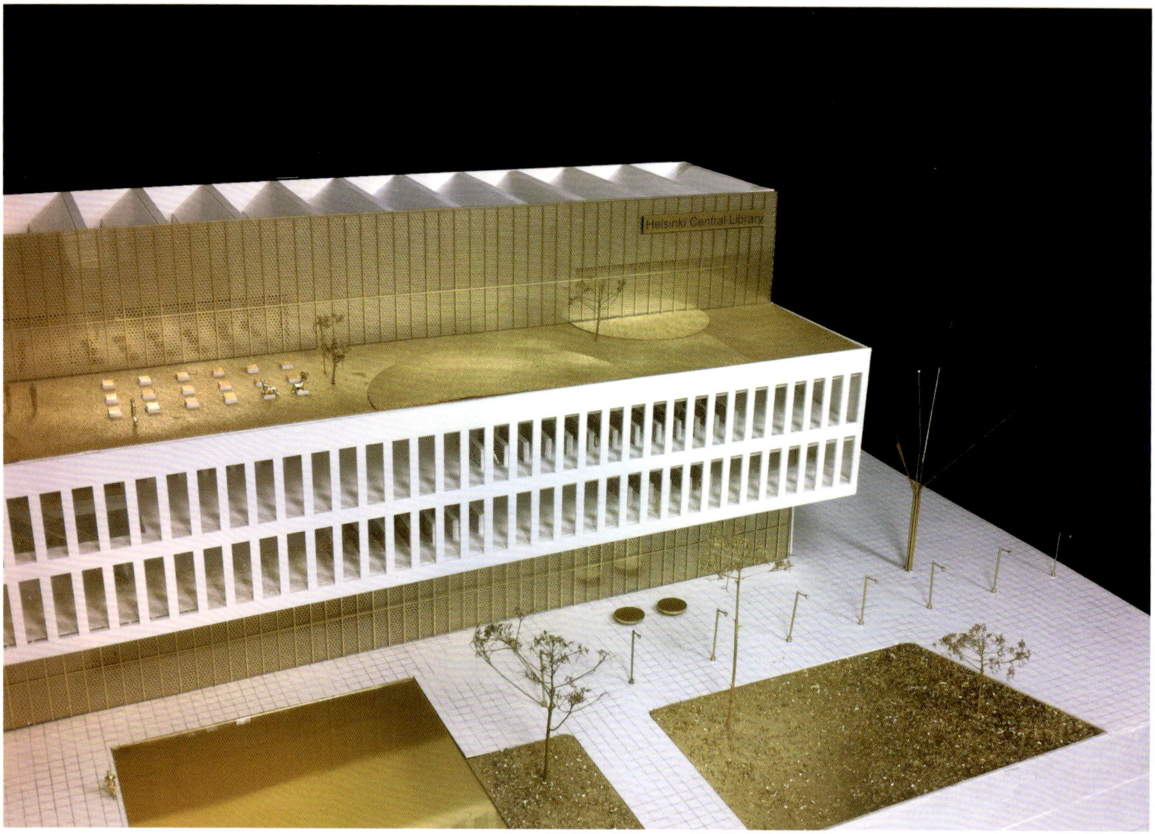


*Above* Model / *Below left* Undergound & ground floor plans / *Below right* Mezzanine & Level 1 plans / *Opposite page below left* Levels 2 & 3 with their adjacent terraces plans / *Opposite page top left* Transversal & Longitudinal Sections / *Opposite page center left* South Elevation, drawing / *Opposite page right top & bottom* Views of upper terraces at day & night

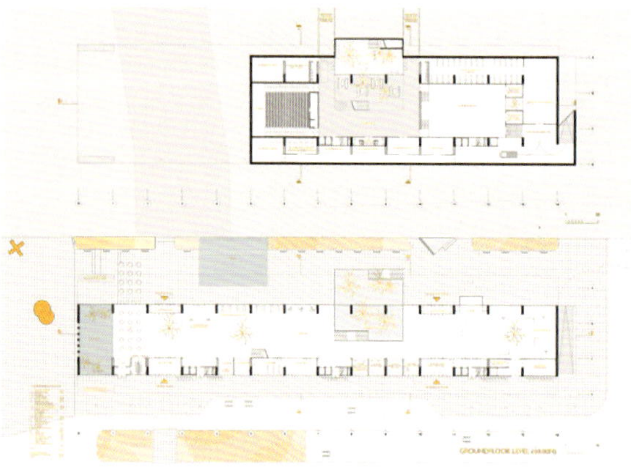

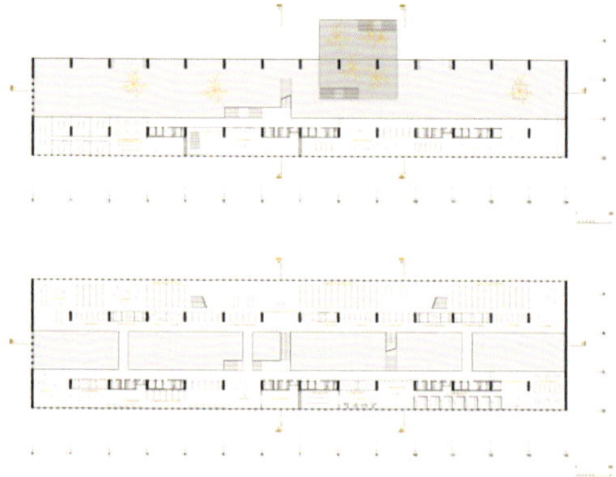

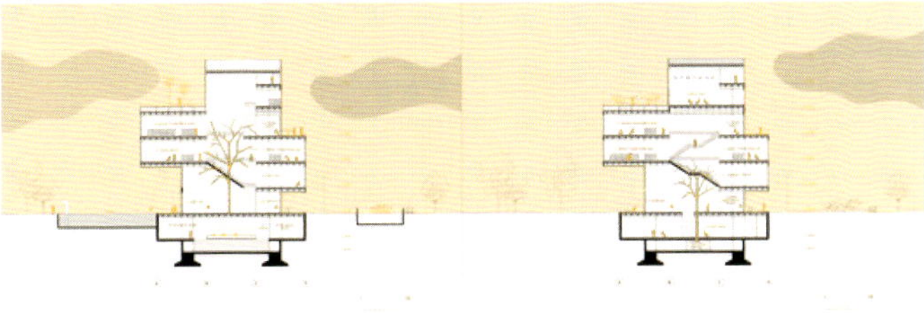

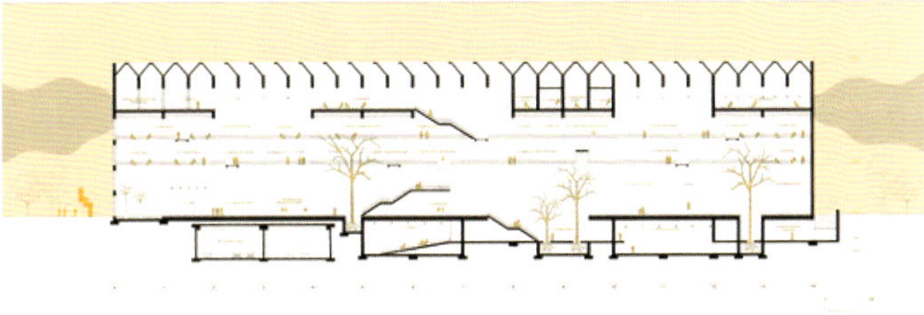

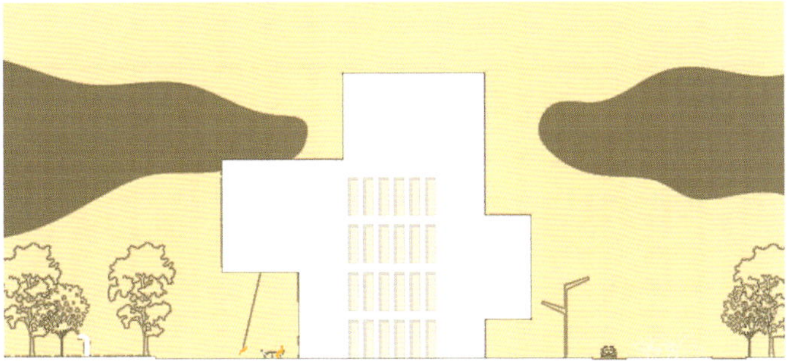

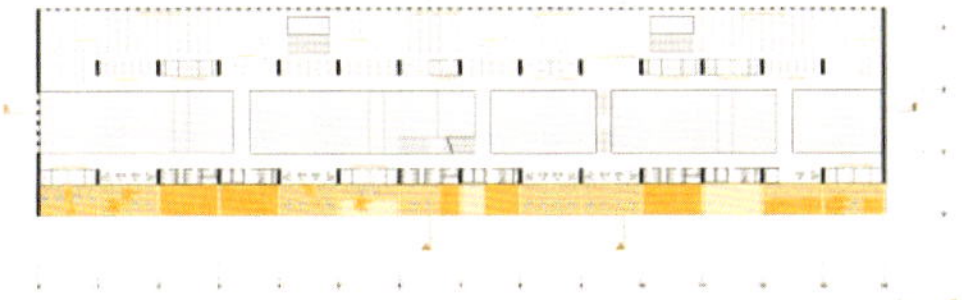

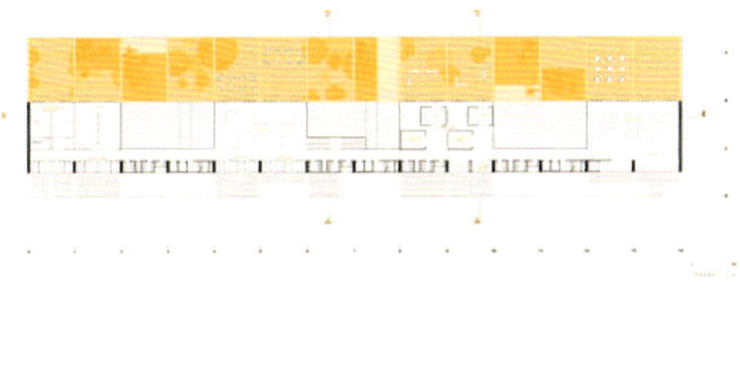

*Below* Drawings of interior scenes / *Opposite page* Central Hall, Rendering

**Thermal Park in Dolores**

*Second Prize - Open Competition*

*Buenos Aires, Argentina, 2011*

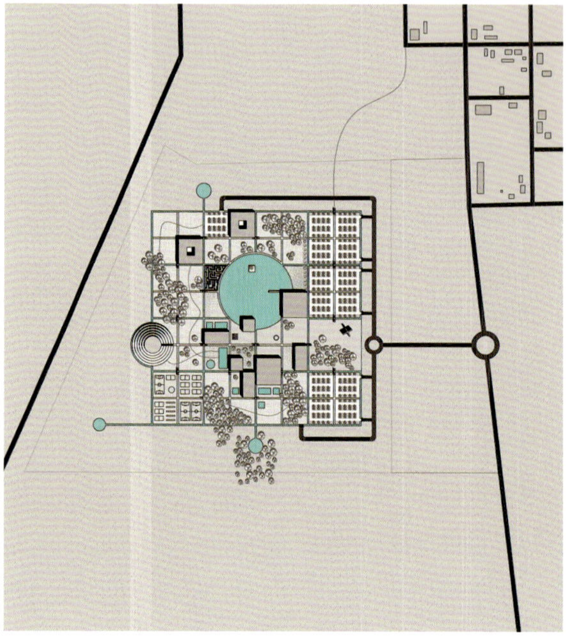

Like the typical urban settlements of the Americas, where a reticular grid is laid-out over virgin land, we decided on a large-scale landscape intervention for the design of this thermal park. Rather than creating a large recreational lake as the competition rules required, we reduced the size of the central excavation and created a grid of water channels to allow the visitors to explore the complex by canoe. The park incorporates elements taken from classical landscape design, such as symmetry axis, an artificial mountain (the land recovered from excavations), follies, water parties, bridges and a maze, reused here in a contemporary park that establishes a new dynamic between program and landscape. The architecture is presented as a harmonious ensemble of stealthy volumes whose serious and repetitive outer appearance houses a wide range of diverse architectural compositions within.

Architectural Design: PRODUCTORA (Carlos Bedoya, Victor Jaime, Wonne Ickx, Abel Perles).
Local partner: Arq. Miguel Alvite.
Collaborators: Alejandra de la Mora, Antonio Espinoza, Diego Escamilla, Ivan Villegas, Uriel Piña.
Location: Dolores, Province of Buenos Aires, Argentina.
Type: Open National Competition.
Organization: College of Architects of the Province of Buenos Aires.

*Opposite page below* Shaded Porches for activities and pools / *Opposite page above* Site plan / *Above & Below* Aerial views of the Complex

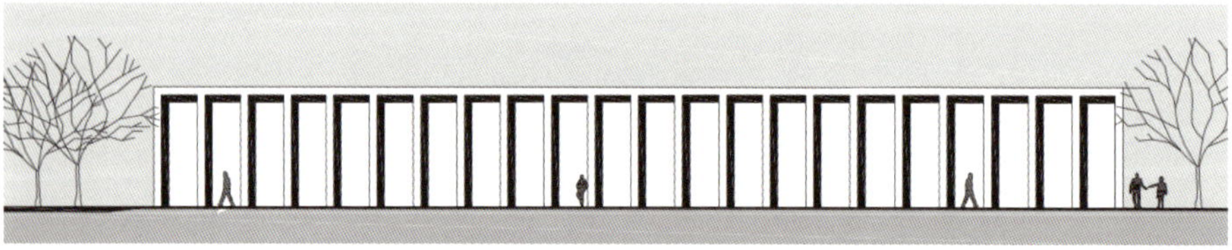

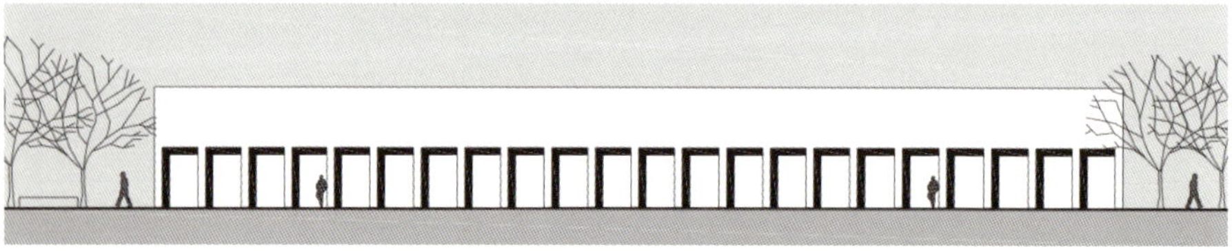

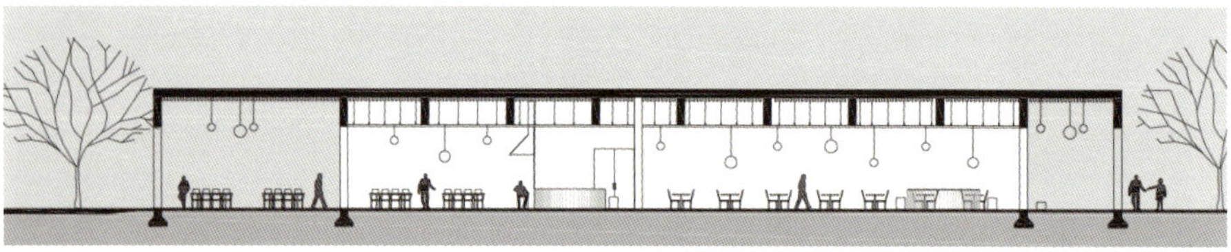

*Above* View of canals and Shaded Colonnade / *Opposite page below* Elevations & Section / *Below* Covered Colonnade overlooking canals

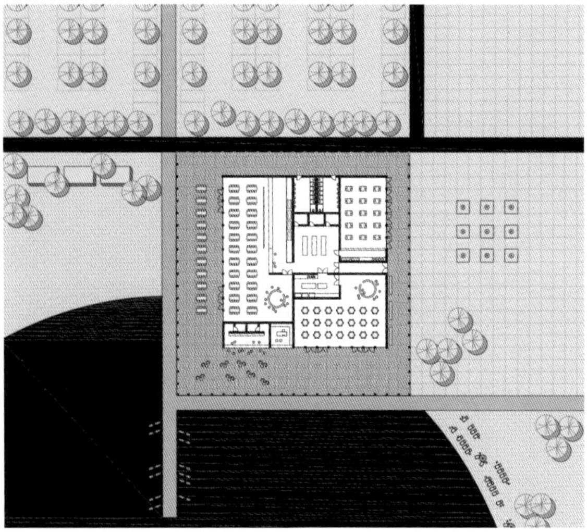

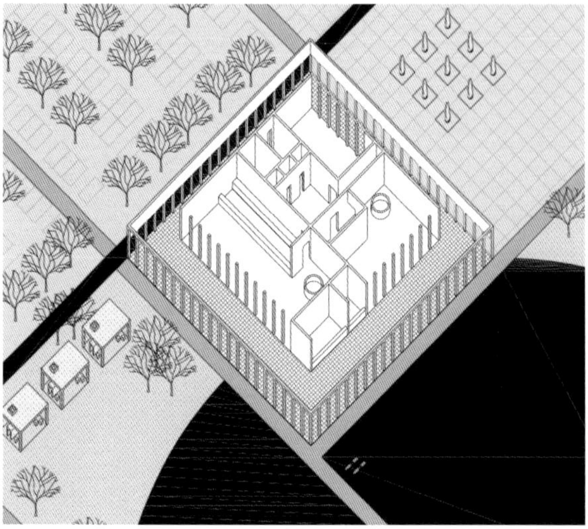

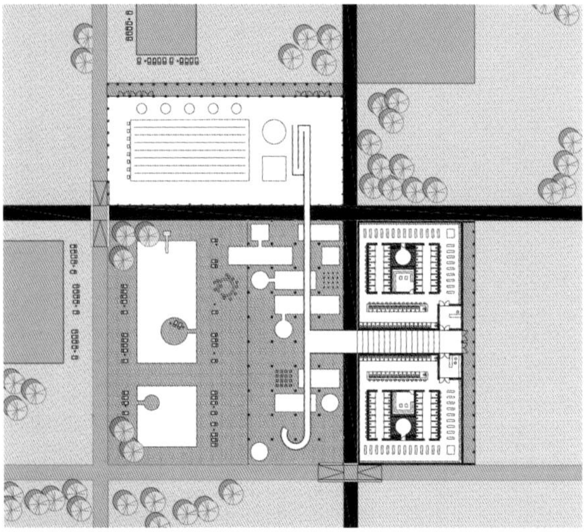

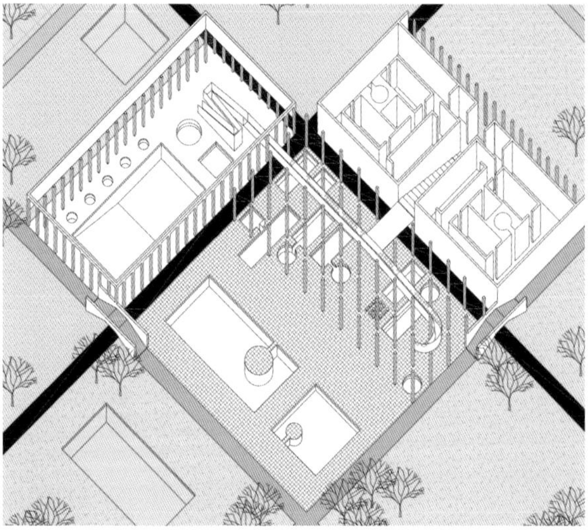

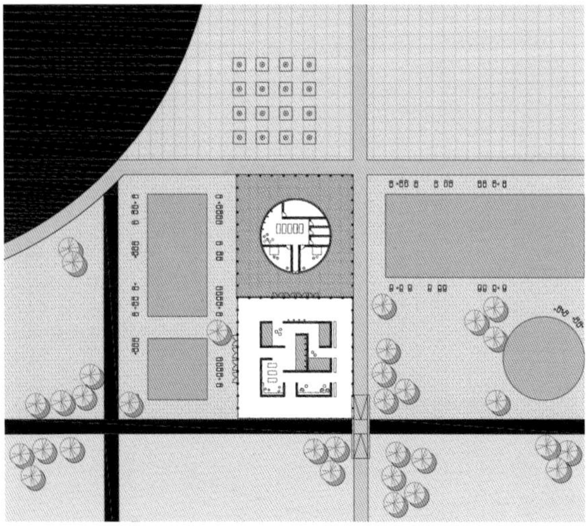

*Opposite page above* Gastronomic area, Plan & Axonometric / *Opposite page center* Pools & Dressing Rooms, Plan & Axonometric / *Opposite page below* Special treatment area, Plan & Axonometric / *Above & Below* Model of the complex

## MPAC Museum of Contemporary Art

*Competition*

*Mar de Plata, Buenos Aires, Argentina, 2009*

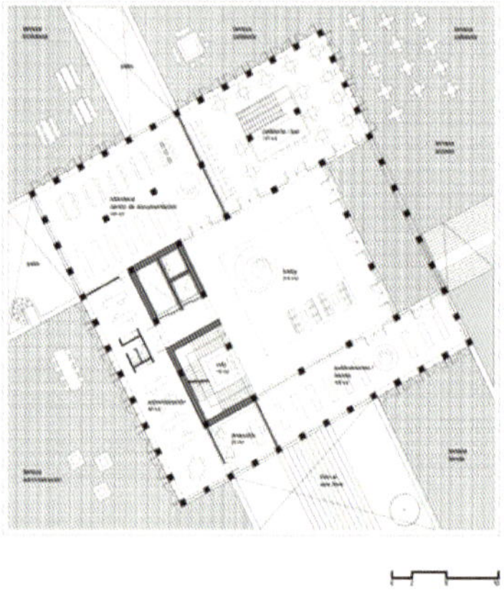

In a landscape dominated by the horizontal line of the Atlantic Ocean, an architectural complex is proposed to highlight this horizontality with a building divided into three differentiated floors. Two entirely closed volumes follow the orthogonal logic of the urban plan while a third, intermediate level is frankly oriented towards the sea. This middle level forms a public, transparent platform that is elevated two meters above street level, allowing open views towards the sea over the traffic on Félix Camet Avenue.

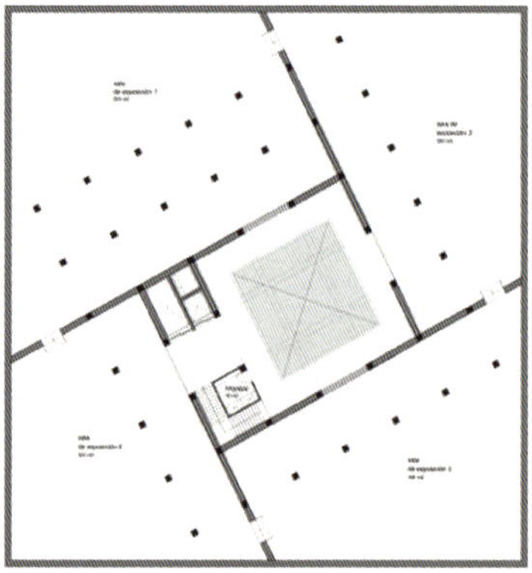

Architectural Design: PRODUCTORA (Carlos Bedoya, Victor Jaime, Wonne Ickx, Abel Perles).
Local partner: Miguel Alvite.
Collaborators: Laura Rodríguez, Gerardo Ramírez.
Project type: open competition for provincial contemporary art museum (honorable mention).
Organization: Ministry of Infrastructure of the Province of Buenos Aires and the Architects' College of the Province of Buenos Aires.

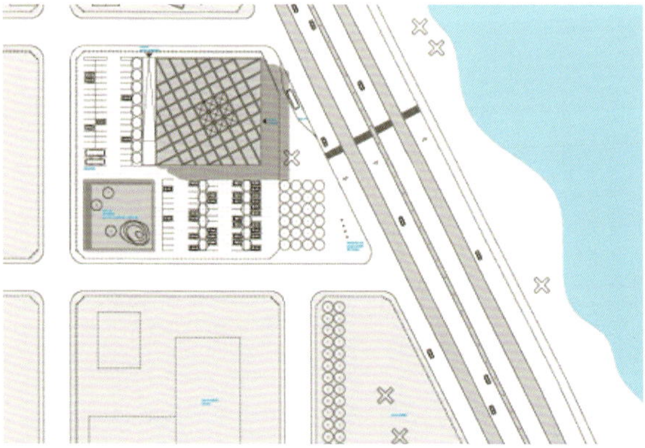

*Opposite page below left* Site plan / *Opposite page above* Entrance Level & Exhibition Floor plans / *Opposite page below right* Sculptures Garden, Rendering / *Above* Exterior, Rendering / *Below* Aerial view, Rendering / *Bottom* Exterior view from street, Rendering

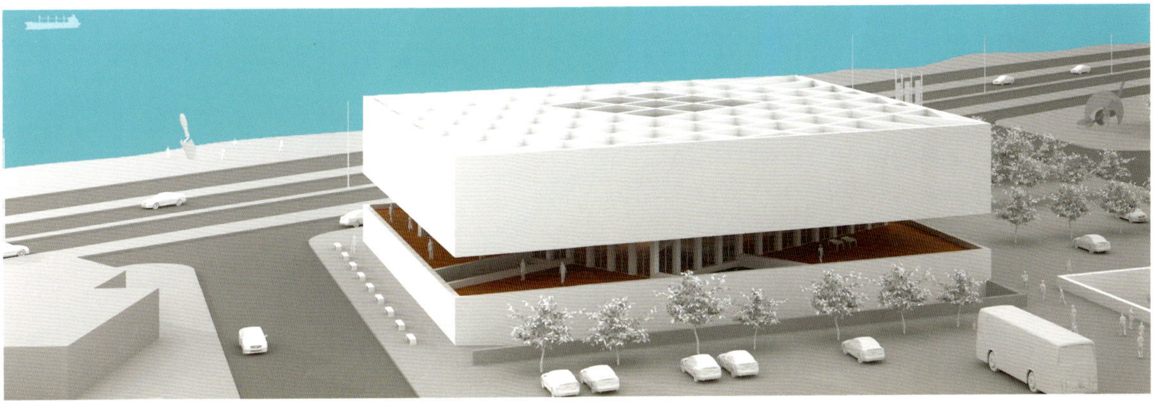

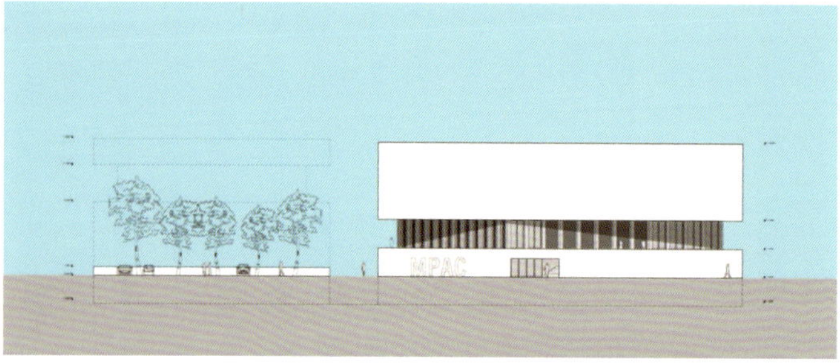
MPAC

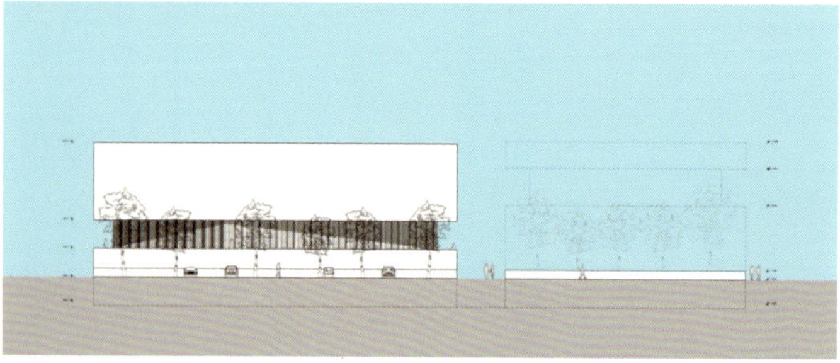

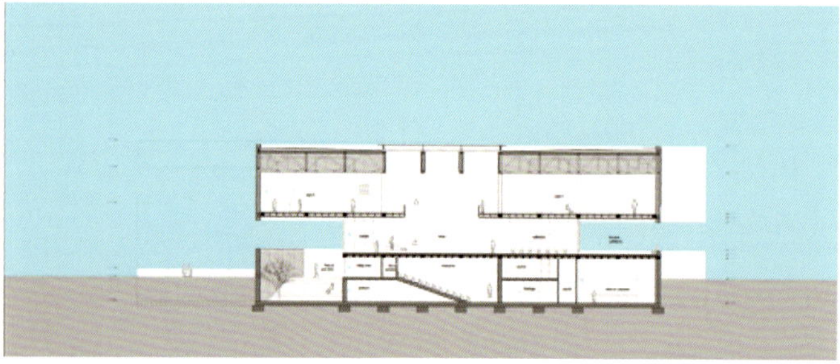

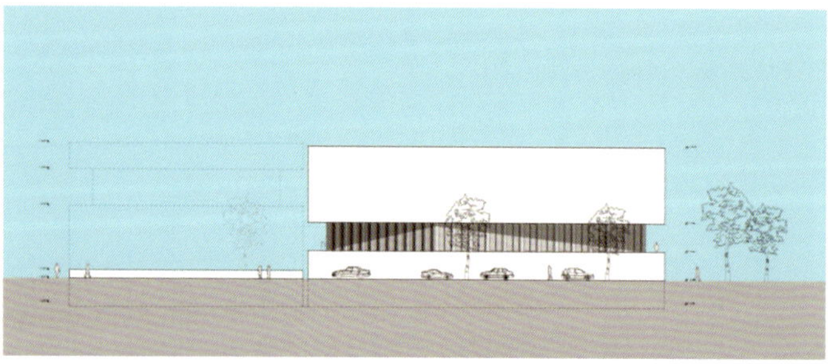

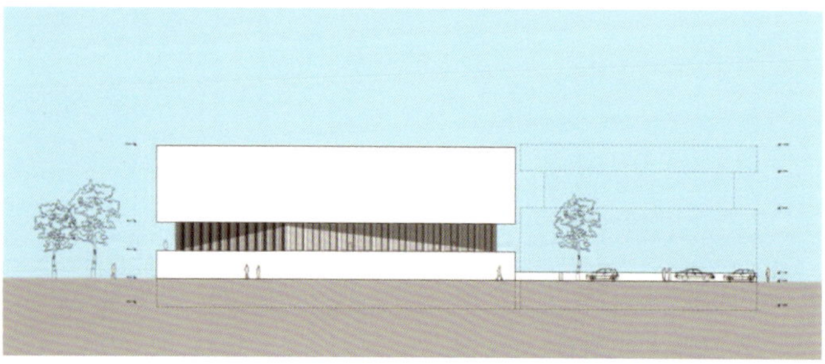

*Opposite page above* Elevations / *Opposite page center* Section / *Opposite page below* Elevations / *Above* Entrance, Rendering / *Below* Sea view from access platform, Rendering

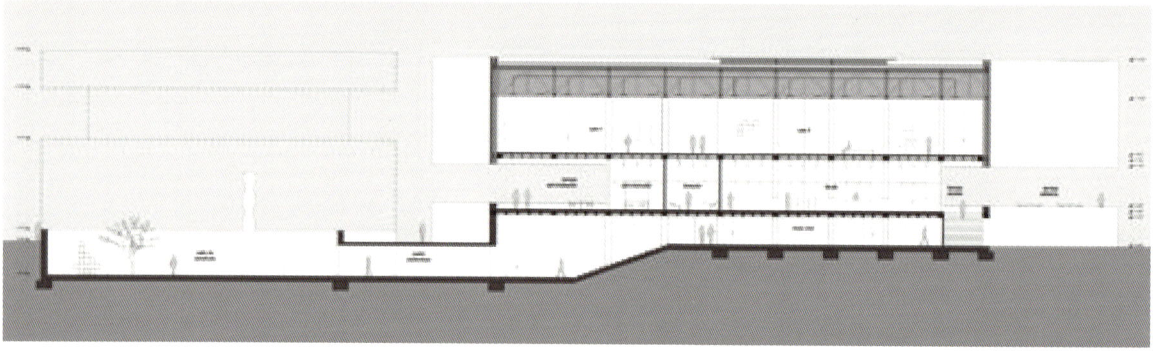

LEÓN FERRARI
OBRA GRÁFICA

*Opposite page above* Central Lobby, Rendering / *Opposite page center* Section / *Opposite page below* Central Lobby, Rendering / *Above* Exterior night view, Rendering / *Below* Exhibition area, Rendering / *Further below* Cinema, Rendering

## Headquarters of the Corporación Andina de Fomento (CAF)

*Restricted International Competition, 1st prize*
*Caracas, Venezuela, 2008*

This project, winner of a restricted international competition, features a slender and elegant main tower which takes up little space and frees up as much street level area as possible to the community. The base of the tower is an open structural grid with a clear relationship to the urban surroundings, while a double façade protects the offices above from the sun. The tower is thus a pristine monochromatic volume sitting on an open and transparent base, a large contemporary obelisk in dialogue with the old obelisk in Plaza Francia. A second open building with a structural grid contains the CAF's more public activities—art gallery and documentation centre—and a third smaller one is the entrance to a 600-seater auditorium in the CAF complex plaza. The project features characteristic elements of Latin American modernity: colour, an abundance of tropical vegetation and the integration of plastic arts.

Architectural Design: PRODUCTORA (Carlos Bedoya, Victor Jaime, Wonne Ickx, Abel Perles) in collaboration with Lucio Muniain.
Collaborators: Jorge Fernández, Gerardo Galicia, Alejandra de la Mora, Antonio Espinoza, Rosalía Yuste, Pamela Martínez, Paul Christian, Lena Kohl, Marissa Nava, Andrés Rivadeneyra, Diego Escamilla, David Ortega, Alfonso Gutiérrez, Jorge Arroyo, Christian Estavillo, Alejandro Zapata.
Maqueta Model: Iván Villegas, Cecilia Ceballos, Begoña Prada, Ximena Maza, Rebeca Laham, Sacnicté Ortiz, Mariana Valdez, Uriel Piña, Abraham Berumen.
Technichal consultants: José Guillermo Frontado (CAF project coordination), Inelectra (project management and engineering development), Óscar Capiello (technical coordination and local architect), Lighteam/Gustavo Avilés (lighting), AKF México (LEED commissioning).
Client: Corporación Andina de Fomento (CAF).

*Above* CAF full view, Rendering /
*Below* Site plan / *Opposite page* CAF Square & French Park, Rendering

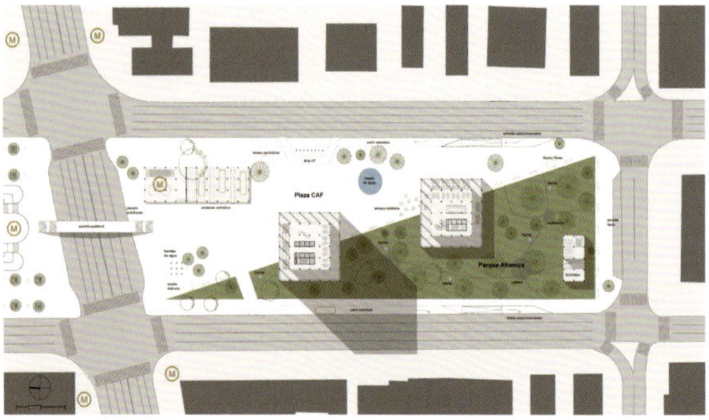

CAF

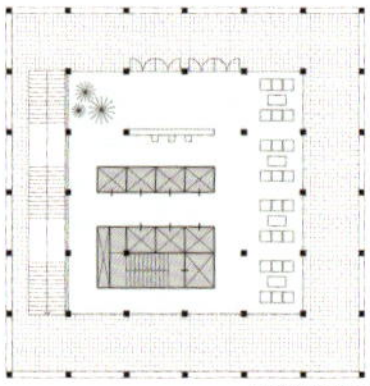

nivel 0 / ±0.00 m
lobby

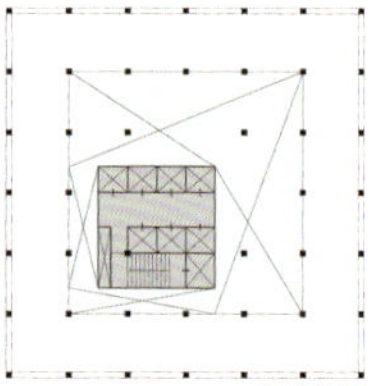

nivel 1 +4.20 m
vacío lobby

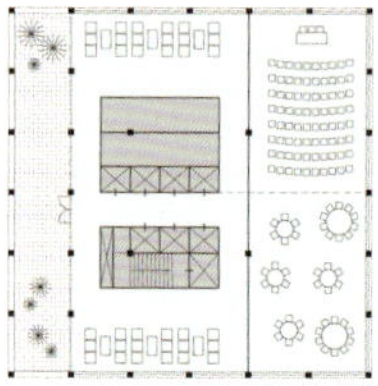

nivel 2 / +8.40 m
sala de usos múltiples

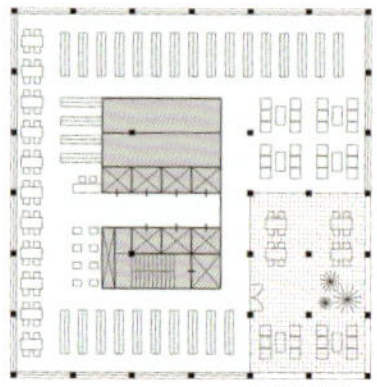

nivel 3 / +12.60 m
biblioteca

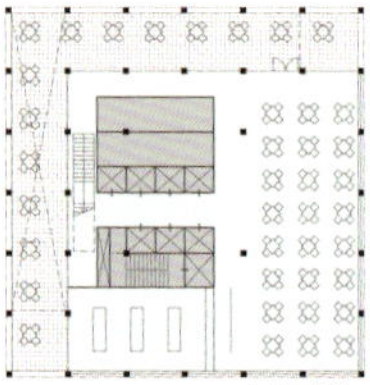

nivel 4 / +16.80 m
comedor menú

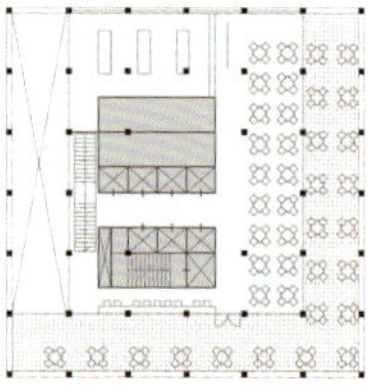

nivel 5 / +21.00 m
comedor a la carta

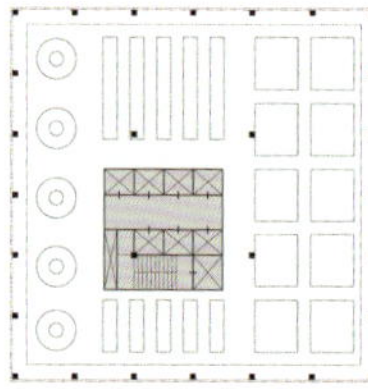

planta instalaciones

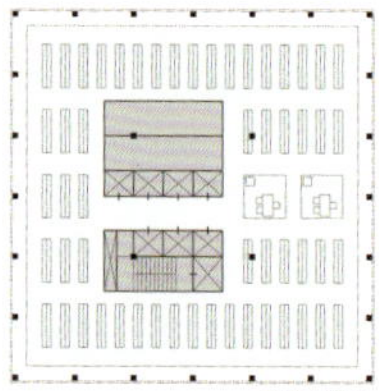

planta archivos

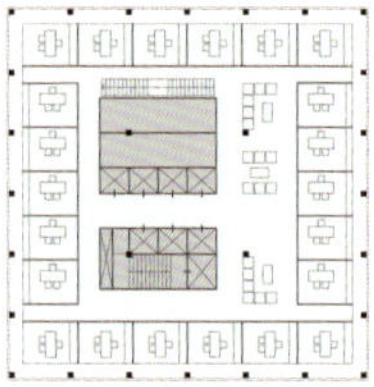

planta tipo 1
22 privados

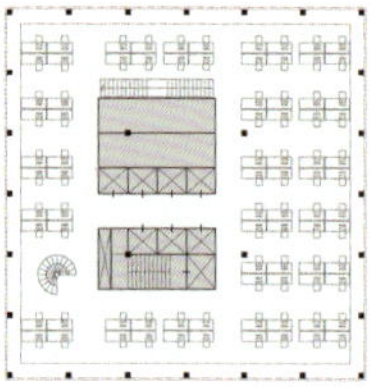

planta tipo 2
84 estaciones

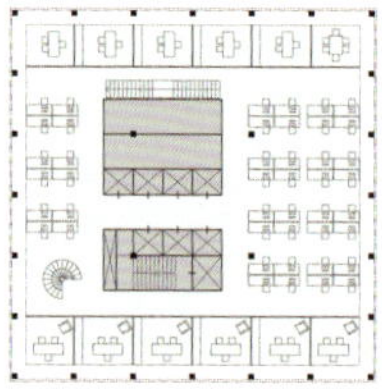

planta tipo 3
mixto

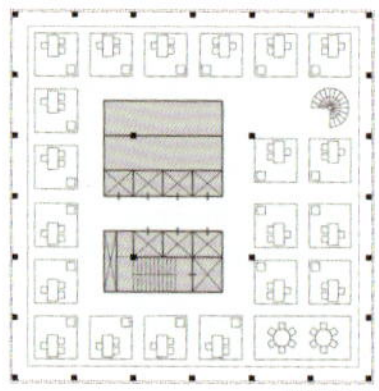

planta tipo 4
gerentes / subgerentes

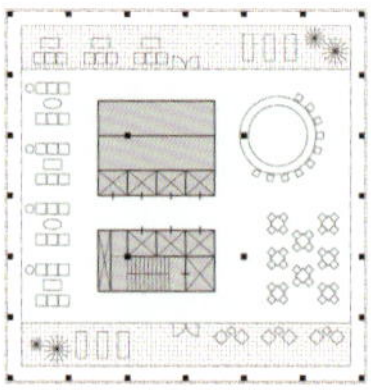

planta café lounge

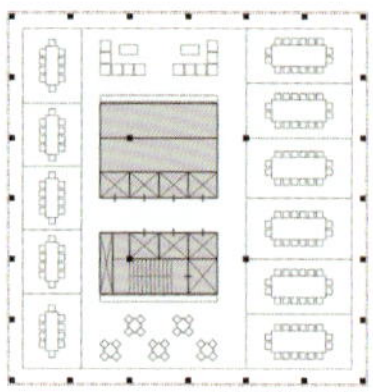

planta meeting rooms

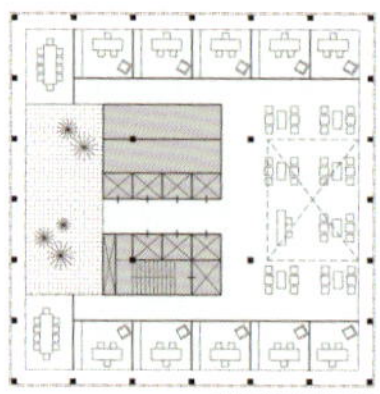

planta vicepresidencia

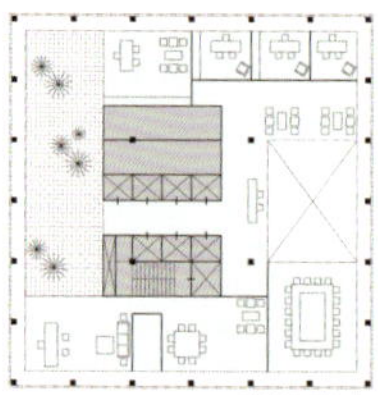

planta presidencia

*Opposite page above* Plans / *Opposite page below left* Transversal Section / *Opposite page below right* Longitudinal Sections / *Above* CAF Square, Rendering / *Below* Porch, Rendering

# CAVEJA STUDIO

Farli, Italy

**Ampliamento Cantina Valpolicella Negrar**

*Cavejastudio in collaboration with Arch. Davide Lorenzato*

*Valpolicella, Italy, 2014 - 2017*

Base – Existing Building: The design for the new winery Negrar Valpolicella maintains the existing building as the basis of the new intervention. We want the identity of the winery to be rooted in the tradition of Valpolicella. All existing functions at levels 0, -1, -2 are maintained, while new functions are integrated to the new level 1 floor. In addition to the existing building and to the office building, the project retains all existing equipment, most notably the silos.

Penthouse – New Building: The new project is placed above the existing building to promote better air circulation, as is the case in the traditional attic floors of the historic, Venetian, countryside estates. As in the Venetian residences, a lightweight wooden construction has been placed atop a solid masonry base. The structure consists of wood trusses that serve as both architectural and structural elements, clearly visible from the exterior. This structure provides a large, outdoor, covered space supported by that recalls the repetition of the rows of vines beyond.

Flexibility – Modularity: The first level is understood as a large flexible space developed along a 2×2 meter grid that can be divided by panels that slide on guides in the ceiling. The panels are opaque or transparent depending on the needs of the various spaces. The floor is ventilated through a series of skylights that can be opened to provide natural light and ventilation.

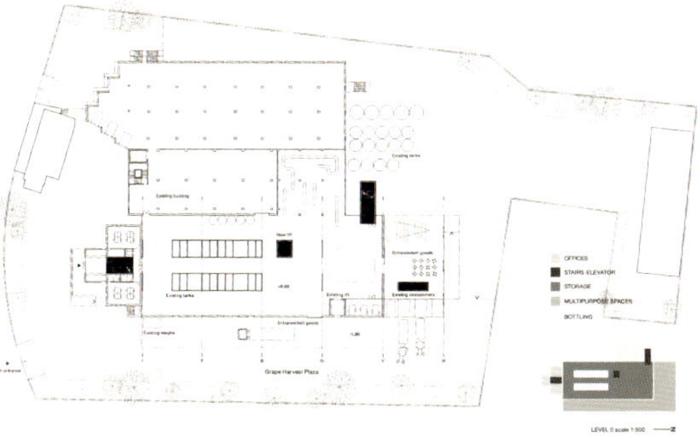

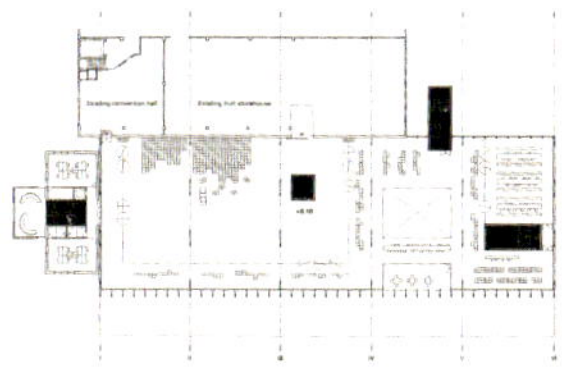

*Opposite page* Building in the landscape, Rendering / *Top left* Site plan / *Above left* 1st Level plan / *Above right* Exploded Axonometric / *Below* Interior, Rendering

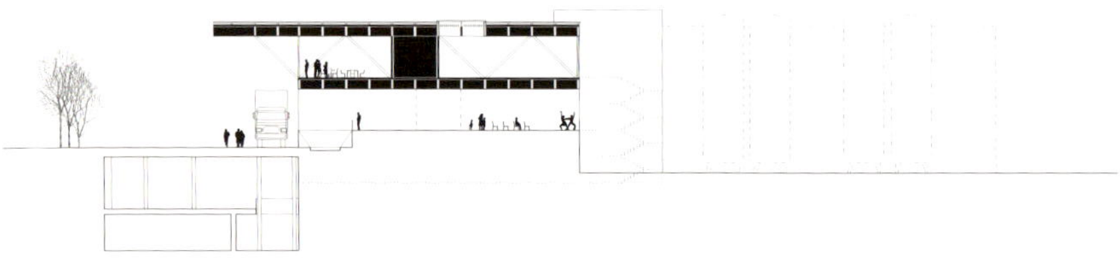

*Above* Elevation / *Opposite page below* Transversal Section / *Below* Logitudinal Section

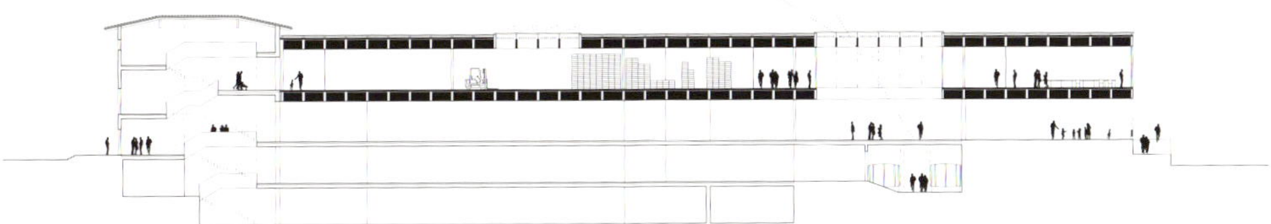

**Nuovo Science Centre di Città della Scienza**

*In collaboration with Arch. Davide Olivieri*

*Napoli, Italy, 2015*

The project is composed of two elements- the basement and the first floor|roof. A dialogue is established between the two parts, while each maintains differing characteristics that relate to specific environments.

The lower level enters into a dialectical relationship with the soil from where it originates. Comparable to a Platonic cave, it is the place from where the inhabitant ascends to the luminous exhibition space of knowledge above.

The stereometric and ribbed base of the ground floor recalls the powerful rustication of the Church of Gesu Nuovo.

While the lower floor is conceptually tied to the ground, the upper floor is linked to the sky and the horizon. This level is fully glazed and open to the sea, sheltered by a projecting metal cover that protects from the summer sun. The upper floor of the new building, flexible and able to adapt to any type of arrangement, is able to accommodate the wide array of museum functions.

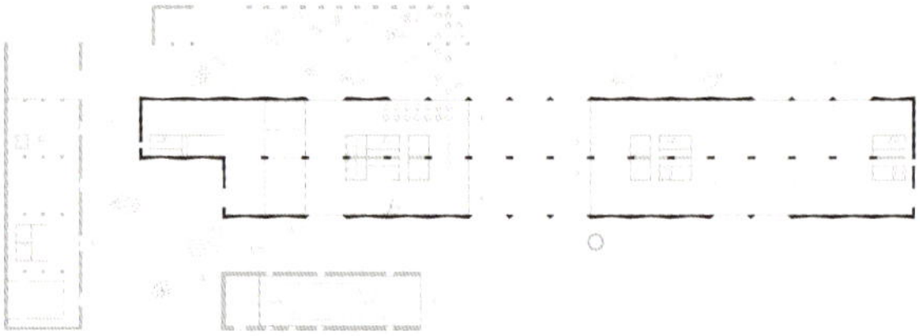

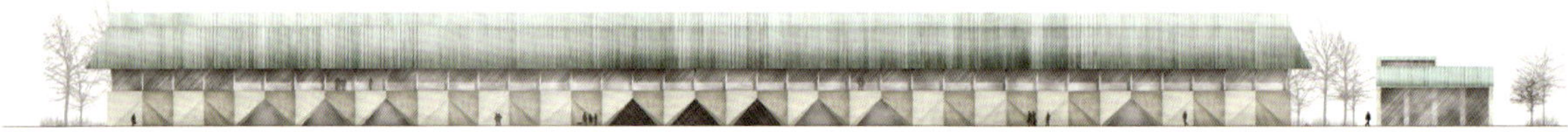

*Top right* Site plan / *Center* Plan & Elevation / *Below left* Structure Model / *Below right* Model / *Opposite page top* Exterior view / *Opposite page center* Building in the landscape / *Opposite page bottom* Interiors / *Following spread* Interior view

# LAURENT DE CARNIÈRE

Paris, France

**Perpendicular - Guggenheim Museum Helsinki**

*Helsinki, Finland, 2014*

The creation of a new Guggenheim museum in the harbor area of Helsinki raises the question of the relationship between art content versus people, between the museum as a building versus the city and its public space. 'PERPENDICULAR ' is a proposal that explores this dialogue in two directions. Horizontality is evoked by the exhibition space, which acts as an extension of the civic amenities by offering the juxtaposition of two rational and geometric areas based on a grid plan.

The choice of using a rational and evenly proportioned system throughout offers flexibility for a variety of uses and programs. Beyond being an efficient and economic system (both in terms of space management and programmatic flexibility), this configuration tends to validate the very nature of museum content and the variety of its manifestations. Within this organization exists a zone covered by over-head lighting that offers a succession of generic rooms attached to each other without corridors. In addition, a variety of performances can take place in an open, interior garden enclosed by a natural stone wall that houses a gallery for temporary exhibits and workshops.

The introduction of a series of simple elements such as beams, columns, or walls, not only provides the necessary structure for the building, but also defines the formal expression of the museum. The details are duplicated and thickened, to heighten its architectural identity. A thin vertical slab, centered on the horizontal slab, rises at the intersection of the network of squares and the enclosed greenery. These two perpendicular volumes form a single entity that becomes a new landmark in the harbor landscape. The upper part of the facility includes high-rise areas for displays, restaurants with panoramic views, shops, and projections rooms. The project does not blend into the terrain, but rather asserts its presence within the port and the skyline of the city, providing a recognizable architectural expression that highlights the richness and variety of individuals and artworks that take place within.

Collaborators: Gerolimetto, Ivana Katuric, Jasna Bajlo, Ranko Lipovac.

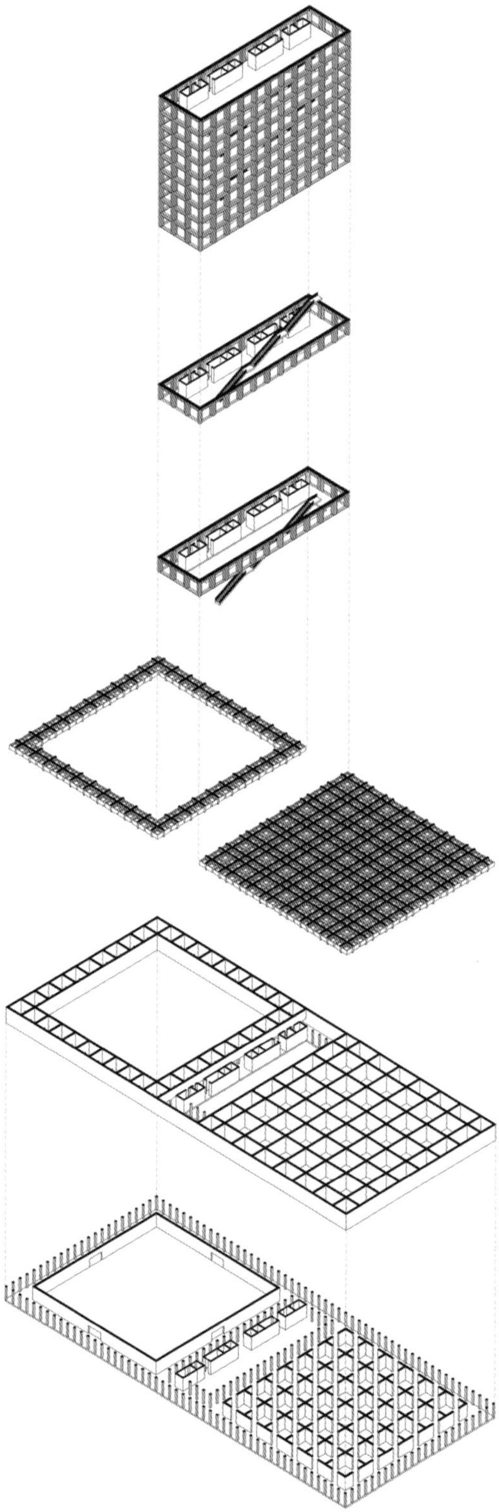

*Above* Exploded Axonometric Diagram / *Opposite page* Building, Collage

*Above* Location map / *Opposite page* Model

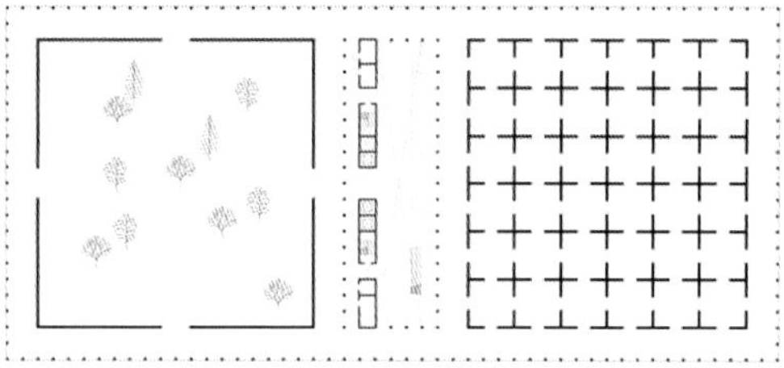

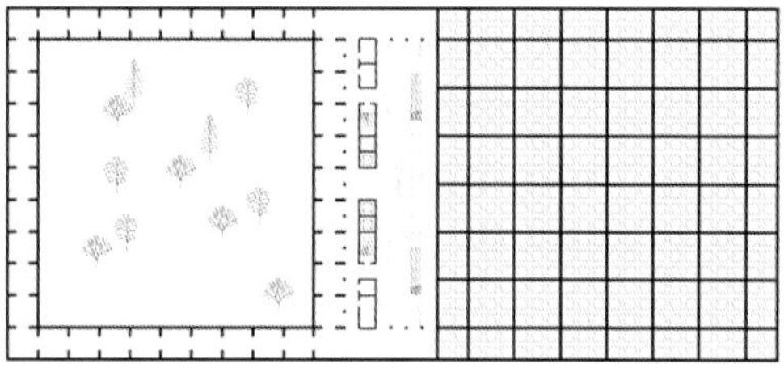

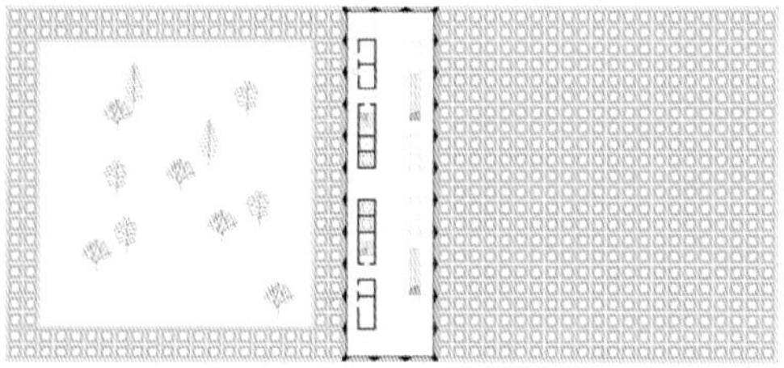

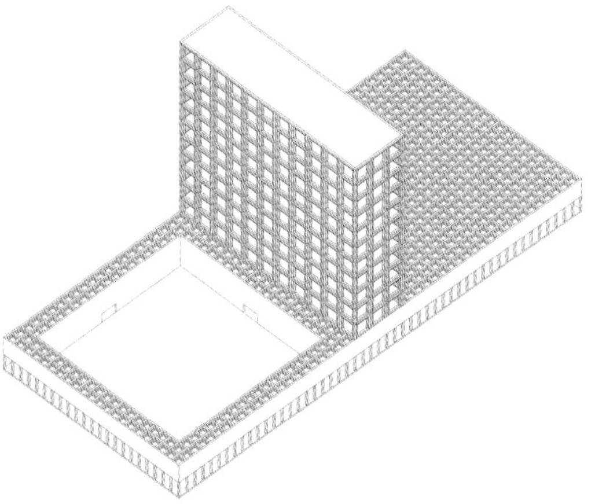

*Opposite page above left* Plans / *Opposite page below* Axonometric / *Above* Project in context, Collage / *Below* Exterior view, Rendering

*Above left* Roof detail, Rendering / *Above right* Project in context, Collage / *Below* Elevations / *Bottom* Sections / *Opposite page* Interior, Collage

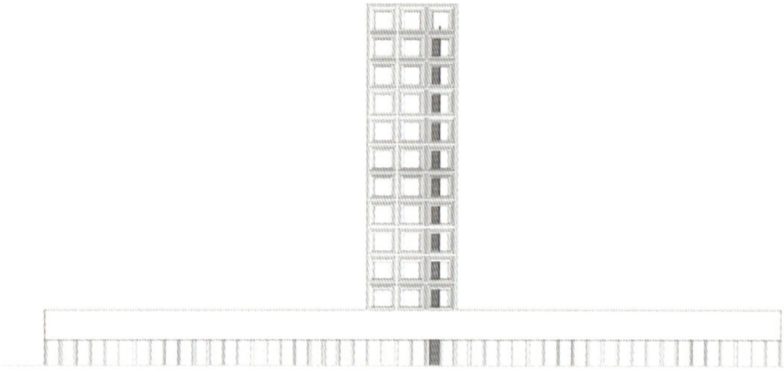

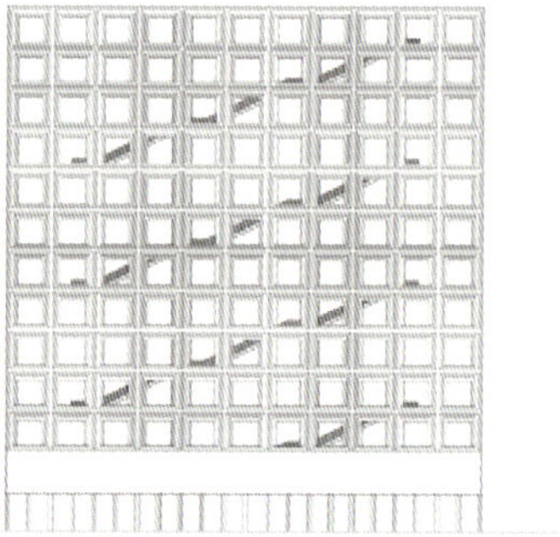

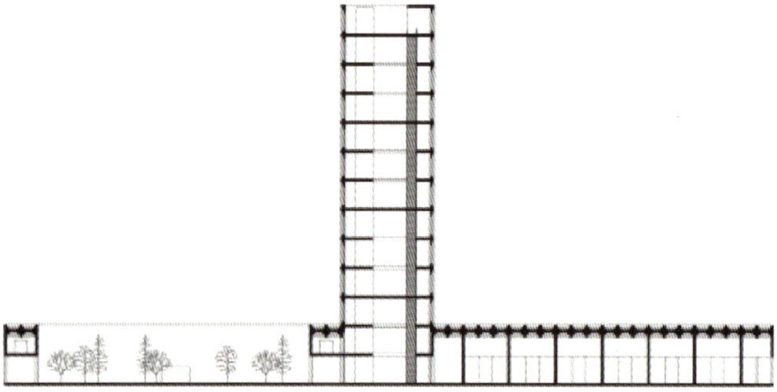

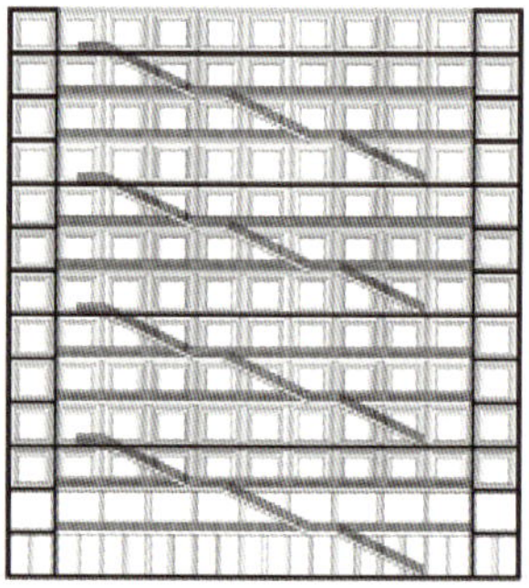

**Morland - Port Vertical Metropolitain -**
**Reinventer Paris**

*In collaboration with Jean-Benoît Vétillard*
*Paris, France, 2015*

"Paris has to reinvent itself at every moment". Anne Hidalgo, Mayor of Paris.

The City of Paris launched a call for innovative urban projects on twenty-three sites. We choose to transform the 40,000 sq.m., administrative, Morland building into a Vertical Metropolitan Harbor.

*Above* Motto of the city of Paris /
*Below* Location map / *Opposite page* Building Structure Perspective, Collage

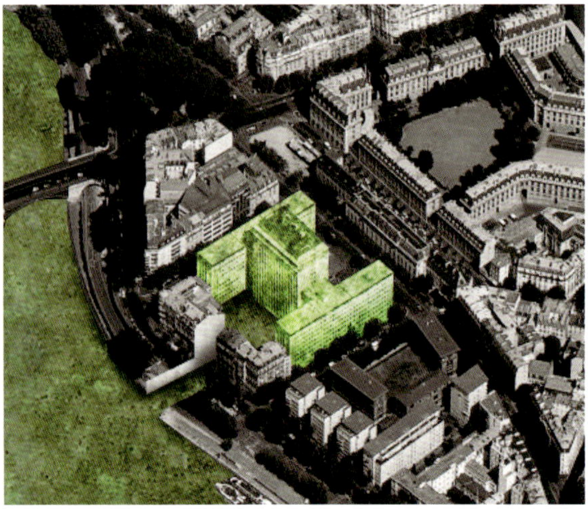

*Opposite page above* Location map / *Opposite page below left* Building in the landscape / *Opposite page below right* Structure, Collage / *Above* Entrance

*Above* Entrance / *Below* City view from pool, Collage / *Opposite page* Interior, Collage

**FUNDAMENTAL ACTS - TERRA INCOGNITA**

Based on a palimpsest provided by Superstudio in 1972, FUNDAMENTAL ACTS proposes a collective reformulation of the five great themes of human existence - LIFE, EDUCATION, CEREMONY, LOVE and DEATH.

FUNDAMENTAL ACTS was conceived by Superstudio as a series of films centered on the relationship between architecture and the acts of human life. The films were sketched in storyboard format and later published as a series of documents on the pages of Casabella.

FUNDAMENTAL ACTS contains the possibility of reintroducing a discourse on the relationship between architecture and ritual. It explores the spatiality of rituals and their structure, focusing on architecture as a technology at the service of memory.

Collaborators: Gerolimetto; Ivana Katuric, Jasna Bajlo, Ranko Lipovac

FUNDAMENTAL ACTS is a project initiated by Salottobuono and edited by Matteo Ghidoni.

TERRA INCOGNITA (Latin phrase meaning 'unknown land') is a term used in cartography to describe regions or unknown territories that have not been mapped or documented.

TERRA INCOGNITA is a series of collages that mixes various floating transportation units with architectural structures in an abstract oceanic context.

TERRA INCOGNITA is a graphic composition that plays upon the confrontation of well-known marine technology and the utopian skyscraper.

Collages

## UHO

Paris, France

**City of Students**

*Closed Competition*

*Tirana, Albania, 2015*

To describe the actual condition of the City of Students is not an easy task. Different layers seem to have been superimposed one upon another without any long-term planning. It is the result of a 40-year process of heterogeneous urbanization; the result is a chaotic and dysfunctional fabric. Aside planned groups of residential and collective buildings, illegal private constructions occupy more than 25% of the total surface of the site. And none of these structures seem to provide the conditions for a sustainable development.

But if we are forced to admit that the whole needs to be reshaped, it is also impossible to completely ignore the existing situation: this would imply a tabula rasa and a build up from scratch.

It is without any form of romanticism concerning the territory and its « natural » aspect, nor with a sincere interest for the current buildings, that we proceed in the following manner. Rather than producing an autonomous object, a new city within the city, we propose a project that is able to manage the inherent complexity of the whole site by extending its logic to fulfill the new expectations of the most important campus of Albania. Rather than submitting a new Masterplan, a new formal layer upon the previous ones, we propose a long-term process, open to the volatility of the urban structures. Realism is understood here as a means to accept the irreducible complex condition of the city. Here, Realism is a detached statement.

Our proposition consists of three-phases.

Phase I

The first phase of our project is dedicated to the renovation of the existing buildings. After a close look at these buildings, it appears that there is an urgent need to renovate them by readapting their internal organization according to their structural capacity. This renovation should take into account that these structures are not able to support every expectation of contemporary student residences. But as mentioned above, we do not want to simply ignore this existing condition by suggesting their demolition. Rather, our proposition tries to absorb contemporary housing needs and transform the existing buildings to accommodate them.

We worked in two complementary directions: at a programmatic level and at a construction level. We decided to remodel the organization of living areas inside these buildings to avoid the strict dormitory function. By

reducing the number of students per room, from 3 to 2 in some cases, by dividing buildings into collective apartments where 10 to 16 students could live together, sharing collective spaces, and by placing public facilities open to every student on the Campus inside the buildings, we completely reversed the current buildings' functions and opened them to a wider use.

At the construction level, we proposed to extend each of these buildings with a new and simple construction that can host modern technical facilities and fulfill European standards of comfort and security. This should solve the visible complications of the current buildings.

Similar to the way we proposed to renovate the buildings, we submitted the idea of renovating the existing landscape by reinforcing its limits. A first belt of trees would be planted on the periphery of the site during Phase I.

Phase II
Possibly overlapping with the renovation period, a second phase would be initiated by the construction of three new buildings that would allow a significant expansion of the capacity of the actual campus. These buildings, designed as a series of large-scale elements, would reaffirm the presence of the campus in the city of Tirana.

The new buildings have been designed to provide different typologies to accommodate a large number of students. These buildings would also host the new large-scale collective facilities such as sports areas, food courts, and a library.

With the construction of these three new buildings, the landscape would be deeply transformed by the planting of a meadow surrounded by a dense concentration of trees. This new landscape would allow the whole site to reclaim its centrality and to introduce different shaded areas to be used by its residents. While the wooded area suggests intimacy and anonymity, the meadow is an invitation to gather and a space of collective expression.

Phase III
The third phase of our project would allow for the City of Students to achieve its ambition of housing 10,000 students with all the necessary requirements. By extending its actual used surface to its legal surface, through recovery of the land illegally occupied today, it will be possible to build new constructions and to extend the new landscape into these reclaimed territories.

Architects: Building Building, Elias Guenoun Architecture & UHO.
Consulting architect : Studio Rebus.
Landscape architect: Camille Fréchou.
Consulting artist: Antoine Espinasseau.
Structural engineer: Bollinger + Grohmann.
Estimator management expert: VPEAS.
Extended team: Nastasia Bettarel, Fatme Hassan & Nicolas Violette.

*Opposite page* Aerial view, Rendering / *Below* Terrace perspective view, Collage

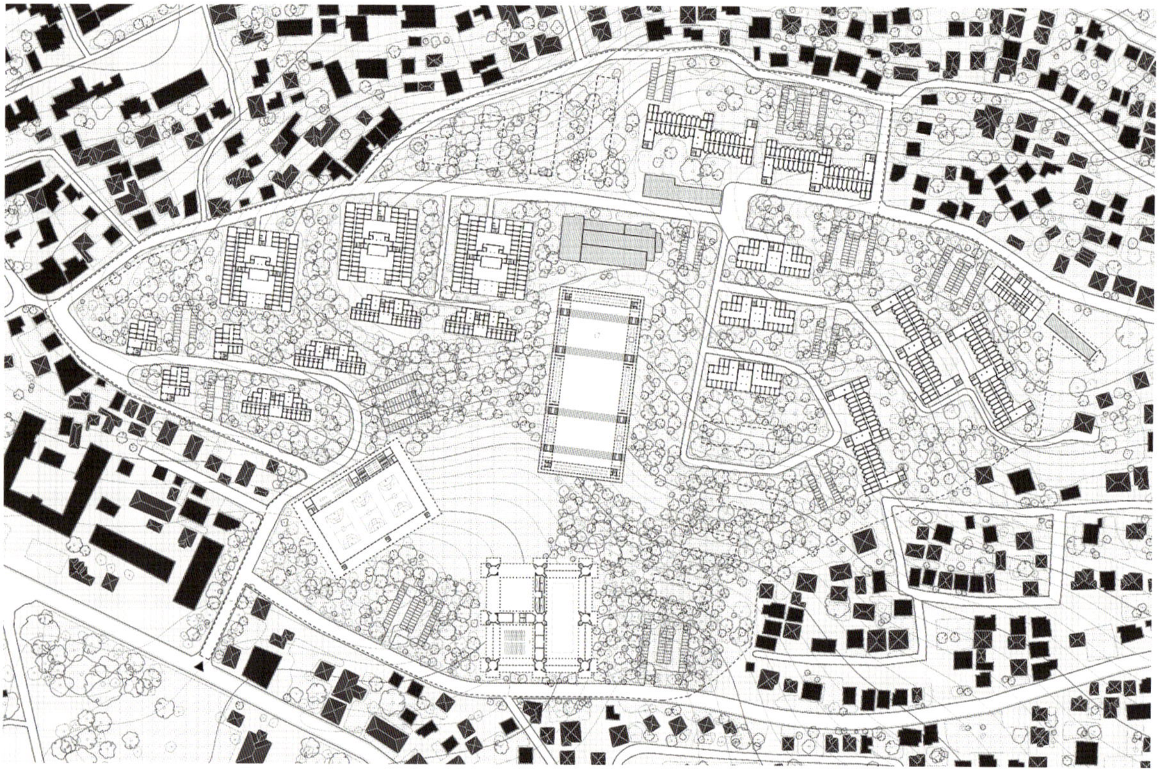

*Above* Site plan / *Below* Overall view, Collage / *Opposite page* Lawn view, Collage

*Above* Sky view from inner yard, Collage / *Opposite page* Plans

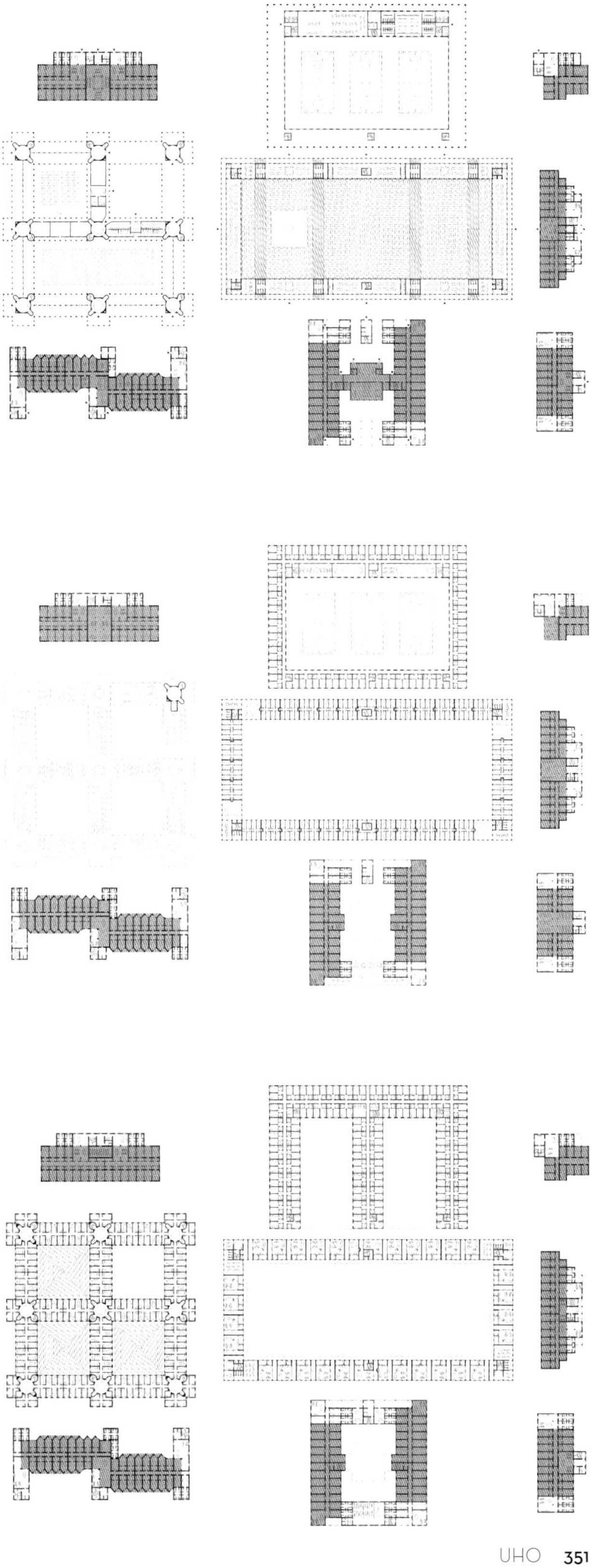

*Above* Lawn view / *Below & Opposite page* Interiors, Collages

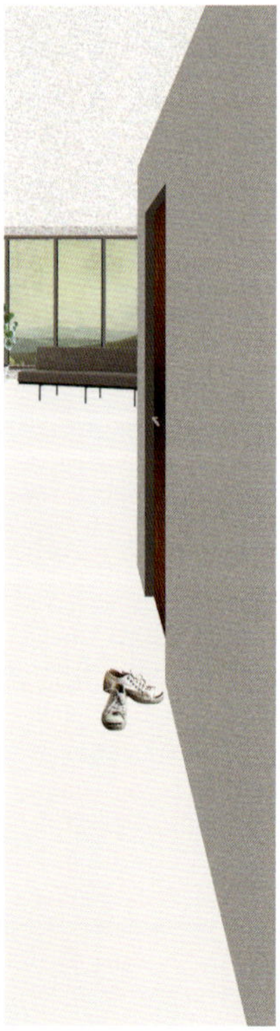

**Lake Park entrance**

*Closed competition, 1st prize*
*Tirana, Albania, 2015*

The project we propose for Tirana's Lake Park Entrance takes into account a local and general approach on the idea of Landscape. We attempt to produce a series of local singular interventions, which, observed from a distance, reveal a border, a clear difference in quality between the Park and the City. This series of singularities includes, amongst others, a playground, a public service building, and the modification of an existing street path.

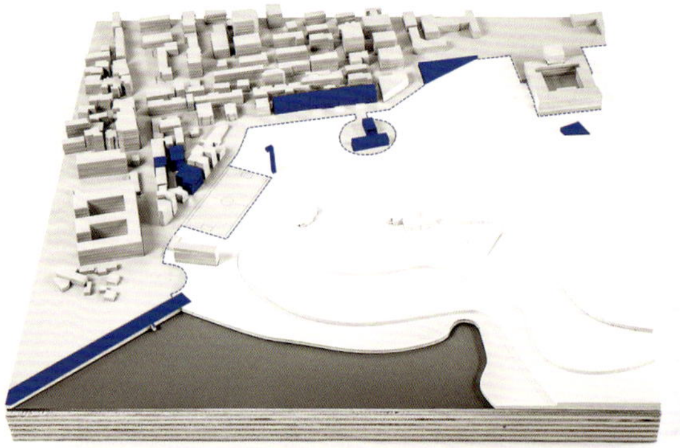

Architects: Building Building, Elias Guenoun Architecture & UHO.
Consulting architects: Studio Rebus, Martin Le Bougeois.
Consulting urbanist and landscape architect: David Levain.
Consulting artist: Simon Boudvin.
Structural Engineer: Bollinger + Grohmann.
Estimator management expert: VPEAS.
Extended team: Nastasia Bettarel, Chiara Buccolini, Fatme Hassan, Manon Lespagney & Adrien Quennepoix.

*Opposite page below* Interior model / *Opposite page above* Site model / *Above* Site Axonometric illustration / *Below* Model

**16 family-housing**

*Open competition*

*Marfa, USA, 2014*

Marfa is an atypical location for a housing project. Indeed, it is home to extreme variations in temperature, but most noticeably it hosts one of the most progressive communities in the United States. Could a prototypical housing project rely on the particularities of this specific locality to enhance the concept of housing?

In our view, housing should:
- allow for minimal disparities in the tenant's living conditions
- act as an integral part of the City

In other words: each housing unit should be as equivalent to the others as possible and the housing project should contribute to the public space.

Architects: Martin Le Bourgeous & UHO.
Extended team: Federico Coricelli.

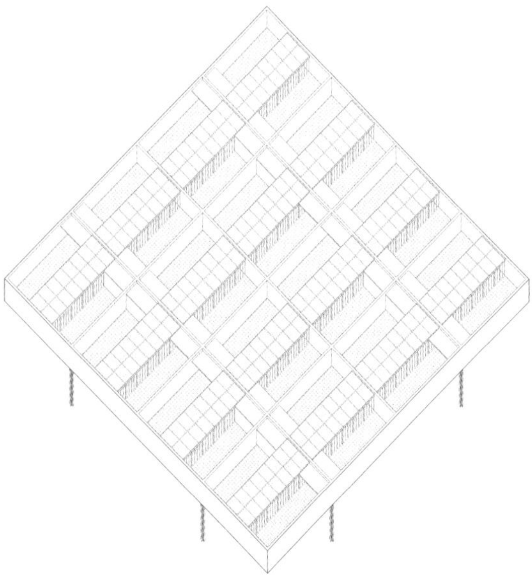

*Opposite page* Axonometric / *Above* Axonometric/ *Below* Elevation

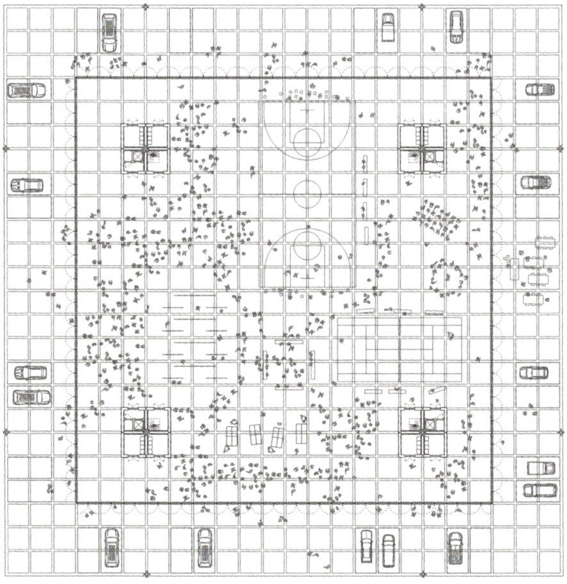

*Opposite page above* Interior, Collage / *Opposite page below left* Site plan / *Opposite page below right* Floor plan / *Above* Interior / *Above* Roof plan

**Public Library**
*Open competition*
*Daegu, South Korea, 2012*

The proposed project for the Daegu Public Library consists of a massive cubic construction, in stark contrast with the surrounding cityscape. The singularity and unexpected nature of this landmark building is legible at once, without bearing the trace of any logo, or distinctive sign of its function. It is its absence of obvious identity – its apparent neutrality and slickness –that consecrates it as a singular landmark. The library projects no further identity than its mass.

The library stands due to its dimensions (34.5 m x 34.5 m x 34.5 m), its sharp edges, and the rupture it generates with its surroundings. The building's cinder block façade is by-and-large blind, with the exception of the entrance. The façade reveals nothing of the building's interior. It is the simplest expression of the space it contains.

A central square column emerges from the entrance level. The resulting continuity is underlined by the use of the same ceramic tiling. The column erects itself over the full height of the library. It lodges the staircases and elevator. The staircase allows a vertical circulation between four levels: 1st floor, 2nd floor, 3rd floor and roof terrace. It is a long ascending pathway to a venture point. It is both intimate and exposes the visitor to views of the building and its grandiose verticality.

While most of the building consists of open plans, two solid enclosures run through the first two levels. They are meant to lodge technical programmatic elements.

The chosen material for this outer wall (cinder block) contributes to producing a sense of enclosure. The entrance door mediates the relationship between exterior and interior. Its off-set position further contributes to dissimulating the scenic attributes of the interior space, and the various modes of occupation that it enables. The resulting interior is self-contained, quiet, and virtually free of external influences.

A 3-dimensional grid structure of 2.75m cubic frames runs through the building, generating interior spaces and supporting its own weight. The assembly of cubic frames makes up the skeleton of the stairway and two decks (the roof-terrace and the main flooring). The cubic frames are paneled with duckboard when they are mobilized as flooring or see-through partitioning elements. The cubic frames can be mobilized as anchoring points for a variety of light partitioning methods (curtains, etc.).

The building's structure provides the necessary space for the allocation of the library program. Most of this space is relatively open and flexible. The plans suggest an illustrative example of such occupation and space allocation for the main (non-technical) programmatic elements, which are deemed to evolve over time.

Architects: École (Nicolas Simon and Max Turnheim) & Adrien Durrmeyer.
Extended team: Ophélie Dozat, Hadrien Gauthier, Gerta Heqimi & Louis Latzarus.

Interior drawing

*Above* Building in the landscape / *Below* Plans / *Opposite page above* Axonometric / *Opposite page below* Upwards view

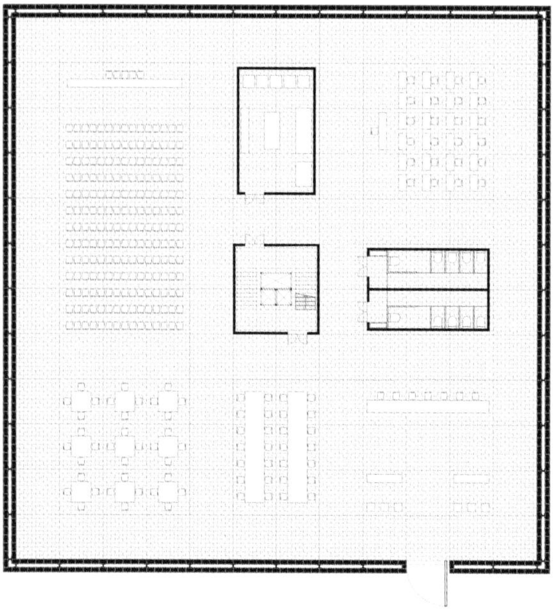

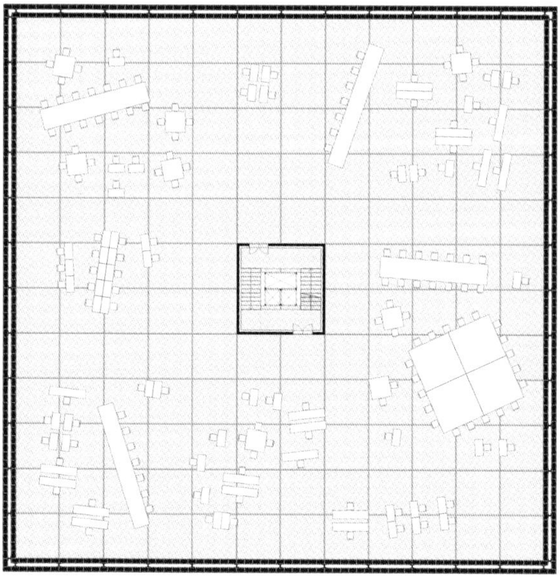

# SALOTTOBUONO

Milan, Italy

### Delta and Porto Baros Area

*Rijeka, Croatia, 2013*

The city of Rijeka is located in a key position. With Ljubljana, Zagreb and Trieste, it creates a cross-national quadrangle. This territorial perspective, together with the connection of Rijeka to the main European infrastructural networks and corridors, opens up the possibility to see the Delta project as a key strategic initiative attracting the interest of a very diverse range of actors.

Public space can be considered the predominant theme of the project. It allows for the systematization of various functions and serves as the mirror for contemporary Rijeka. From the park, public space is defined first with a large market square, then along the docks, and inside the inner courts lined with commercial spaces. The city of Rijeka rediscovers its identity as a port city with a variety of activities.

This international design competition was sponsored by the Fine Art Academy, Zagreb Croatia. The project program included exhibition spaces, an entrance hall, gallery shop, coffee bar, educational workshops, library, archive, storage spaces, and technical areas.

Collaborators: Matteo Ghidoni, Andrea Piovesan, Francesco Zorzi, Annapaola Busnardo, Caterina Gerolimetto, Ivana Katuric, Jasna Bajlo, Ranko Lipovac.

Collage

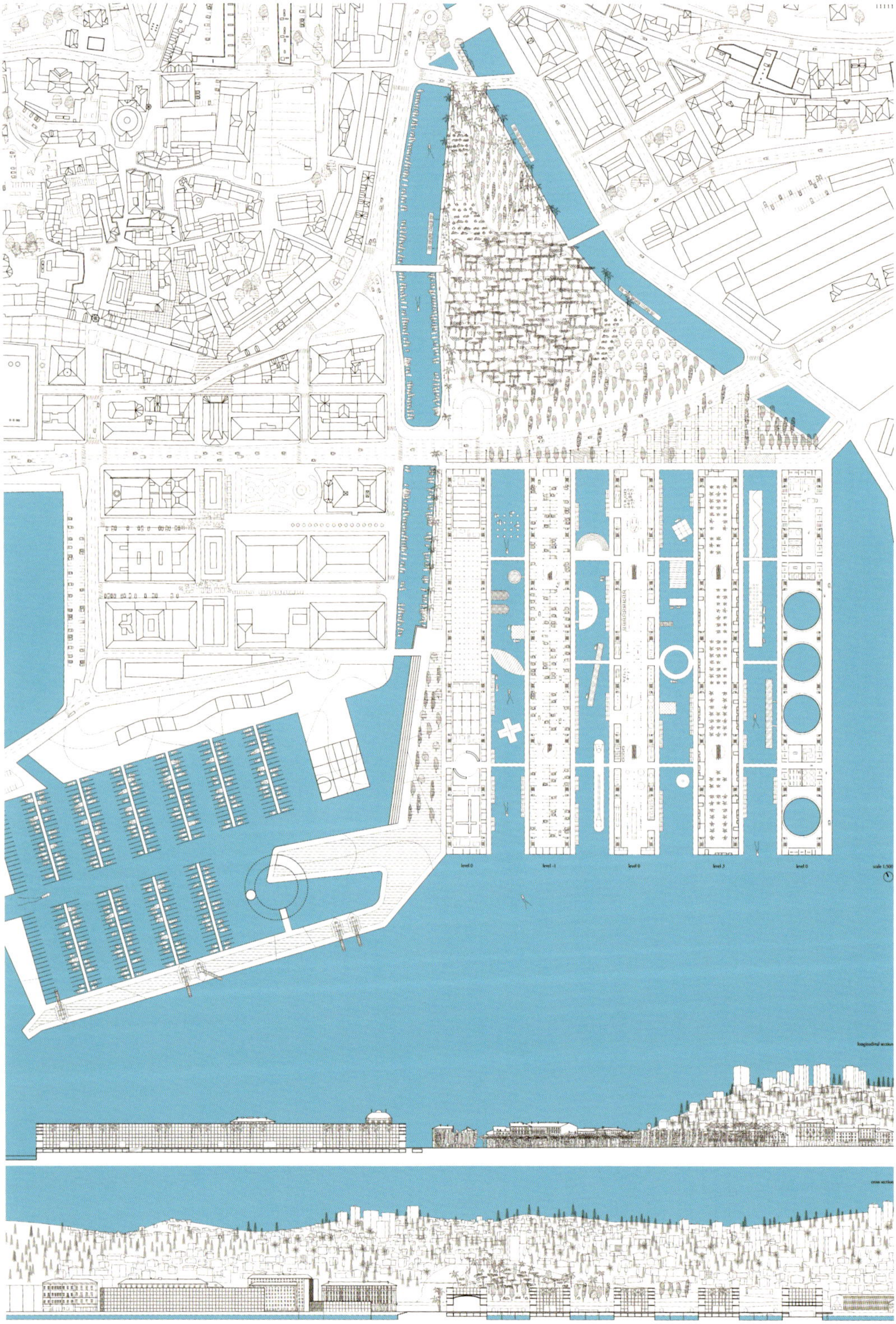


*Above* Site plan and sections / *Opposite page above* Section perspective / *Opposite page center* Axonometric / *Opposite page below* Section

cross section

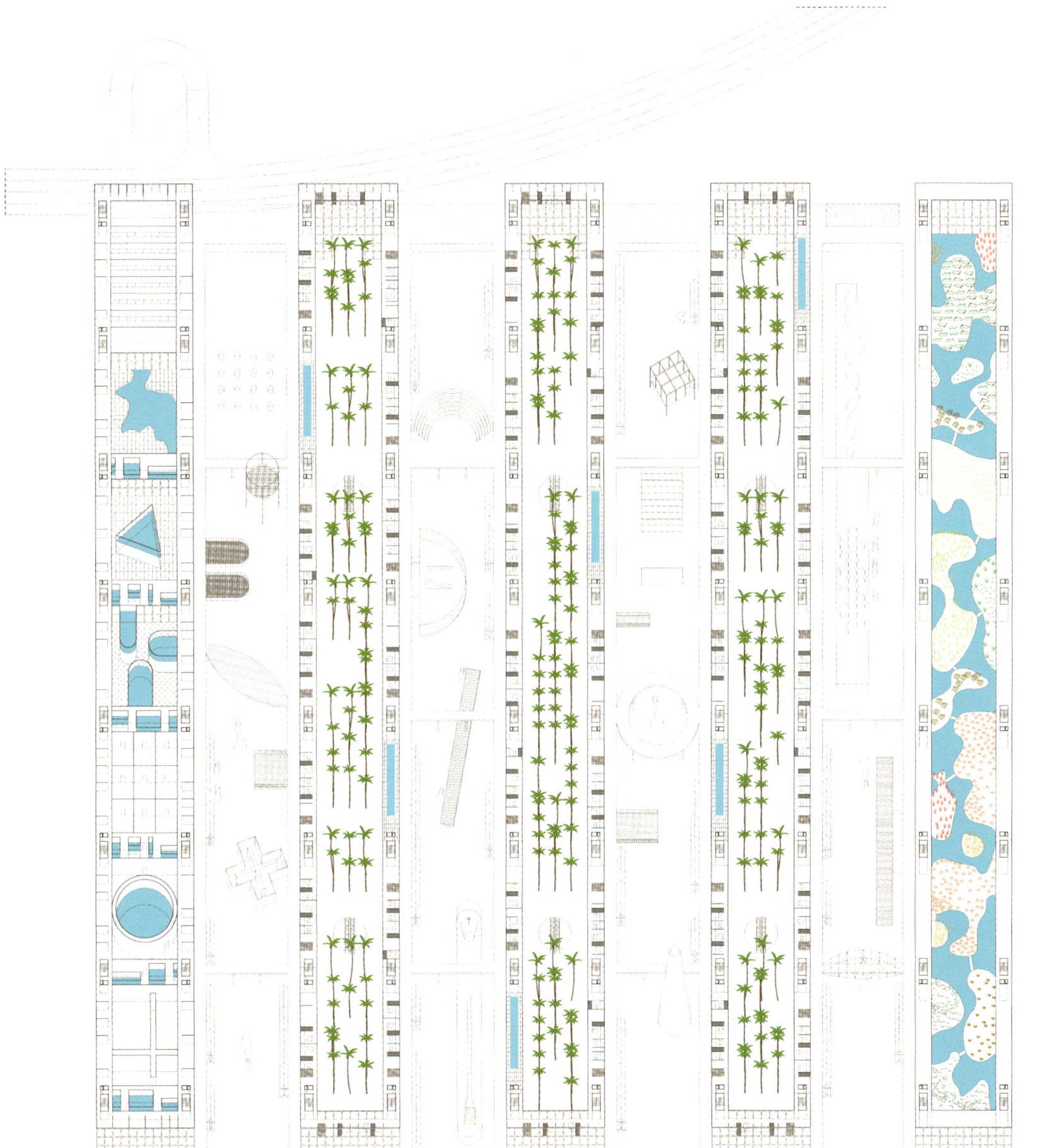

axonometric plan

scale 1:500

longitudinal section

**Civic Center**

*Competition*

*Milan, Italy, 2014*

The form of the contemporary city is the material and imaginary result of a multiplicity of actors, each one with its own rhythms and needs.

The contemporary city, discontinuous, heterogeneous, and impoverished of easily recognizable rules displays distinct forms and different techniques that have been established in different eras. The particular Milanese urban condition, where the fragile relation between public space and the undefined urban texture deeply influences most of the city's urban structure, is highlighted in our project. It creates a paradoxically autonomous work that fits into the area and creates a polarity deeply integrated into the new Porta Garibaldi development. Ultimately, the project operates within a duality of built space and green space and between landscape and artificial object, a tradition that comes from historical gardens that display how the disposition of an open and immersive space can lead to a condition of intimacy and insulation from the city.

Collaborators: Matteo Ghidoni, Francesco Zorzi, Paolo Migliori with Andrea Belosi.
Promoter: Municipality of Milano.

*Left* Day view / *Right* Night view

*Above* Axonometric / *Opposite page* Plans, sections, elevations

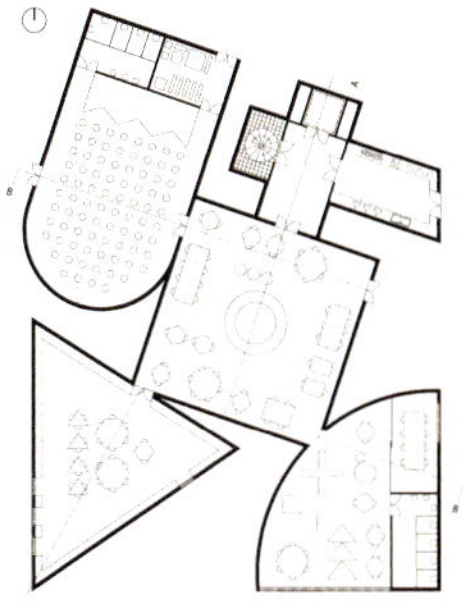

Pianta piano terra

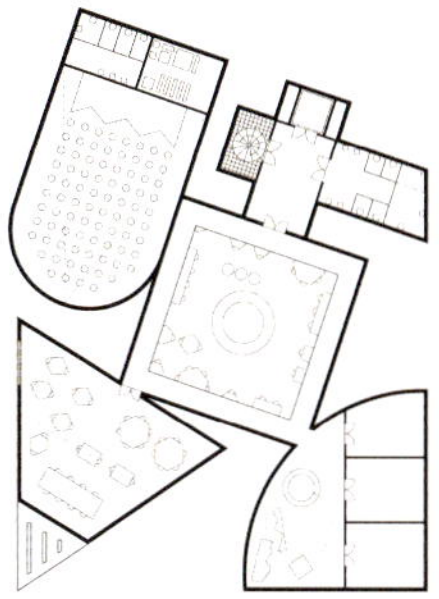

Pianta primo piano

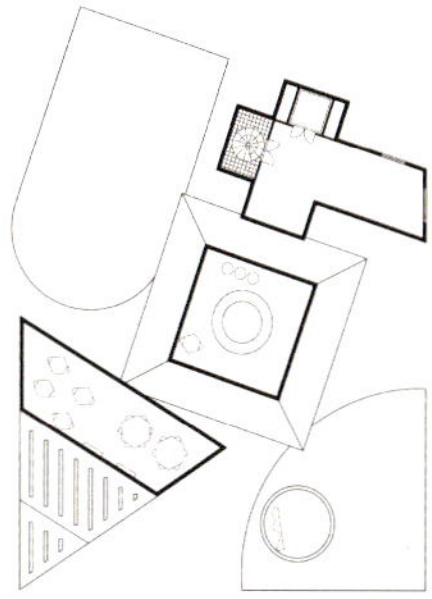

Pianta secondo piano

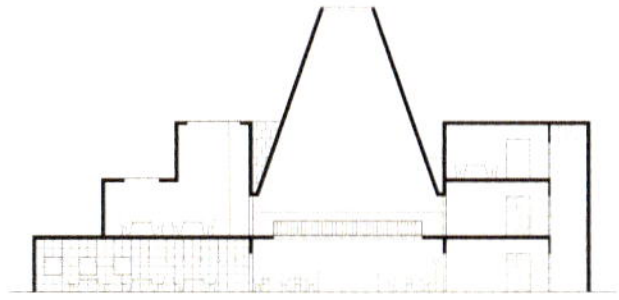

Sezione A-A

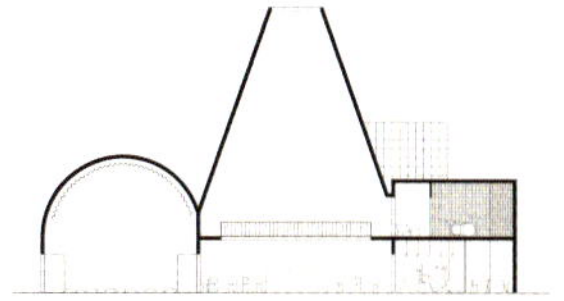

Sezione B-B

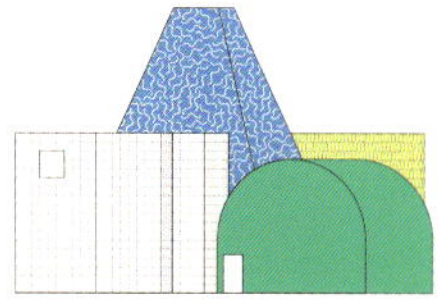

Prospetto Nord

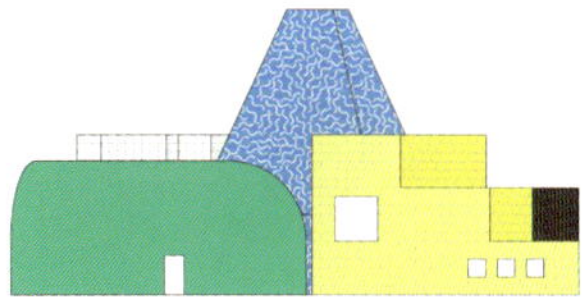

Prospetto Ovest

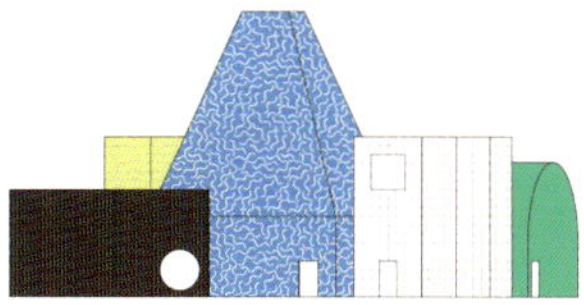

Prospetto Est

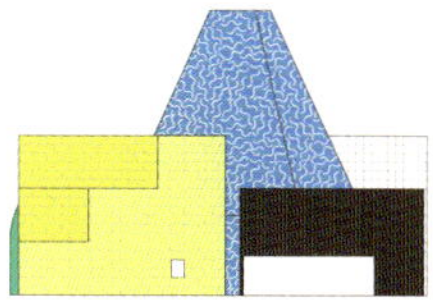

Prospetto Sud

977B9QM4

# MOS

New York, United States

## House No. 2 (Floating House)

*Ontario, Canada, 2008*

The Floating House is part of a master plan including five proposed guest houses based on the repetition of a generic vernacular house. Located on a remote island in Lake Huron with a harsh seasonal climate, an on-site construction process would have been difficult, so the 2,200-square-foot house was built on a floating steel pontoon structure at the contractor's lakeside workshop and then towed and anchored to the final site for the installation of finishes. The front of the house faces the water. There is a loose symmetry in the plan. The entrance opens onto a landscaped path that passes through the building and down the stairs, wrapped behind a screen of cedar siding. This path connects the two sides of the U-shaped island.

The house is clad in a cedar plank rainscreen that visually unifies walls and roof. The spacing of the planks varies around openings to admit light and air. The rainscreen provides air movement between interior and exterior, dissipating heat gain and reducing wind load. Anchored to the granite lakebed, the house moves with the changing water level. The architecture floats; it is an abstraction of the vernacular house, displaced onto the lake.

Project Team: Michael Meredith, Hilary Sample, Fred Holt, Chad Burke, Ryan Bollom, Forest Fulton, Temple Simpson, Martin Kedzior, Jimenez Lai.
Structural Engineer: J. David Bowick, Blackwell Engineering Ltd., Toronto.
Photography: Florian Holzherr.

*Above* Exterior view / *Below left* Site plan / *Below right* Floor plan

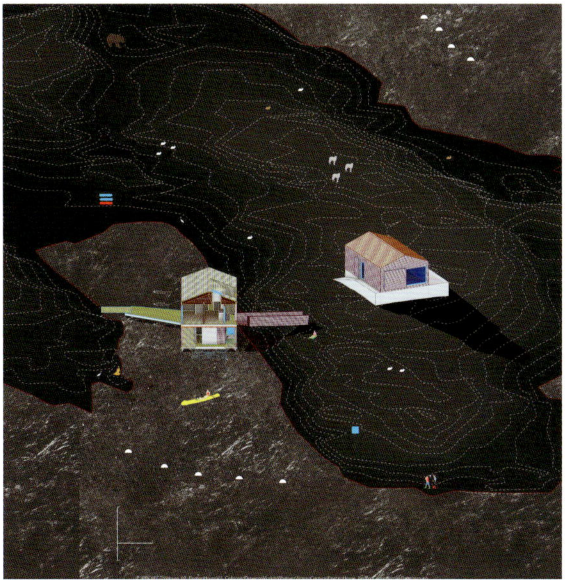

*Opposite page above* Exterior view / *Opposite page below* Entry and cladding detail / *Above* Interior view / *Below* Stair detail / *Following spread* Night view

**Store No. 1 (Miami Facade)**

*Miami, Florida, United States, Under Construction*

Spanning across multiple retail stores in Miami's new Design District, this facade design was developed using Software No. 13, FACADE. Marble-veneer panels create the appearance of a monolithic volume punctured with 24 square openings. Windows and doors are given a similar treatment with all fenestration set back three feet from the marble facade to give the appearance of deep holes. Recessed lighting is integrated into the window setbacks so that the openings are illuminated at night, not just shaded during the day. The arrangement of the holes is based on a simulation of gravity. Falling squares are frozen in the process of collapse, and become openings through which an anonymous public looks through the facade at an unknown tenant. The facade is just a single material with series of openings, each framing something provided by the unknown tenant. Maybe they will fill the windows with stuff. Or maybe not.

Project Team: Michael Meredith, Hilary Sample, Carson Russell, Phi Van Phan, Thomas Heltzel, Ivi Diamantopoulou.

*Below* Model / *Above right* Collages / *Opposite page above* Elevation / *Opposite page below* Axonometric

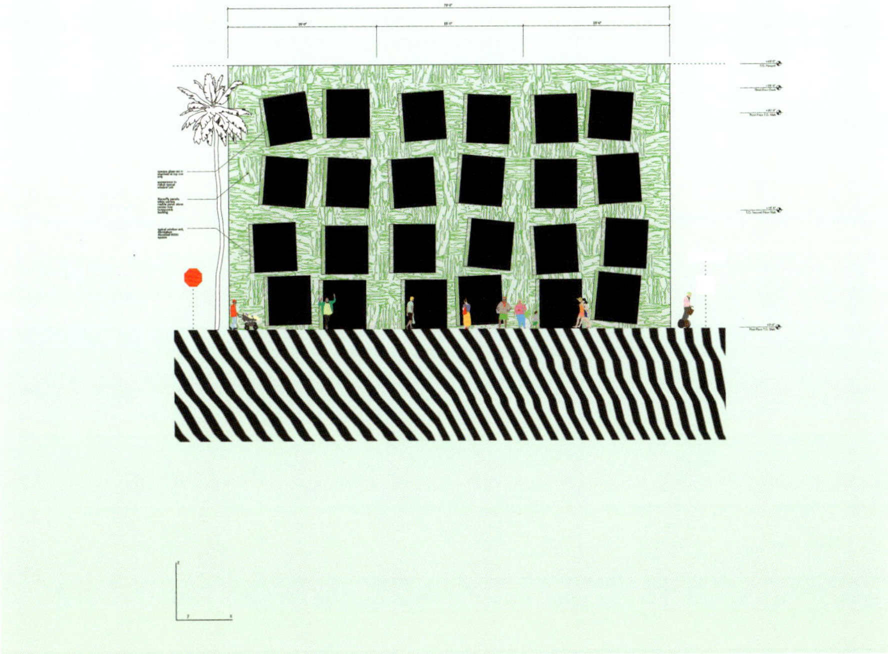

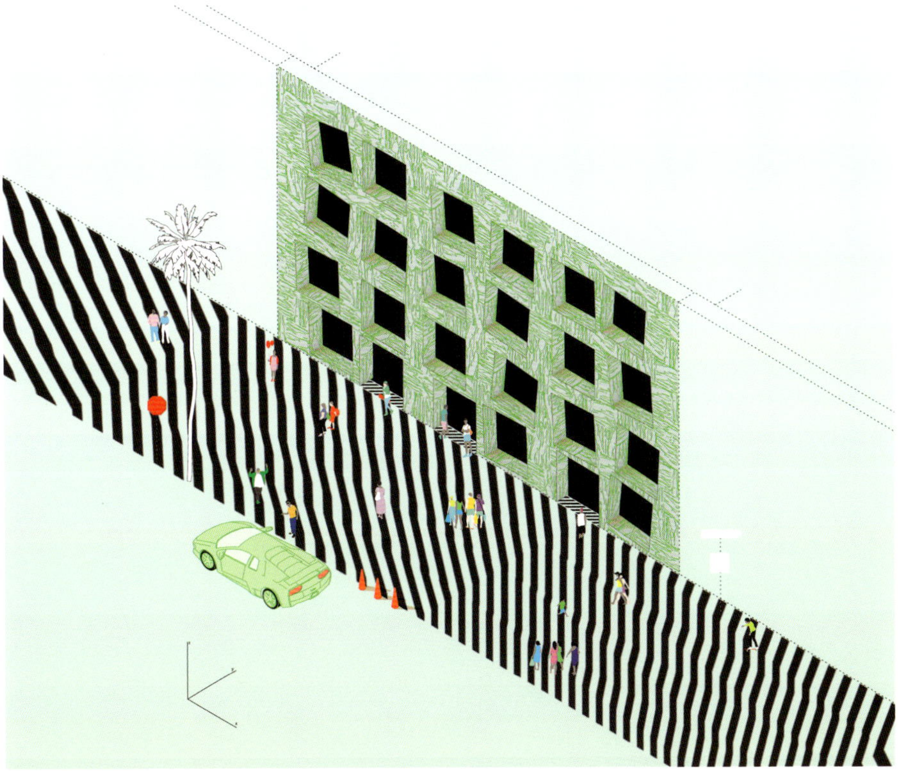

**House No 8 (Ramp Hill)**

*Upstate New York, United States, 2015 (proposal)*

This single-family house is located within a forest surrounded by farms in Upstate New York. It is a singular building, programmatically stratified within the steeply sloped landscape. Built into the side of a hill and partially buried in the ground, its three distinct levels are all individually accessible and all open onto the landscape. The four pavilions above are both connected to and separated from the house, allowing them to operate autonomously as cabins, guest spaces, greenhouses, and studios. The lower level, buried in the ground, is a large ceramics studio that opens onto an adjacent pond. The main living space is organized one room after another, and connects internally to the levels above and below with a small secondary stair. In this way, three relatively disconnected programs are unified into a singular geometric figure. The abstract figure for the house allows for a double reading: either as a serial system, one part after another, or as a singular crenellated figure, an exaggerated fragment of a castle.

Project Team: Michael Meredith, Hilary Sample, Tim Brennan, Ivi Diamantopoulou, Yann Gay-Crossier, Ceri Edmunds, Igsung So.

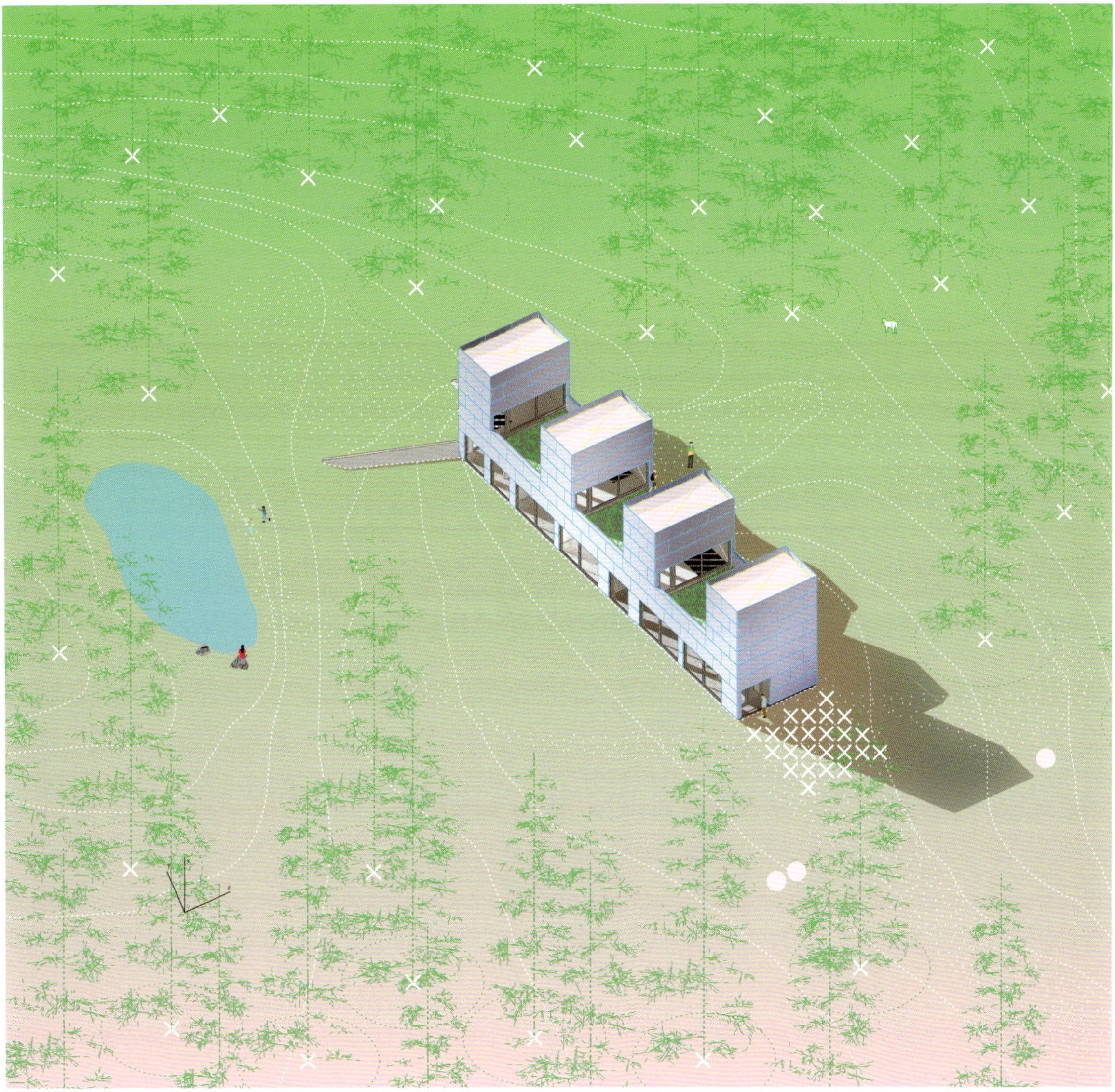

*Opposite page* Frontal Axonometric / *Above* Axonometric / *Below* Plan

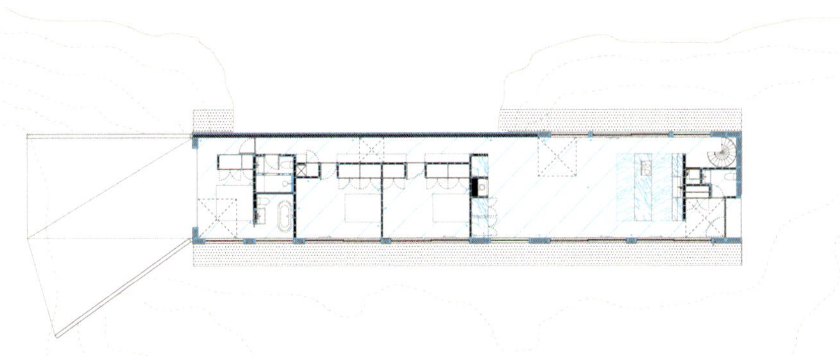

*Above* Model / *Below* Model in the landscape / *Opposite page above* Oblique views / *Opposite page below* Worm's-eye axonometric

# JAIME CORREA & ASSOCIATES

Miami, Florida, United States

### Mobile Stage

An ephemeral pop-up performance space. It brings awareness of the necessity of public cultural spaces all over the American territory. The project is meant to be assembled on residual spaces and no man's lands; given its dimensions, 24 ft. X 44 or 64 ft., the project can be easily accommodated on asphalted parking areas or as an infill condition on small urban lots.

The proposed performance space is composed of two volumes and a central space; the two volumes, configured as a cube of half the size on each side, contain a stage and a sitting area; the central space separates the two volumes with a peripheral bench and serves to create a community "third place". Upon disassembling, the entire project can be stored as a full cube.

A colossal lantern illuminates the stage; the rear of the stage building contains a digital screen to accommodate larger audiences or to show movies as a drive-in theater; the sitting area is composed of three over-sized benches with a board and batten wood system articulating the base of the interior space and its corner window; the base of the buildings serves as the project datum line and as the informal bench for the central public space. The whole composition is set on a raised black deck.

*Above* Plan and elevation drawing / *Below left* Axonometric drawing / *Below right* Reversed section drawing

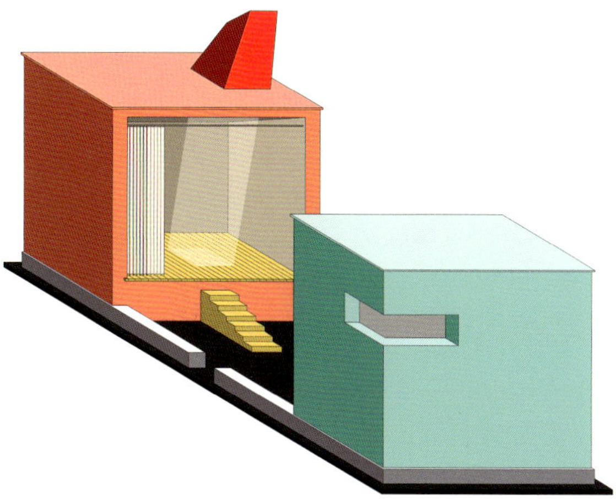

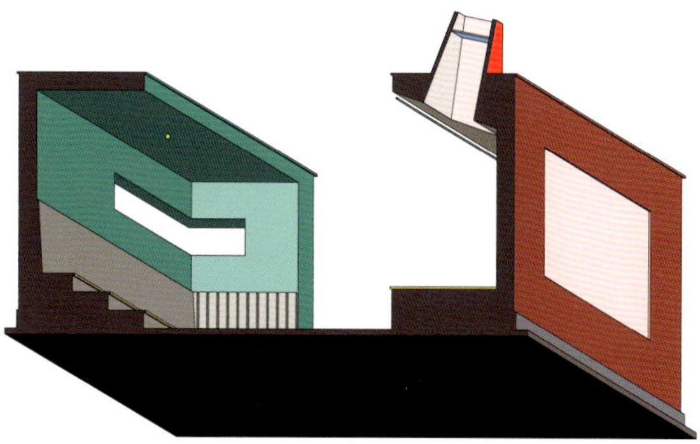

## Red Square

A social housing project arranged in a traditional "English Close" configuration. The project includes 22 single-family houses with garages and granny apartments to subsidize the mortgage payments. The plan of each first floor may be easily adapted for partial retail uses. The placement of these housing units generates a square perimeter where a tree-lined central lawn space emerges as the core of the project.

The lack of ornamentation is supplemented with an abundance of color and iconography. Red façades are drawn against the public square; perpendicular ochre planes surround the private gardens; a volume with a circular eyebrow is colored in rose/peach natural tones; pools and grassy areas add color values to the general composition.

Chimneys of air and light, providing natural ventilation, crown the red square façades. A white bench surrounds the perimeter of the central space. Private second-floor loggias add to the repertoire of public/civic elements. Garden walls delimit the privacy of the lot surfaces and the realm of the tree-lined central space. The houses have lateral yard retention pools for purposes of sea-level rise resiliency.

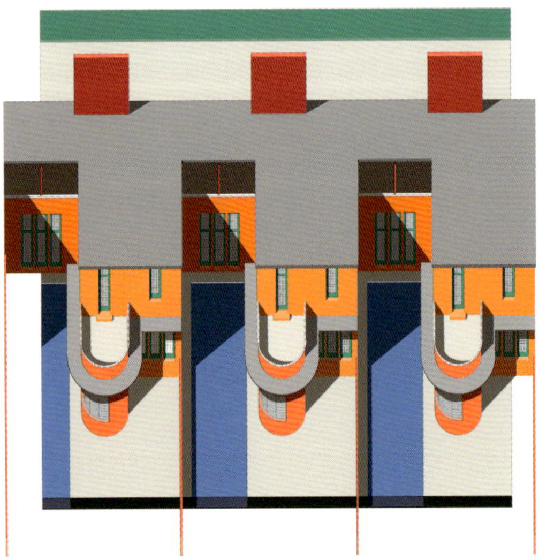

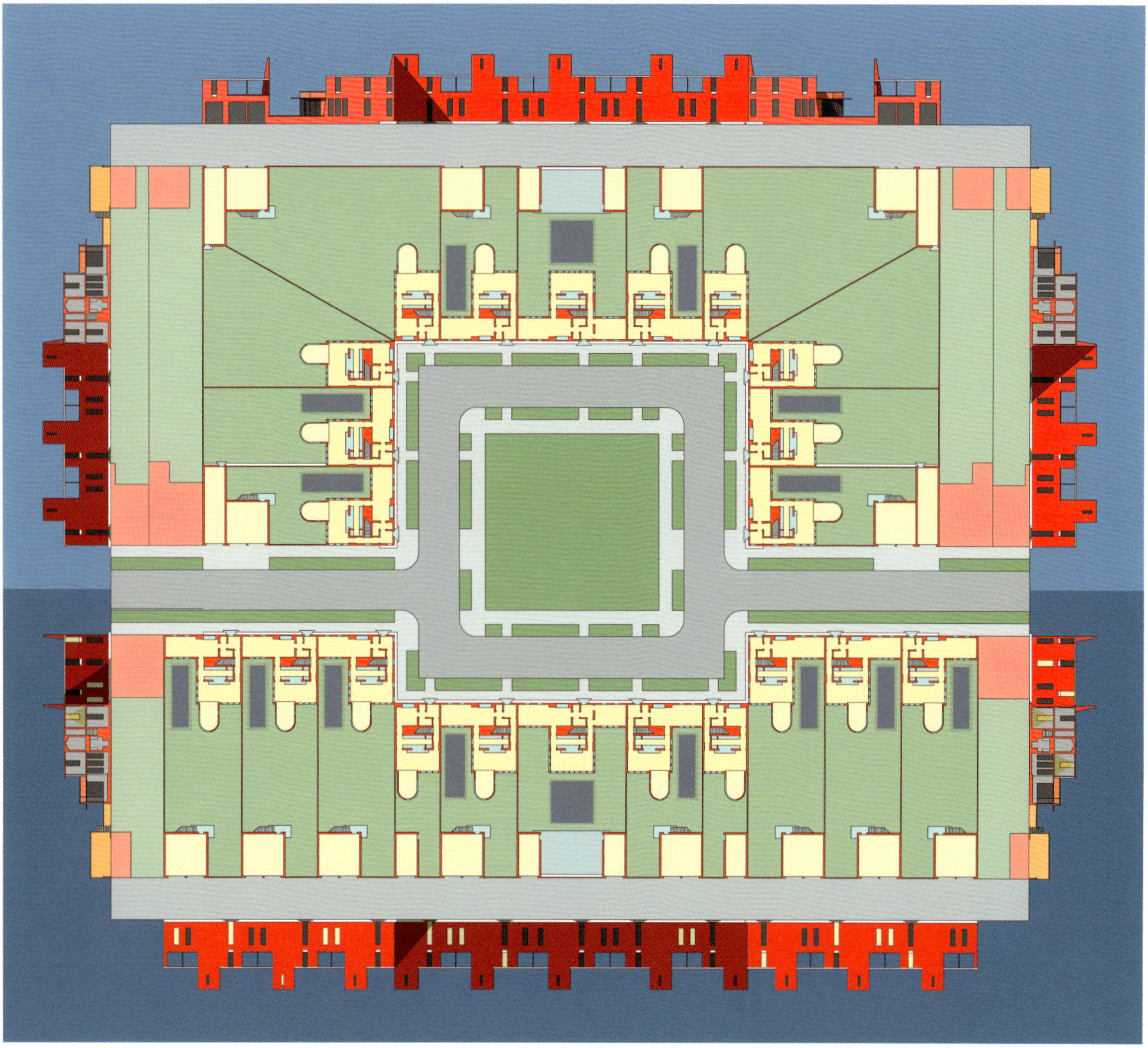

*Opposite page* Axonometric / *Above* Composite drawing

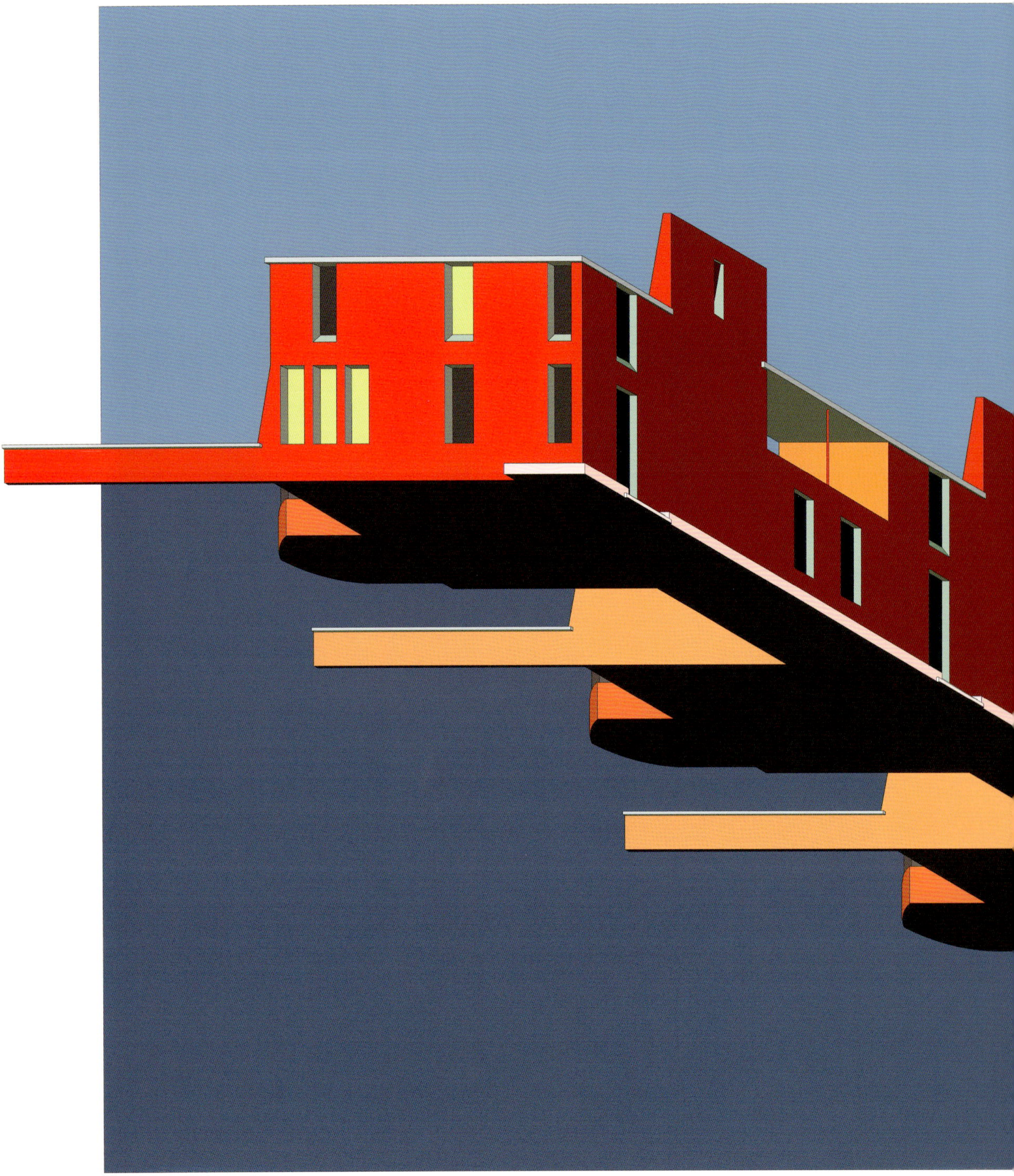

Oblique

# LOEB SARLI ARCHITECTS

Miami, Florida, United States

**Tirana**

*Filling the Gaps*

*Tirana, Albania*

For the naive reading of our foreign eyes, the city of Tirana presents itself as a physical testimony of its political development. One of its distinctive characteristics is the existence of several voids, the gaps, deployed throughout the urban territory. The gaps are a direct consequence of the intricate relationship the political culture of the city has had with "private property" and "land distribution" policies during the different governing regimes.

In our opinion, these gaps offer valuable opportunities for the future development of the city. Considered as a whole rather than a random distribution of empty parcels, the gaps suggest the possibility of overlaying a poly-nodal structure on the existing urban tissue. The nodes would replace the gaps to become microcosms in the city that live from and for the city. We imagine the nodes as areas where contemporary questions and needs such as sustainable design could be answered. Sustainable design in its broadest meaning: in the relationship of the intervention with the environment and context, in the relationship of the public and private realm, and in the relationship of different programs capable of generating the necessary spaces for citizens to live, work, think, entertain, wander...

Our proposal is based on the mixture of apparently antagonistic elements such as Agriculture + Housing, Civic Space and Commerce.

Agricultural land is to be placed over housing and commercial structures, becoming a green roof, a protective mantle for the "city". It offers the possibility of renting agricultural land and cultivating goods to be commercialized in the proposed market, or to be used privately by the residents as rooftop gardens. The market would generate jobs, formalize the casual commercial activity currently existing on the site, as well as activate the use of the existing train station.

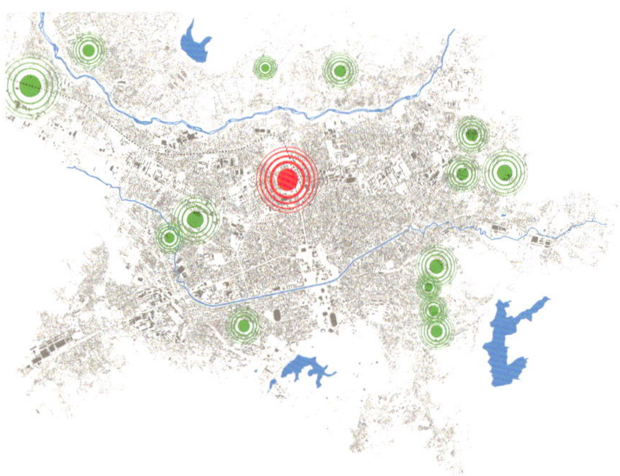

*Opposite Page* Site plan polynodal / *Above* Axonometric / *Below left* Ground strategy/ *Below right* Roof strategy

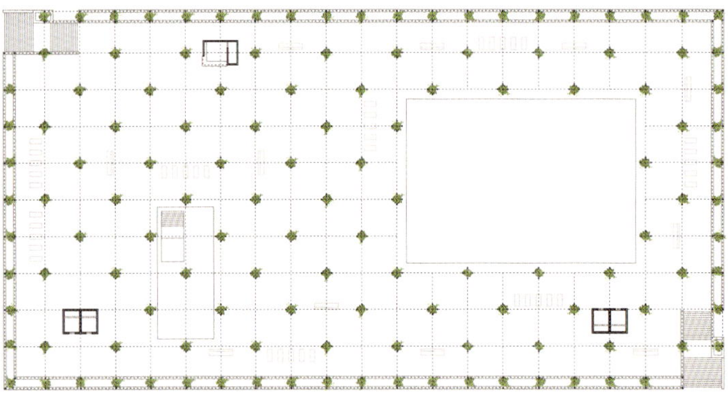

*Opposite page above* Housing Plan / *Opposite page below* Plan of elevated park / *Above* Axonometric / *Below* Housing elevation

## KJPK - Children's Psychiatric Center

*Basel, Switzerland, 2011*

Located on the northeastern edge of the Universitäre Psychiatrische Kliniken campus in the city of Basel, the new Children's Psychiatric Center seeks to establish a straight forward relationship with the orthogonal arrangement of the existing buildings. A walk around leaves behind an understanding of the campus as a composition of an infinite repetition of 90 degree angles in the shape of two and three story buildings, in contrast with the impactful lush vegetation significantly higher than the modestly scaled structures. In this repetitive tempo and the tension between built and natural forms, the new center finds its narrative.

Programmatically, the center consists of conventional uses found in a psychiatric clinic such as offices and therapy rooms, as well as housing facilities and a school for the patients in need of long term treatment. In order to be consistent with the surrounding building heights, the clinic and the school were separated into two different structures. This would drastically change the daily routine of the young patients staying for extended periods of time. In order to attend school they would have to leave the clinic, perhaps establishing a rhythm closer to their daily lives when staying at home. In between the school and the clinic a large playground welcomes the children staying at or visiting the clinic, as well as the community at large.

The school building is organized along a single loaded corridor with generous windows that allow for direct views to the playground and the park-like campus. Its oversized dimensions, along with a large open area at one of its ends could sustain active playing during breaks when the weather would prevent the children from being outside. On the western side the classrooms receive the afternoon sun. The construction method of the school is exposed cast in-situ concrete.

While the school's typology would present it as a slender volume when seen from the street, the large rectangular body of the two story clinic would be perceived as excessively horizontal and well grounded. The cornice line is endlessly parallel to the ground. Vertical fiber cement paneling and windows evoke the verticality of the surrounding "forest." The apparent dullness of the exterior wall is juxtaposed to a series of sculpted circular voids that unexpectedly animate the interior. On the inside, the voids dominate the composition. They are defiant and do not conform to the orthogonal matrix. Finished with oak, their geometry is clear and soft. The intention is to create an opportunity for the children to pause in their routine visits to the clinic.

Architect: Loeb Sarli Architekten GmbH, Tamar Loeb and Edgar Sarli; Landscape Architect: SKK Landschaftsarchitekten AG. Structural Engineer: Aegerter & Bosshard AG; Mechanical Engineer: Suiselectra Ingenieurunternehmung AG. Energy and Ecology Consultant: AAB Architekten.

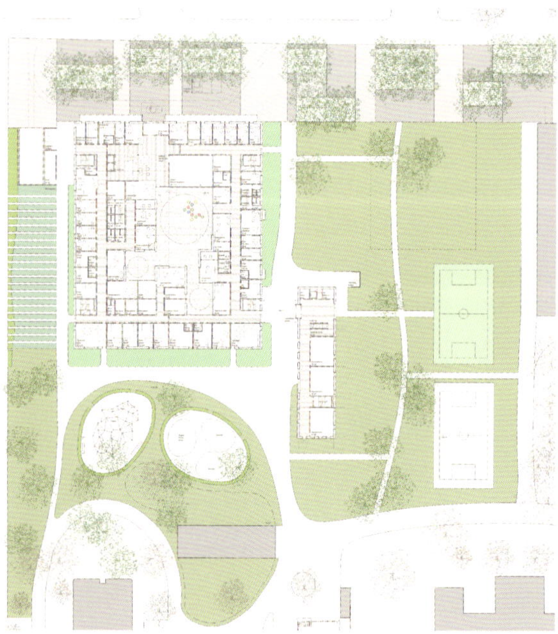

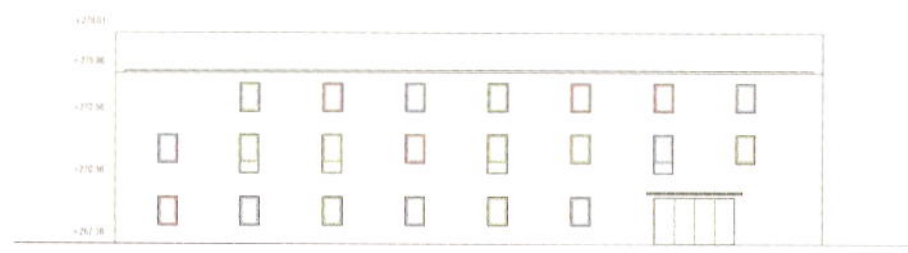

Fassade Schule NO 1:200

Fassade Schule SO 1:200

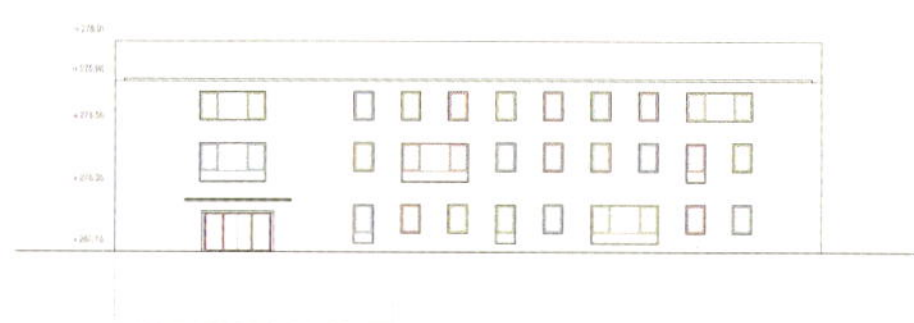

Fassade Schule SW 1:200

*Opposite page below left* Site plan / *Opposite page below right* Elevations / *Above* Entrance view / *Below* Garden view / *Following spread* Yard

# LEDERER RAGNARSDÓTTIR OEI

Stuttgart, Deutschland

**'Annexe to the annexe' of the Sparkasse**

*Ulm, Germany, 2008*

The building has a distinctive presence, with a high arcaded brick base, its piers gently flaring out, giving a sense of the building raising itself on "tiptoes". Above, dense strips of small triangular oriel windows project, the chromed zigzagging stainless steel of their frames explaining the shifting dappled reflections as you approach – giving the effect almost of shimmering scales.

Photography: Roland Halbe.

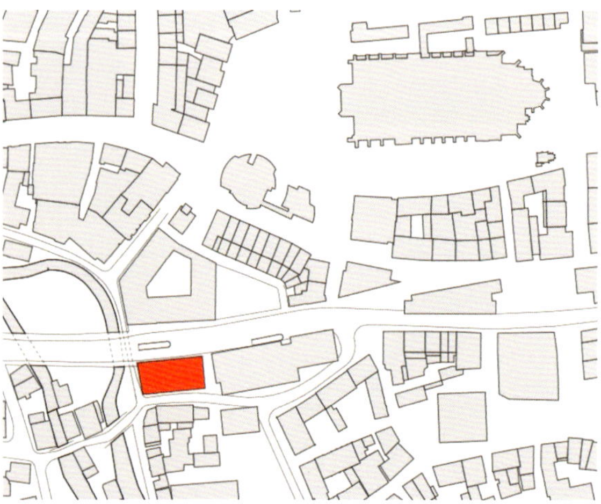

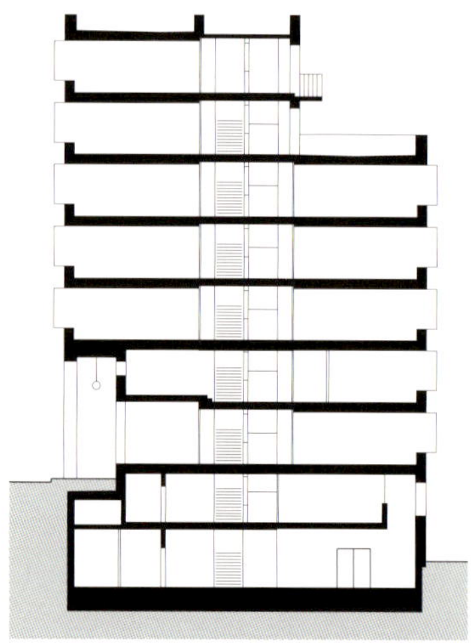

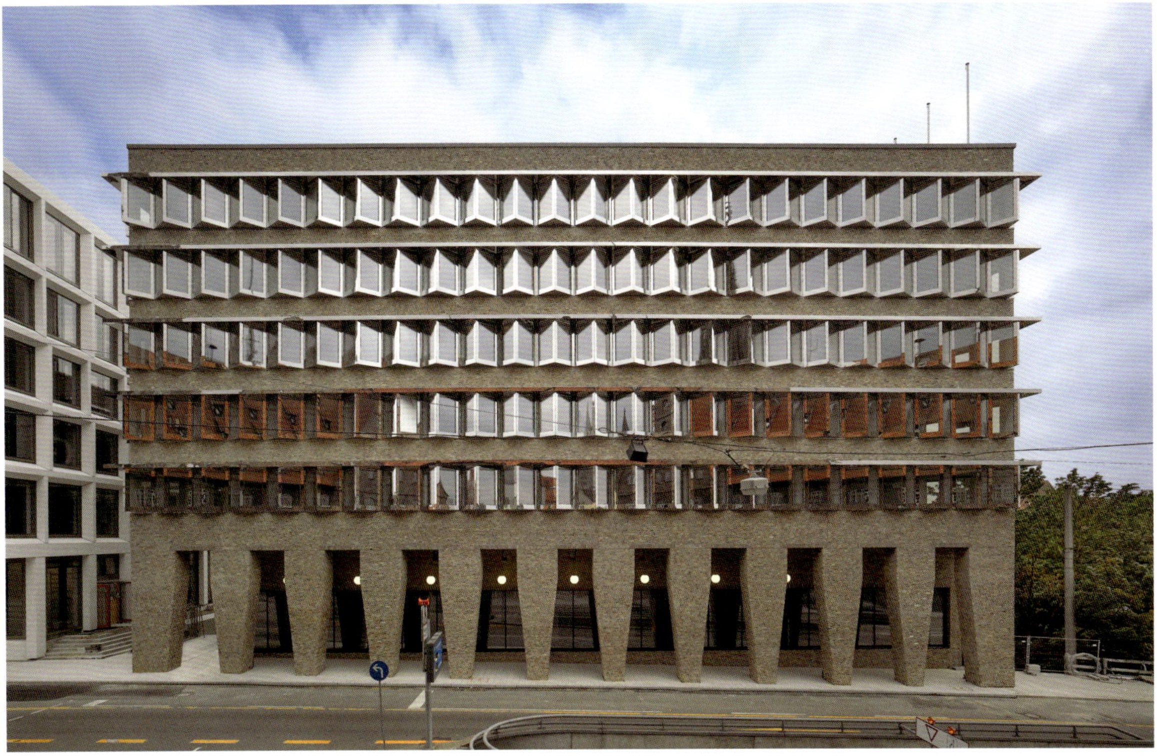

*Opposite page above* Section / *Opposite page below left* Window detail / *Opposite page below right* Site plan / *Above* Exterior view / *Below* Plan

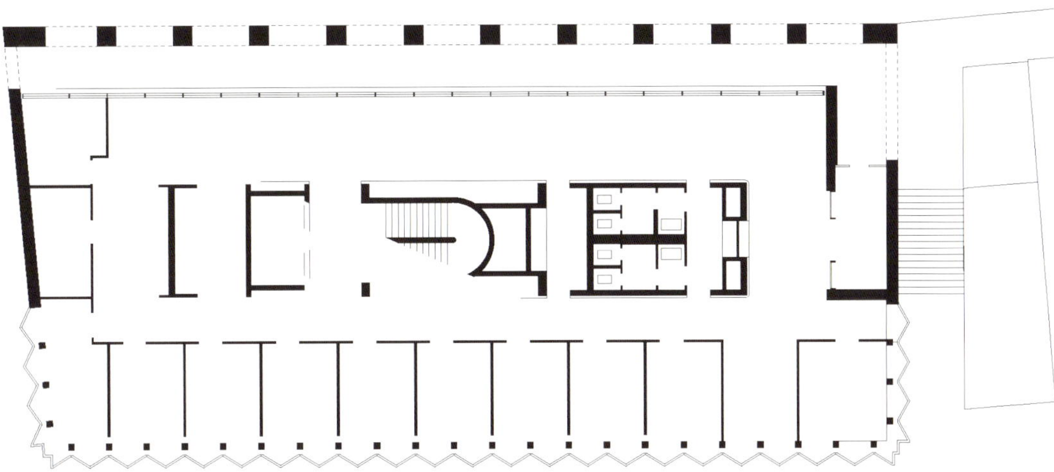

*Above* Wall detail / *Below* Interior detail, bay window

05.

# Conversations

Matteo Ghidoni
Nader Tehrani

# Matteo Ghidoni

The following is a conversation between Matteo Ghidoni, Chief Editor of San Rocco Magazine and principal of Salottobuono and Carie Penabad, Director of Undergraduate Studies at the University of Miami and principal of CÚRE & PENABAD.

**CP** **Can you tell us a bit about your background?**

**MG** I began my formal studies at the Venice School of Architecture in the early 1990s. At that time, Aldo Rossi, Manfredo Tafuri, Vittorio Gregotti and Gino Valle were still teaching at the School; and yet you could sense that the institution was entering a period of decline. These important figures had spawned followers that were attempting to take over the School, trying to replicate their masters' ideas quite nonsensically; and this created a sense of disillusionment and criticism among the student body. With the death or departure of these key figures, there came an architectural and intellectual void that was difficult to fill.

Upon graduating, I started collaborating with Stefano Boeri, in Milan. He was a Bernardo Secchi scholar; and Secchi had been my mentor in Venice. I believe Stefano was a key figure for many involved in the editorial board of San Rocco as many of us had the opportunity to work with him on a variety of projects. I participated in academic collaborations with him in Venice, Mendrisio and at the Berlage Institute. Later, I became a partner in Multiplicity, an agency for territorial investigation he founded in Milan; and finally I worked for him at Domus and in a more sustained capacity at Abitare, while I founded my own office Salottobuono.

**CP** **You have stated that the production of San Rocco surfaced as a critique of the contemporary architectural magazine. Could you elaborate on this?**

**MG** Yes. Initially, San Rocco surfaced as a critique of the contemporary architectural magazines. However, this was not the main reason for its existence. In 2007–2008, the majority of the members of the current editorial board were working on editorial projects in collaboration with leading, Italian, architectural magazines. It was a moment when these publications were beginning to face the financial challenges connected to the broader economic crisis. Funding from leading advertisers was disappearing; and the magazines had to reevaluate their publishing strategies. Many decided to enlarge the spectrum of topics covered to be able to attract a broader audience. So they began to focus on issues of society, economy, geography, politics, lifestyle. These factors are certainly related to the making of cities and the production of architecture; but at the same time, they diluted the magazine's ability to focus on a conversation about architecture and its intrinsic characteristics. We were disappointed with this direction. We were also a bit nostalgic for the Italian magazines produced during the 1960s and 1970s. These publications were able to produce a debate that had the ambition of spreading internationally. In some way, we wanted to recover this.

**CP** **How would you describe the project of SAN ROCCO?**

**MG** I would put it in very practical terms. It is a magazine about architecture. From the beginning, it was conceived as a finite project with 20 issues; and we are in the process of making this a reality. We wanted the magazine to be published in English because we wanted to generate a new platform for an international debate on architecture. This began with the magazine and has extended into exhibitions, the summer school, the Book of Copies, and other projects that are currently being developed. Finally, I would say that the most important aspect of this project is the unique collaboration between the four architectural offices, two photographers and one graphic designer that form the board and all those that have responded to the Call for Papers.

**CP** **Where does the title for the magazine come from?**

**MG** San Rocco is the name of a project produced by Aldo Rossi and Giorgio Grassi in 1971. It was a competition entry for a housing project near Monza. It did not win the competition; so in a sense it was a failure. Yet it was a unique collaboration between two personalities that decided to renounce their own distinct and individual authorship to produce a more fragile and hybrid project. They never collaborated again. Nevertheless, we found the project inspiring because of its brave attempt to produce a shared product.

**CP** **Can you describe the importance of collaboration, both in the case of the magazine and by extension for architectural practice?**

**MG** Collaboration is crucial in both cases. I think that it is the continuous underlying idea that we are trying to promote with the magazine. For the 2012 Venice Biennale, we attempted to make this more explicit by producing an issue on collaboration. We identified two types of collaboration: synchronic and diachronic. The former is concerned with a collaboration that exists at one point in time, while the latter focuses on something that has evolved across time. A classic example of diachronic collaboration would be the design and construction of St Peters Cathedral, a project that extended beyond the life of any single architect involved.

In our opinion, these two realities are intrinsic to architecture. We are able to collaborate simply because we work on something that we can share. This idea of collaboration reveals the very public nature of architecture.

**CP** **In a digital age, why are you committed to the production of a paper magazine?**

**MG** Paper is but one of the possible choices today. I do not see the digital publication as an evolution of the paper one. There are many possibilities. At one time we were used to receiving information about architecture once a month in the form of a magazine that was delivered to our houses. Today we can find information about architecture everywhere.

In any case, producing information is not our job. We're not interested in novelty or the latest architectural project. These topics are covered excellently through other media such as blogs or architectural websites. Instead, we wanted to construct a slower project that did not have to follow day-to-day events. We wanted to give ourselves the luxury of being slow to be able to think about what we were producing and writing. At the same time, we wanted to assume responsibility for a project that was developed through time with a specific print rate, number of issues, etc.

In recent years, we have seen the appearance of many printed architectural magazines. This is quite impressive as it was thought that the economic crisis of 2008 was going to put a halt to paper publishing. Many examples were included in the recent Archizine exhibition, curated by Elias Redstone, anticipated by Beatriz Colomina's Clip/Stamp/Fold, that put together all the experimental independent publications from the 1960s and 1970s.

Yet despite the increase in paper magazines, many have been published only once or twice and then have disappeared. San Rocco is conceived differently. From the beginning, we laid out a five-year plan; and we felt that paper was the best medium for this sustained endeavor. Finally, the choice of paper was also about the pleasure of the tactile experience and to be able to see the work in print, a reality that is still all together different from a digital production.

**CP** **Does the project of San Rocco argue for an idea about architecture? If so, how would you describe it?**

MG I think that the most honest way to express San Rocco's idea about architecture is to say that architecture is the architectures built through time. If you look at San Rocco as a magazine, it is nothing more than a folder of projects each expressing certain ideas about architecture. We are not interested in stating ideas about architecture in general or abstract terms. Instead, we always refer to existing projects that have been built or drawn.

**CP** **That is pretty radical because it implies that history plays a role in the study of architecture. This is not a position that would be advocated by many leading architects, especially those that advance an architecture of novelty. Can you say a bit more.**

**MG** History is important for us; yet we do not want to construct a historicist discourse. We see all buildings as possible material to be used in our work. The production of new projects relies on the existence of a collective knowledge that is constantly explored, and then redefined through our work. In this sense I use the tautology Architecture is Architectures. We cannot talk about architecture if we do not talk about specific architectures that have been produced through time.

**CP** **Some critics have argued that SAN ROCCO promotes a move away from a theoretical discourse and towards a pragmatic position that reattaches architecture to a broader cultural discourse that includes history, form and type. Would you agree with this?**

**MG** No. I do not see any contradiction. A theoretical discourse includes history, type and form. Perhaps the work that we are trying to do is a bit more humble and related to an architecture that is the product of a specific condition, of specific requirements, clients etc. It is not a theoretical construction detached from reality.

As architectural practitioners, we want to learn something about how architecture is produced; and we want to enrich our catalogue of examples. At the same time, we want to rediscover lost issues and architectural knowledge that was erased by the modern movement or by some interpretations of the modern movement. In this sense, I suppose San Rocco is also a project of rediscovery.

**CP** **The editorial board appears to have a shared fascination with the architecture of the 1960s and 1970s avant-garde, a sensibility that extends itself to the work of the firms associated with the magazine. What underlies the interest in recuperating this period?**

**MG** This is true. But I would say that this interest is not homogeneous. We share an interest in the period when modernism was radically put into question. Both The Architecture of the City and Complexity and Contradiction in Architecture were published in 1966. These texts radically criticized functionalism and its role in the erasure of architectural knowledge. The heroes of modernism took the books of architecture and threw them away, wanting to restart from scratch. In time the potential of this radical act was weakened; and we felt the need to rediscover a critique of this phenomenon.

There may be other reasons for this shared interest. For Italians, the 1960s was a moment of promise, a moment of optimism, a rebirth of the country. The architectural discourse was politically charged; and you had the feeling that people believed in architecture as a political act. This period also exemplified an alliance between architectural production and dissemination that was difficult to achieve in latter decades.

**CP** **Several firms associated with the production of SAN ROCCO (including your own) were featured in the CALL TO ORDER exhibition here at the School. Can you identify any shared sensibilities between the work of these various practices?**

**MG** There is a shared sensibility that is difficult to describe because I think it is based on differences. It is easier to talk about the differences than the similarities. Your question reminds me of an anecdote.

In 2008, various members of the current editorial board were invited participate in the Venice Biennale. Baukuh and Salottobuono took part in the Italian pavilion, OFFICE was in charge of the Belgian pavilion, and 2A+PA had its own section within the main exhibition space. To celebrate, we decided to throw a party together and designed the invitation as a *Cadavre Exquis* (a surrealist technique where a collection of words or images is assembled collectively). Our drawing was composed of four parts of a plan made by the different offices in sequence. It was only at the end—when we opened the invitation—that we knew what the final product looked like.

In a sense this drawing describes our attitude towards working together and our shared sensibilities. We work on different themes but we share an interest in developing our own ignorance or what we ignore about the other and what we ignore about architecture.

**CP** **Could you replace the word ignorance with naïveté?**

**MG** I use the word ignorance to refer to the removal of a body of knowledge that was once known but is now forgotten. Thus the information that we have today is incomplete. We wanted to rediscover this information and reinterpret it.

For instance, my generation could not speak of Rossi, Grassi or Canella because they were part of something that had to be forgotten, something that was no longer accepted. Our naïve rediscovery of this body of work, allowed us to reinterpret the knowledge of these subjects and make it new, acceptable, fruitful, productive and even promising.

**CP** **For some issues of the magazine, the voice of the editorial board appears more neutral. However, in the fourth issue (perhaps the most radical in the series to date) you express a clear position against the idea of Concept as a means to justify design solutions in the absence of what you describe as "proper architecture" or "real design". What do you mean by this?**

**MG** I don't agree that some editorials are more neutral. I believe they all express a clear position. However, in the case of Issue 4, the message was communicated with a sort of rage. We simply felt "Enough is enough" with this idea of concept. Here I am referring to the oversimplified use of concept as a way to communicate what you are trying to do in a work of architecture. It serves a role in selling a project or speaking to clients in a way that they can understand and accept it. But it does not have to be expanded to permeate all forms of architectural discourse. This implies a surrender to the logic of the market.

This oversimplification of the discourse allows us to avoid the responsibility of talking about space. Space is certainly more complex and difficult to describe, but it is our role as architects to discuss it. I believe that we are asked to be able to defend this idea of talking about architecture, which is nothing more than the discipline of shaping space and giving form to specific conditions.

I would like to put it another way. I believe that this oversimplified mode of talking about architecture hides a necessity to justify the architectural act with words that are not directly linked to it. It is a form of hidden guilt or the necessity to justify and explain to a broader audience what we are doing because we do not really believe in our role.

The public character of architecture lies not in the fact that it is communicating public values but that it is open to generously accept people's actions, movements, rituals. An architecture defined by a simple concept is not generous. It is obliged to be simplistic; and it is not open to transformation. Once again, the life of a building is longer than that of its producers and inhabitants. Thus one of the unique qualities of architecture is its potential to accept changes in use not foreseen by its makers. This is why we hate concepts so much: they imply a rigidly defined idea that is given once and for all.

**CP** **Do you see concept different from diagram or would you say that the diagram is a graphic representation of a simplified concept?**

**MG** Diagrams are something different, connected to a machinist vision that sees buildings as apparatuses. Diagrams read architecture as a system of connections and overlapping functions. In doing so, they tend to erase the spatial qualities. They describe factors that can be removed from a building and yet the building remains. You can describe the Baths of Caracalla with a diagram as it was used in Roman times. This diagram no longer exists but the architecture is still (partially) there; and it is something else. I think architecture should be good brave and generous enough to overcome functional schemes or diagrammatic descriptions.

**CP** **Drawings play an important role in the graphic culture of SAN ROCCO. What inspires the commitment to the minimal black and white axonometric line drawing?**

**MG** Some of our offices have been producing this kind of drawings since the early 2000, when they were not very fashionable. I would call them non-impressive, or rather "objective" drawings. We were looking for an exact, measurable system of three-dimensional representation. And we wanted to detach as much as possible from renderings and photo-realism. We resurrected these drawing techniques, that very popular in the 1970s and 1980s before the outbreak of digital tools, because they corresponded to our desire of precision, erasing any indulgence in the "gesture" and the authorial signature.

Now it seems that the black and white axonometric drawing has become very fashionable, at least in Europe. We feel a bit guilty when we visit European schools and realize that everyone is representing projects in this way. For us, this drawing type finally became an iconic sign for the magazine, being the protagonist of the cover. But initially it was a way to work on the projects: to rework existing drawings in a way that we could manipulate them to better understand the work. We also wanted to produce a set of comparable objects that we could put on the table to form a sort of strange taxonomy. We wanted to detach the original drawings from their specific authors and time, and re-propose them as material that we could use today; and for us the first act of appropriation is redrawing.

**CP** **The magazine resurrects the model of the practitioner | writer in opposition to the professional scholar or contemporary critic. What drives this desire and what do you believe it offers?**

**MG** We want to re-affirm the role of the architect as an intellectual who is able to express a clear position and participate in a public debate. The division between these roles is clearly a stretch that corresponds to a rigid and artificial specialization of labour. The average reader or contributor of San Rocco is a practicing architect, who also teaches in some European school, gives lectures, conducts independent or academic research, writes essays and contributions to many publications, participates in exhibitions and biennales around the world... You cannot separate all these activities, and you have to take responsibility of the coherence between your ideas and your designed and built work.

**CP** **Can you tell us a bit about the current issue under production?**

**MG** We are in the process of final editing of our issue on clients, whose main question is—why should people pay for architecture today?

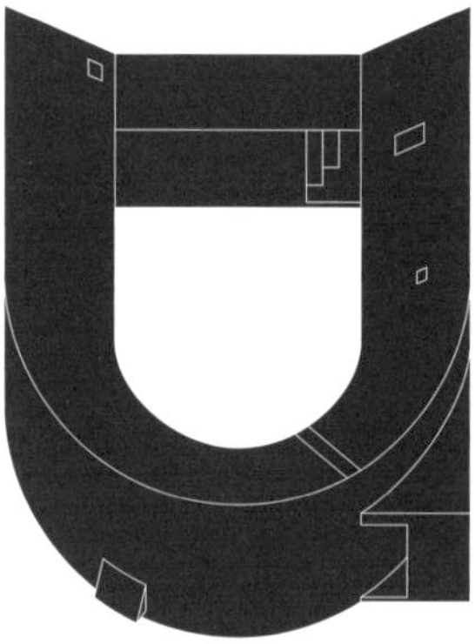

Issue 00

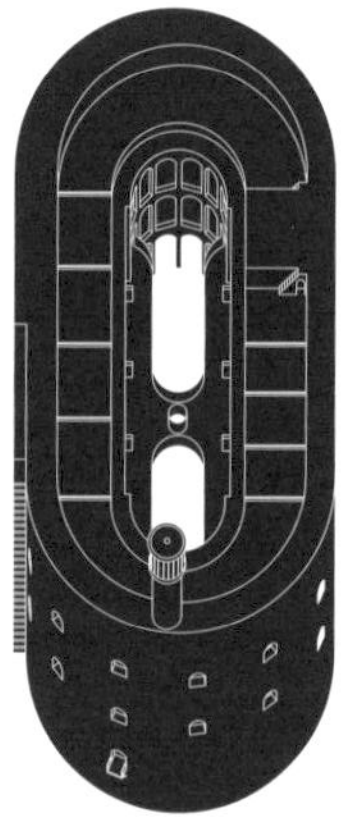

Issue 01

Issue 02

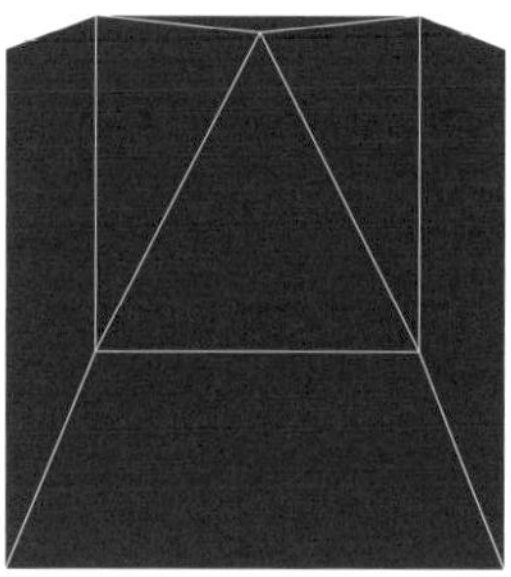

Issue 03

Issue 04

Issue 05

Issue 00 Innocence
Issue 01 Islands
Issue 02 The Even Covering of the Field
Issue 03 Mistakes
Issue 04 Fuck Concepts! Context!
Issue 05 Indifference
Issue 06 Monks and Monkeys
Issue 07 Happy Birthday Bramante!
Issue 08 What's Wrong with the Primitive Hut?
Issue 09 The Client Issue
Issue 10 Scary Architects
Issue 11 Collaborations
Issue 12 Ecology

Issue 06

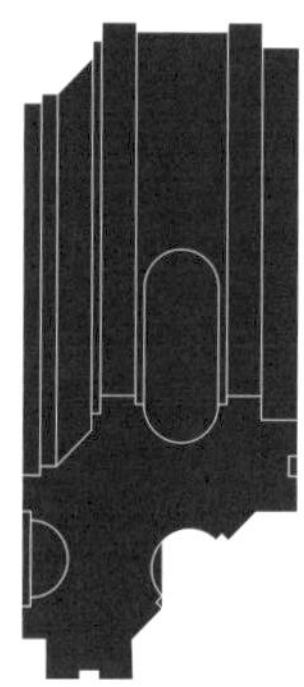

Issue 07

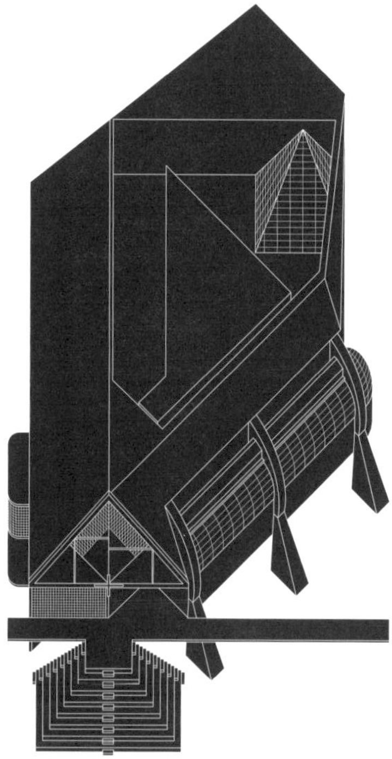

Issue 10

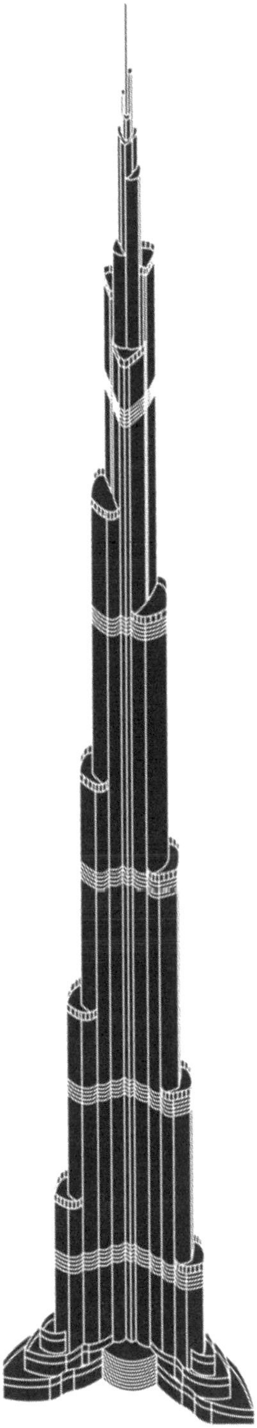

Issue 09

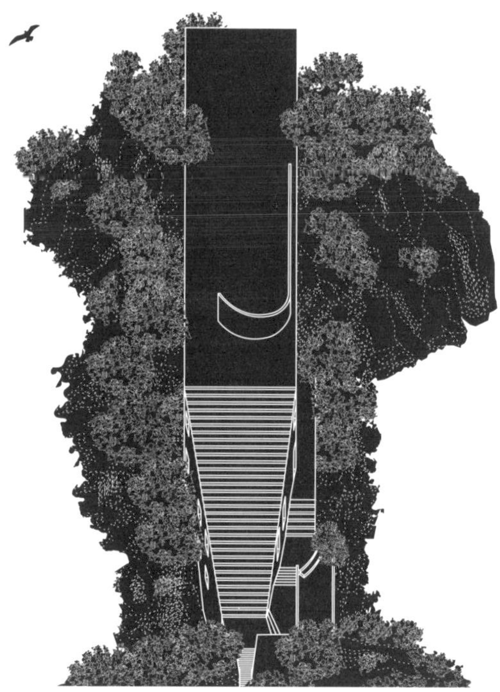

Issue 11

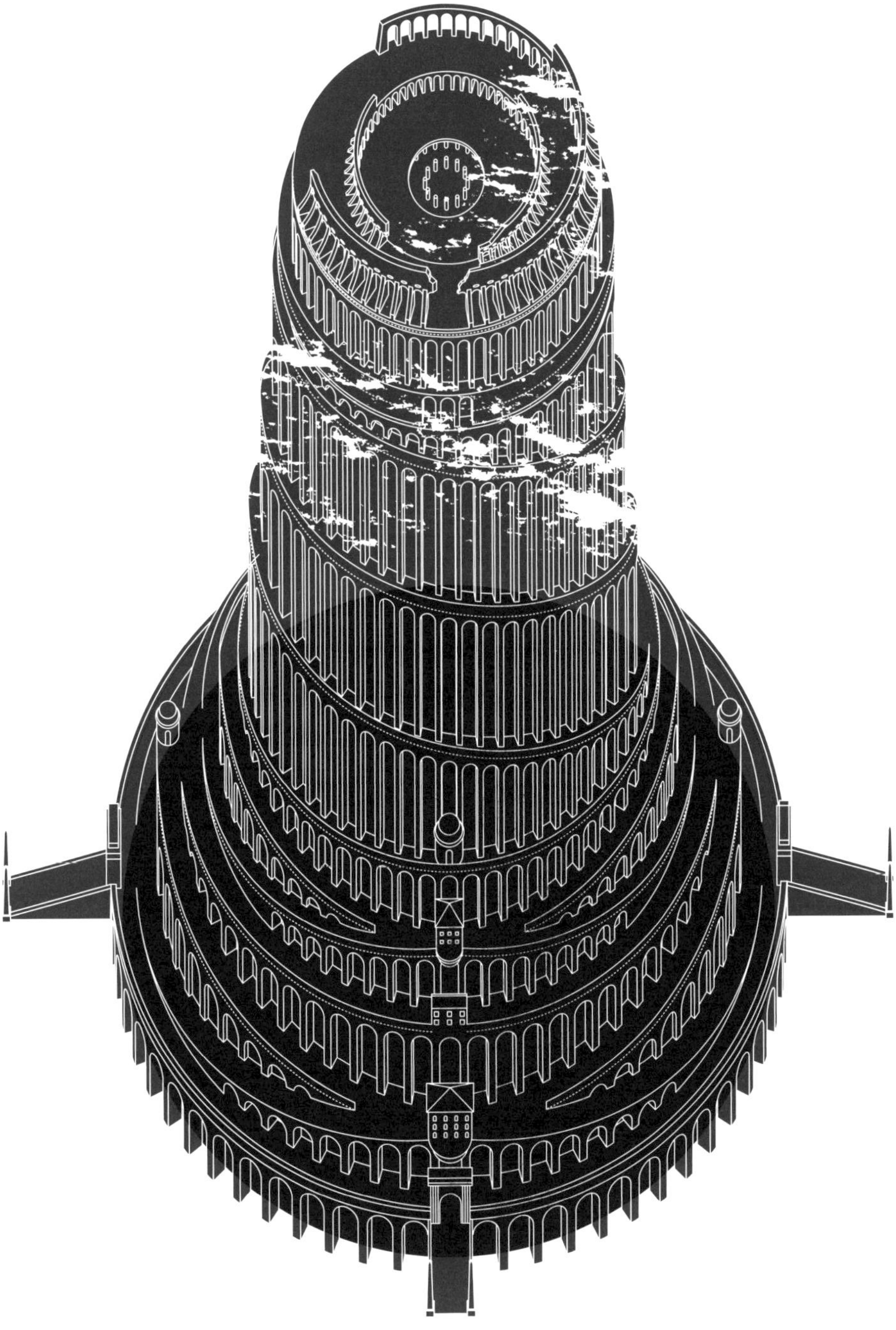

# Nader Tehrani

The following is an interview with Rodolphe el-Khoury, Dean of the University of Miami School of Architecture and Nader Tehrani, Dean of the Irwin S. Chanin Cooper Union School of Architecture and principal of NADAAA.

**Introduction**
Your lecture inaugurates a series titled "Call to Order". It is premised on an observation: It seems that the pendulum is swinging back in favor of a minimal and quasi-naïve architecture.

Just as digital media and CNC fabrication are demonstrating that lines don't have to be straight, that building components don't have to be linear nor standardized, that freeform is possible and even economical, that in fact anything is possible, a number of architects around the world are deliberately choosing the linear, the orthogonal, the generic. They are saying that precisely because buildings could have any form that they shouldn't.

Now I don't think this ostensibly applies to NADAAA and you may be wondering why we invited you to inaugurate this series? And you would be right in suspecting that we see you aligning with the "Call to Order" on another more fundamental level. While you may not share the formal language of many of the other speakers in the series, you do converge with regards to history, typology, and urban morphology.

**REK** **Could you comment on the new phenomenon that we are observing, and then perhaps confirm or deny our assumption about the orientation of NADAAA?**

**NT** First, it may be important to say something about our trajectory of work over the first twenty five years of practice, much of which took canonical organizations as a starting point, but then placed emphasis on elaboration and mannerism. Also, as a process, we always started with material studies as the foundation of architectural actions, with the aggregation of building blocks as basis for configurations that would, in turn, enable architectural forms—whether they be simple, complex, whole or fragmented. This resulted in a very productive generation of work that ended around 2010 as I dissolved Office dA; however, with the launching of NADAAA, while we still had the arsenal of techniques we had developed prior, we placed more emphasis on critically evaluating our own process. This began a new generation of work that is now focused more on the editorial process, on curation and establishing what is irreducible in each work.

You'll note that even though there are continuities in relation to history, type, and urban morphologies from the prior work, the recent work is more selective, sparse, judicious about what is and is not included if only to underline what matters. It is not so much an economic imperative, but a value engineering that is intellectually motivated.

Thus, what seems important to me in your question is how any work finds a way to underline what matters with brevity, clarity, and relevance.

It also has to do with maturity.

When you are young, you need to flex your muscles to build an argument, but there also comes a time when you can self-edit to demonstrate a different type of confidence about what is necessary. Some people come to that age much earlier in their architectural career. In my case, because of my own fascination with Mannerism and the Baroque, it led me down paths that were almost always about surplus, excess, and elaboration –even when their point of departure was a mere detail. The linguistic flourishes that were the rhetorical hallmark of the early work have now given way to a more judicious reduction of that which has most agency. Thus, in this case, the Call to Order also has a deeper biographical reflection.

**REK** **One way to see the dialectic is in a tension and oscillation between type (Rossi) and diagram (Koolhaas). Where do you situate the work of NADAAA between those two poles? [Or perhaps we need a third paradigm to address the work of NADAAA: the organism?]**

**NT** I like the reference to the organism because it does go back to the trajectory I just described between our past and our present. In the earlier phase, I talked about the tell-tale detail, the generative seed of where we began with material units as the building block of larger scale organizations, where one builds an organic relationship between part and whole. Much of that earlier work also reflects the challenges of developing a systemic organization for building construction, not only to develop 'smart' building blocks (how a system turns corners, caps a building, meets the ground, etc.), but also to recognize the exceptions within the very systems one launches.

In the case of Rossi and Koolhaas, there are many other ways to look at the question of type and diagram that flatten the apparent dichotomy: the construction industry as standard, social and cultural conventions, the objet trouvé or the generic object; all of these form a constellation of references between type and diagram that remain relevant for us because they are ready-mades that have a priori cultural significance. Often we will deploy them for pragmatism, as ready-made matter that requires no added emphasis as such, but also matter that is already a language from which to depart. Thus, it is also a foil for those moments of elaboration that make part of what is necessary to emphasize; that which we underline, transform, or invent. And so for me, the type and he diagram, despite their theoretical distinctions, come together in the way they define a ground zero: a clear foundation from which invention and transformation become distinguished.

**REK** **It is interesting because you underline the similarities as opposed to the tensions.**

**NT** Exactly. I think that despite the necessary differences between type and diagram as conceived by Rossi and Koolhaas, neither are convincingly relevant for the area of emphasis we bring to our work. If anything the type is adopted as raw matter, and the diagram as a morsel of clarity, as parti, and neither are used to authenticate our strategies, per se. It is what happens next that matters: I am interested in that moment where architecture becomes something else, when it is de-familiarized, dismantled, transformed or transported to another state. In the best instances of our own work, there is that moment when the building is no longer that which we readily know.

**REK** **The diagnosis of the emerging sensibility is primarily based on a formal observation; but much like their predecessors in the sixties and seventies who were primarily invested in urban morphology, the new protagonists are basing their project in an urban vision, in ideas for sustainable and livable cities. Do you think the diagram has failed the city? Is type and the intelligence sedimented in it better equipped for the complexity of the city?**

**NT** The idea of type as strong form on its own is not, in and of itself, sophisticated enough to deal with some of the complexities of the emerging city; but also that is not to say that a simple diagram cannot resist the apparent complexities of a city to coalesce in something larger than the sum of the city's parts. In that sense, the clarity of a type may have a radical impact on the transformation of the city.

As you suggest, on its own terms, the idea of type is invested in layers of complexity such that it cannot be reducible to a diagram, but also to a layering of systems—if one deems the material, infrastructural, and organizational breakdown of the building as importantly as one does to its "gestalt". Even the simplest building is the result of a layered and complex organism.

I suspect that much of what drives the current sensibility and the reappraisal of type is the result of what we have lost as a discipline in engaging the city. That which has been taken over by real estate forces, privatization, community participation, or any other such force that tends to marginalize the disciplinary priorities of architecture, can now be counter-acted by the power of the type: sometimes using the power of strong form as symbol of what architecture can do at the urban scale, but also sometimes as a supple system that engages the complexity of the city around it.

Consider our own Melbourne School of Design project. From a typological perspective it is a simple atrium building, not significantly different from the building it replaced at first glance. However, once one digs deeper, one realizes that the significance of the new building is how it absorbs and engages the context within its doughnut organization. The street that runs through it, the way in which the Joseph Reed façade is redeployed not as icon, but a functioning threshold, and the inside-outside spaces that are activated by programs such as the fablab – all these suggest a transformation of the purity of the type that exceeds its formal autonomy.

At the same time, in an act of resistance to the very context, the invention of the suspended studio within the core of the atrium is not only a reimagination of what studio culture can be today, but the adoption of a powerful iconic strategy that underlines the formal autonomy of the atrium as a public space, not just a benign interior. In this sense, I can see the MSD project as a bridge between that which performs as urban scenography with that which weaves itself into the infrastructure of the city in deliberate and transformative ways.

REK **There are two instances where you neatly align with our agenda, if not when surely with the School: It is with regard to the vernacular and to drawing. Since the Office dA days, you have**

Interior, Melbourne School of Design, University of Melbourne, NADAAA & John Warde Architects, 2014, photograph by Peter Bennetts

**been interested in teasing out formal innovation from vernacular building traditions and you have been consistently committed to the drawing as the site of invention in design. The vernacular and the drawing are of immense interest to SoA as you already probably know. At this time we are looking at them not only as anchors for the discipline but as the means for moving discourse and practice forward, very much like they function in your work. Could you please elaborate on this?**

NT At the time that I gave the lecture, I was not at Cooper Union. In hindsight, it was a timely question because my own investment in the protocols of representation had a lot to do with my move to Cooper Union, where its curriculum is punctuated by many areas of research in varied media of representation and generation.

The transformative moment of architecture, more often than not, occurs in the act of drawing. I often describe the way in which we drew the Weston House. The line at the top of the corrugated wall was the same length as the line at the bottom of the corrugated wall, which demonstrates that drawing in architecture is not an illustrative process but is already an act of construction. In that instance, that corrugation can produce a ruled surface is its thesis: the vertical ribs offering structural stability to each line connecting top to bottom coordinates, while the horizontal malleability of corrugation offering its flexibility to undulate at a larger scale. Drawing that elevation was very much our first act of fabrication, with the drawing as proof of its "buildability", which was summarily proven through the very model that was its mock-up.

The other aspect, which is admittedly metaphoric but important, is that drawing always involves acts of projection; and the idea of projection, beyond its agency through geometry, is also about how reality may be transformed, and even challenged, through disciplinary media.

Your question curiously connects drawing through the vernacular, and I wonder if these two are inextricably bound?

In the same way that we adopted typology, we also engaged vernacular building traditions if only to launch our research in material systems. Clapboard siding, running bond brick, butt glazed curtain walls—these are all building system conventions that are widely shared. In our work, they also become the site of transformation and invention. We did not so much represent these materials, but treated the aggregation of lines as construction systems in their own right.

Our first projects were each dedicated to dismantling different construction typologies, one by one: The Mill Road house in terms of vernacular wood construction, Casa la Roca in transforming stacking to variable bonds, the Issam Fares Institute through geometric subdivisions for structural proliferation, etc. We adopted the vernacular not so much as historical matter, but to establish critical building practices through the drawing process, and challenge how construction protocols may transform the ways in which we deploy the means and methods of fabrication.

To this end, it is important to link drawings to construction, where most of our energy has been invested. Not only through digital systems of fabrication, but also in collaborations with the building industry, much of our work on drawings has been to appropriate the process of generation to short-circuit the shop drawing process, and develop a level of control over design intent to absorb the means and methods as part of the critical part of the design process.

**REK** **In your role as both a teacher and a practitioner, could you say something about this idea of projection as it relates to drawing by hand versus drawing by computer?**

**NT** The great thing about Cooper's traditions is that it has never constructed an opposition between drawing by hand and computer. To that end, it never really participated in the paperless studio as Columbia did some years ago; nor has it neglected it in fruitful ways. Visualization and generation are part of a research process that occupies many media concurrently, and is a central part of the pedagogical process.

Our own working process is very sympathetic to this, as we work in non-linear ways. Drawing, modeling, fabricating mock-ups, and toggling between digital and hand based media, we adopt a more strategic use of techniques as they become relevant for the questions we are developing.

I like to think that there are ideas in architecture that are captured by the long durée of history such that they can anticipate the invention of a certain architecture for which we do not yet have the right tools to draw. When we first drew Casa la Roca and the MOMA Fabrications projects, we drew them with pencil even though those projects were completely digital, and parametric, in their conceptualization.

On the other hand, there is the notion that the instrumentality of the means and methods of drawing is really the foundation of what is possible in a certain medium. The idea that you draw a line by hand in a certain way, or that the spline—in a digital capacity—enables a different spatial and architectural speculation. These two phenomena are not necessarily opposing each other, but they demonstrate a design process that is at once alert of the longer arc of history and disciplinary conventions, while also focused on the agency of contemporary media as a sight of exploration.

Many architectural ideas have a history and a future that is relevant far beyond the immediate technique that is available for their implementation. At the same time, think of those paradigmatic moments where a vision comes to fruition as a direct result of the invention of a technique. Think of the technique of perspective and a project like the Teatro Olympico, a building that is imbedded in an idea about representation. Our own MOMA fabrications project is, in fact, a response to that very phenomenon, adopting the anamorphic projection not only as representational challenge, but as a test for construction tolerances in the digital age.

**REK** **From your perspective, do you have any general observations about the group that has been compiled for the Call to Order exhibition and how they might contribute to the contemporary architectural discourse?**

**NT** There is great variety in the group that you have assembled, and thus trying to unify them may be unnecessarily forced. I am reminded when they curated the Deconstruction show at MoMA, they amassed a great many tendencies, and yet somehow they all had a tangential link to some interpretation of Deconstruction –through philosophy and semiotics, through Constructivism, and through visual tendencies that provoked a more literal 'dismantled' reading of buildings.

Maybe the more interesting part of your list has to do with how the relationship between forms and ideas play themselves out, between words and images; this tends to be the most polemical aspect of the architectural discipline, as the slippage between the literary and the visual always promises a loose fit, and therein lie many debates. Within that debate, that which matters emerges.

Let me offer an anecdote.

I am sure you followed the ascent of Alejandro Aravena to the Pritzker award; and you have also witnessed the backlash of many critical essays against him claiming that he is riding the train of a social project, in many ways abandoning the project of Architecture. This is ironic for me because this is not a person who has not dabbled into the complexities—and even frivolities—of playful form. Quite the opposite, though he has undertaken a social project of some political complexity, what is striking is actually the range of formal, spatial and material tropes he has deployed in the purest sense of the term. That he has been able to merge the interests of the former and the latter is maybe what distinguishes him, and absolves him of the guilt with which we conventionally target the Formalists.

Somehow, though, Aravena manages to speak in two languages concurrently, taking that which is irreducible to Architecture's agency and translating it into what matters more broadly at a political and cultural level.

What is important to the Call to Order occasion, might be to re-evaluate what matters, and how we may overcome easy polarities to disentangle the conventional oppositions between different forms of debate.

Longitudinal Section, Teatro Olympic, Ottavio Bertotti Scamozzi, 1776

06.

# Round Table Discussion

Young Architects Symposium

The following is a transcription of the Round Table Discussion that took place after the Young Ancient's Symposium held on January 21, 2015 at Glasgow Hall, University of Miami School of Architecture.

Participants: Wonne Ickx (WI) Adrian Phiffer (AP)
Carie Penabad (CP)
Moderator: Rodolphe el-Khoury (REK)

**REK** I really enjoyed this. And I am happy to see that we have the right intuition in putting the three of you together, because I find interesting similarities as well as divergences that may provoke discussion. I want to start with the most obvious, what is ostensibly a similarity between the three of you and the work that we saw, basically the formal affinity, the predilection for the orthogonal, for the simple geometries and forms. Just as now we know that we can do anything with digital fabrication; that anything goes; that freeform is possible and also economical; that when we know that we can do anything, you are telling us precisely why we shouldn't; and you deliberately choose to demonstrate discipline by restricting the palette.

I would like to know more about this.

Is it a moral position?

For instance, the recent Helsinki Guggenheim competition generated a great deal of interest, something we should all be excited about and yet there was a backlash, in part because of the seeming orgy of invention, the formal intricacy, the virtuosity was just too much. Your proposal, which I see as a recycled artifact is a resistance to this consumerist frenzy.

**AP** Our choice to work with simple straightforward forms has to do with a reaction to the excesses of contemporary architectural culture and is often dictated by the conditions of the project including budgets, site, and program. The Helsinki Guggenheim project was a strategic one, an effort to stand out in a sea of over 1700 entries. In reusing an existing ship, we believed that we could push the idea of a new type for a contemporary museum.

**WI** I would like to comment on what you said earlier regarding the use of free forms as not only possible but also economical. I don't believe this is the case. In fact, it may be just the opposite.

After many years of experimenting, we have seen that free form is neither easy nor economical. This is an important thing to consider. Having said this, I do not believe that this is the reason that we have these affinities with platonic forms.

If you give my friend Adrian an enormous budget he will still make an orthogonal object; and this ethos is not merely the result of a disappointment with digital culture but a willful aesthetic act.

**CP** I think for me it has to do with thinking about the individual object in light of the overall city. Seeing architecture through this broader lens influences your formal decisions, your choice of geometries, materials etc. You realize that the majority of the city is composed of discrete and often anonymous fabric buildings whose sum adds up to more than any of the individual parts.

**REK** I would say that another common denominator of the work presented here tonight is an investment in the generic and the commonplace. In our mission statement here at the School, I was reading about how we are more interested in fabric buildings than monuments. I find this extraordinary. It is courageous to say that; but I think it goes against the false dichotomy that we see now rehearsed time and again, especially in the ongoing debate in the New York Times between building and architecture, which I think bares more scrutiny.

**CP** When referring to fabric buildings earlier, I did not mean to suggest that the monument is not important or that the role of the architect is not critical in the making of cities. I merely wanted to cast a broader lens, to understand the city across time. What is it that has permanence? What is it that continues? What is it that remains after the latest fad has passed?

**REK** As far as I'm concerned I am not willing to relinquish the monument.

**CP** Neither am I. I simply do not believe that every building should be designed as one. This is when we get into the territory of excess, something all too prevalent in architecture today.

**AP** Just to point to something else, I think that right now there is the danger that the platonic forms are becoming the new trend. I am seeing this increasingly in European schools of architecture, particularly in places such as the AA.

**RK** So are you saying that it is not so much a critical impulse driving this new sensitivity but rather the desire for a new style?

**AP** Yes indeed. It can be seen as the pursuit of an alternative, without a real understanding of the multiple meanings implicit in those formal choices.

**REK** Perhaps; and this could be very problematic.

Yet I feel that what brings you here is a core commitment to the type of city that you are envisioning. For instance, the image you showed of the cover of the Rossi monograph, was extremely powerful. It crystalized a whole idea about the city, where the architecture provided an enduring framework that enabled certain things, like the flow of life, but at the same time was indifferent to it.

Alternatively, Rem Koolhaas's notion of the city of congestion and his ideas promoted in Delirious New York, depict his thinking of architecture as something that is more than a backdrop or framework but something that is much more of an orchestrator of the culture of congestion. From this notion he has developed an architecture that is actively and completely committed to the staging of the active flow of life. The idea of type, as proposed by Rossi, is completely opposite to this.

I believe this is an important issue. To think that the notion of the diagram, or the idea that a building emerges from the forces that shape the site and is very much responsible for precisely orchestrating its use, the inhabitation of the program, etc. has failed the city in a certain way.

To provoke your challenge, your method returns to a more mute framework, where types have evolved over millennia let's say, versus buildings that have to be concocted as solutions to particular circumstances.

**AP** I think there is a big problem with the notion of diagram as building, where every building and every project is explained by way of diagrams or better yet is a three dimensional representation of a diagrammatic idea. Ironically, in my opinion, despite the desire for variation, the results are always the same. They produce similar outcomes despite being very different architectural projects.

**REK** You could argue that there is still a typological foundation in this approach.

**WI** I think we are in a moment where the central position of program and spectacle as developed by Rem Koolhaas has lost its power as a generator of architecture. I think that we have returned to the idea that buildings should exist beyond the realm of being a direct response to a specific program.

**CP** Ultimately architecture is always a formal act, even if it is veiled in a quasi-scientific discourse dominated by the idea of the diagram. In the end, the architect works with a series of forms that they have selected, reacting to a given program and site.

The recent obsession with the diagram has led to a diminished conversation about architecture. We spend more time talking about how to diagram an idea than how to construct a meaningful building.

**REK** You said something provocative earlier, about how architecture is an autonomous discipline.

Round Table Discussion: Left to Right: Wonne Ickx, Adrian Phiffer, Carie Penabad, Rodoplhe el-Khoury (moderator)

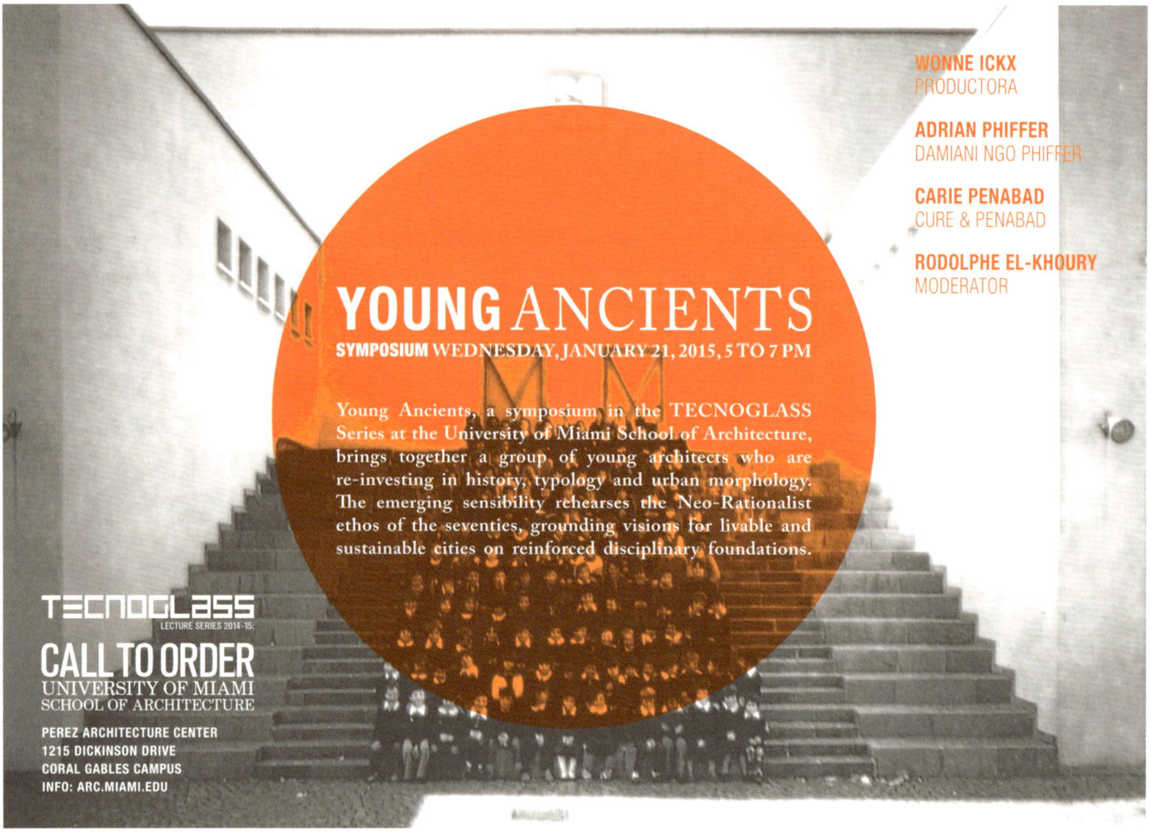


Call to Order Poster, University of Miami School of Architecture Tecnoglass Lecture Series, 2015-2016

That claim was made by the neo-rationalists of course but this is the one claim that I have a hard time accepting. What about ecology, cybernetics, system theory thermodynamics? Do you think they have no place in Schools of Architecture?

**CP** There are extraordinary investigations taking place in a number of parallel fields. As architects and urban designers, we should be open to this complex world; to listen to experts in other fields and to collaborate in interdisciplinary endeavors that can enrich all. At the same time, I don't believe that we need to abandon the language of our discipline to incorporate these new ideas.

For instance, we can find design inspiration in an understanding of ecological systems without feeling the need to design buildings that look like trees; a building can be inspired by Nature and still look like a building.

**REK** I like this.

[laughter]

**WI** I have a simple observation. When preparing the work for this presentation, I sometimes had the feeling that we have been doing the exact same thing for the last century. The same topic and the same solutions, come up, again and again... I find this to be problematic.

**AP** Why is this problematic?

**WI** I guess for me it can be a source of frustration. I admire the way that you so comfortably refer to your sources and your mentors.

But when I discover a reference that is too close to my own work... I sometimes find it very troublesome. Imagine we are doing a fantastic landscape design, and we are really enthusiastic about it,... and then you suddenly stumble upon this piece by Carl Andre which is probably forty years old and which did the same thing twice as good as we did.

**REK** The rhetorical sense in this statement is that it is taking a position against the fascination with originality and making an argument about knowledge building upon elaboration of precedents.

**WI** Yes but I also don't want to discover that we're running in circles. I believe that architecture is no longer autonomous. We have incorporated other disciplines; we have gotten smarter. I want to discover how we have gotten smarter than what people were doing forty years ago. I think it is very important because otherwise we will simply applaud the critical culture that existed in the seventies, and superimpose it over today's culture. I want to try to read where the differences lie.

**REK** In order to acknowledge it, you need to see it as a legacy.

**WI** Of course, of course.

**AP** I don't think that the architects from the seventies were original, they had similar preoccupations but presented it differently, at least that is the way I see the work.

**WI** So it's about universal truths that come back continuously?

**AP** I think your struggle that we are running around in circles is the result of being bombarded with visual imagery. You can go to a blog like ArchDaily and see everything you could have ever imagined and it is so well designed that in order not to get lost, you need to strongly embrace your own set of references.

**RK** Every school has its vicissitudes in history; and our school's defining moment was that period where the school was an active participant in the creation of that culture. The school made a huge contribution to that moment in history. So the danger in organizing Call to Order and these lectures is to think of this as an "I told you so" and "you were right all along". The point is to see how we can do it differently now because now we have learned new things about how we can push the discourse. I believe that these presentations have begun to point a way forward.

07.

# Postscript

Elizabeth Plater-Zyberk

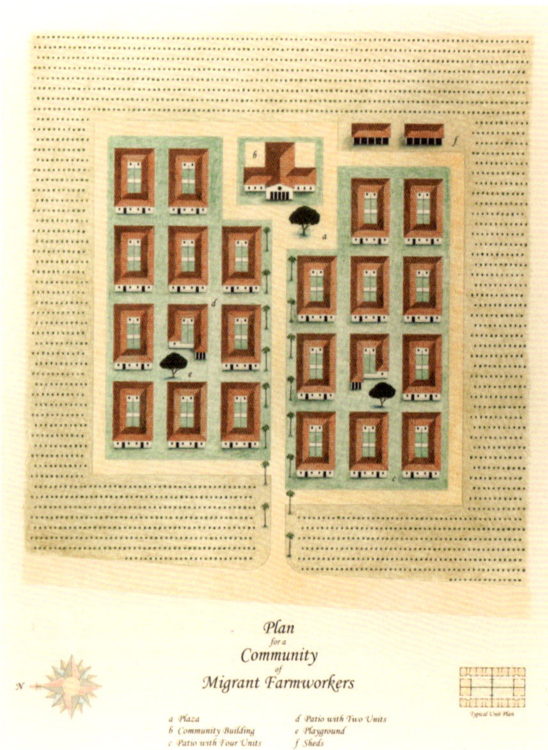


Axonometric of La Estancia, Duany Plater-Zyberk

The exhibition *A Call to Order* marks a transition for the School of Architecture, inaugurating Dean el-Khoury's leadership, seeking impetus from the School's first quarter century. The work of the faculty and others like-minded, was selected with a mind that a return to basics yet again is indicated for the profession.

'One can offset ... excessive compulsion toward the spectacular with a return to simplicity,' the words of Rem Koolhaas opened a recent issue of the Spanish journal *ARQ*, also titled "A Call to Order".

Recalls in the air notwithstanding, the inclination toward the rational and essential has been a long-defining characteristic of the University of Miami School. Its roots lay among the particular influences specific to a *time* and a *place*.

The *time*, beginning with the School's establishment in 1983 (emerging from a program accredited since 1963), gathers three decades of the intellectual fall-out from visitors to Miami. The *place* regards two factors of regional context: the materially modest but visionary origins of South Florida architecture, and the current faculty practices (some represented in the exhibit) that evolved as a response to the realities of Florida and the Caribbean.

To elaborate on the time, the turn of this century obviously gave rise to images of 'starchitecture', but also to an oppositional position—a growing oeuvre of architecture and urbanism, grounded in preservation, emerging from Post-Modernism's renewed respect for history. This dedication to continuity brought historian Vincent Scully to the School for two decades as a professor, co-authoring the manifesto-like *Between Two Towers: the Drawings of the School of Miami.*

The consonant visitors to the School during these years are too many to list. Notables included: Aldo Rossi (originally commissioned to design the school's new building); Rodolfo

Machado and Jorge Silvetti; Javier Cenicacelaya and Inigo Salona; Maurice Culot and Caroline Mierop; and Leon Krier, whose *Rational Architecture* of 1976 proposed the idea that tradition and innovation could be linked through type.

The resulting hybridization of European ideas with the Caribbean defined the place. The region's austere touchstones could translate easily into a rational practice: Key West, a townscape of wood houses; Miami Beach, an amalgam of beaux-arts and international style; Coral Gables' unique imposition of the Mediterranean on a tropical landscape. The city's first architects were the program's founding faculty.

The regional context was enriched by the faculty's interest in the inaugural building of emerging cultures, and those in transition elsewhere—the vigorous building of colonial Hispanic America—in which limited local means are contaminated by the finer things of predecessors.

Such are the Marion Manley buildings that house the School and that could not but be an influence—their spare post-war functionalism, dimensioned to avoid material waste. And the malleable South Florida landscape, undistracted by topography, inspired the very original drawing techniques developed by the faculty.

The region's creation through speculative development led to a critique of suburban sprawl, a degradation of the early town founders' vision. The School's emphasis on urbanism emerged, its role in the New Urbanism, the pioneering research on health and the built environment, and initiatives such as the Center for Community and Urban Design (CUCD), the Knight Program in Community Building, and the Master of Real Estate Development and Urbanism. All recognize that each building contributes to a larger whole, and that the experience of a place may be most satisfactorily derived from the harmonious ensemble rather than only from individual expression.

Attending to pressing problems—post-hurricane and post-earthquake rebuilding, and now sea-level rise—has further encouraged faculty dedication to the simple and durable. The assumption is that beauty and utility can co-exist toward a civic contribution. As Abbe Laugier's *Essai sur l'Architecture* comes to mind, the first call to order, one might imagine the 18$^{th}$ century contest of the romantics and the classicists repeated today in a pluralistic architectural discourse. Most take sides, exhorting their camp to dominance. Others, such as our school, display an open mind, despite risking a discount of their efforts by the opposing sides.

In this vulnerable position the School of Architecture faculty embraces the contradictions, with optimism, courage, civic responsibility, engagement with community, enriching even the most humble building endeavors.

The work may be seen as a negotiation between concept and implementation, global context and local practice, community identity and individual expression, universal influences and specific culture—presenting a robust prospect for the years ahead.

# BIOGRAPHIES

## COLLABORATORS

### 2A+PA

2A+P/A is an architectural office based in Rome established by Gianfranco Bombaci and Matteo Costanzo. The office works on architectural and landscape design and urban planning with a particular interest in the nature and conditions of public space. It engages in a broad range of projects including public and private buildings, housing complexes, urban spaces, event pavilions and temporary installations. Their writings and productions have been published in a variety of international books and magazines such as A10, Abitare, a+t, A+U, Architecture d'Aujourd'hui, Architectural Review, Domus and Volume. The architects of 2A+P/A have publicly presented their projects at and realized site-specific installations for several international exhibitions, such as the NAI in Rotterdam, the 13th and 11th Venice Architecture Biennale, the 5th Brasilia Biennial of Architecture, and Shanghai Expo 2010 inside the Italian Pavilion. Their work was also showcased in a solo exhibition in Rome entitled "The Pop Out Show."

### Caruso St John Architects

Since its foundation in 1990, Caruso St John has been pursuing an architecture that is rooted in place. The practice resists the thin-skinned abstraction that characterises much global architecture in favour of buildings that are perceived slowly over time and that have an emotional content. Its work is enriched by an on-going dialogue with the European city and with history—that of architecture, art, and culture more widely—traditions that bring an accumulated richness of expression to the work • Following the practice's rise to prominence with the winning of the international competition for the acclaimed New Art Gallery Walsall, its engagement with the art world has been notable for the creation of museum and gallery environments that enjoy the confidence of artists. The practice has also assembled a portfolio of projects that intervene in a city's urban fabric at the scale of an urban quarter • The practice is consciously international in its outlook, with approximately 25 people working from an open studio in a 1930s factory in east London that the practice converted for their use. In 2010 a second office was opened in Zurich. Caruso St John were awarded the RIBA Stirling Prize for the UK's best new building for the Newport Street Gallery in 2016.

### Caveja Studio

The caveja is the most eloquent symbol of Romagna, an emblem tied to the land and its traditions. Caveja Studio intends to enhance this tradition, while maintaining an open perspective towards Europe and the World. The starting point for the work is the understanding that through the careful study of local knowledge, one can arrive at universal answers • Alessandro Pretolani studied architecture at the University of Bologna where he graduated in 2006. Following, he was a research fellow at the Faculty of Architecture of Cesena and in 2009 he enrolled in the PhD program in Architectural Design at the University of Bologna. During the same period, he participated in numerous international seminars and spent time as a researcher at the Canadian Center for Architecture in Montreal (CCA) • Filippo Pambianco studied architecture at the University of Bologna where he graduated in 2006. While there, he received a Leonardo scholarship to study the work of Spanish architect, Guillermo Vazquez Consuegra. Upon graduation, he worked for Tomaso Trombetti and Guillermo Vazquez Consuegra from 2007 to 2011, collaborating on numerous international architecture competitions. Currently he is Assistant III for the planning workshop at the Department of Architecture of the University of Bologna.

### CÚRE & PENABAD

Founded in 2001, Cúre & Penabad aspires to create an architecture of place. The practice seeks to find beauty in differences and is drawn to what makes an environment unique. Inspiration is found in both the vernacular and the academic; in the ancient and the contemporary; in the commonplace and the extraordinary. As such the architectural output of the firm is eclectic, molded by the particular circumstances of each setting and client • The Miami-based practice has won recognition, receiving numerous national awards, among them over ten American Institute of Architects design awards and a Silver Medal at the Miami Biennale. Most recently, the firm was nominated as a finalist for the prestigious Marcus Cooperation Architectural Prize for emerging architectural talent • Penabad and Cúre received their Bachelors of Architecture degrees from the University of

Miami School of Architecture and their Masters of Architecture in Urban Design degrees from Harvard University. They are both currently faculty at the University of Miami School of Architecture and held the Louis I. Kahn Visiting Assistant Professorship at Yale University in 2013.

### Jaime Correa and Associates

Jaime Correa and Associates is a peer-to-peer collaborative urban and architectural design firm operating from the City of Miami. Its professional work focuses on the tactical applications of complexity theory and environmental theory in the reconstitution of cities and liveable public spaces. The latest projects include: three public space interventions in the City of Lauderdale-by-the-Sea, redevelopment of the Upper Riverside Industrial District in Miami, eight mini-skyscrapers in Medellin, five counter-proposals to the Sea-Level-Rise status-quo in Miami, urban design collaborations in Central and South America, and the master planning and implementation of "The Wave," a 50,000-people new town in Muscat, Sultanate of Oman.

### Johnston Marklee

Founded in 1998 by principals Sharon Johnston and Mark Lee, Johnston Markee's projects vary in scale from master plans to buildings to temporary installations. Johnston Marklee has a substantial architectural portfolio including residential, commercial, institutional, and exhibition environments with a particular focus on the arts. Current projects include a new studio campus for the UCLA Graduate Art Program in Culver City, California, DEPART Foundation's Grand Traiano Art Complex in Grottaferrata, Italy, Poggio Golo winery in Montepulciano, Italy, Vault House, a private beachside residence in Oxnard, California, and Chile House/META, a community arts center in Penco, Chile, for the Chilean government. The firm has garnered many notable awards including Progressive Architecture Design Awards, AIA Los Angeles & AIA California Council Honor Awards, an American Architecture Award, and an AR Award for Emerging Architecture.

### Khoury Levit Fong

Khoury Levit Fong, founded in 2006, brings together three partners with diverse professional and academic backgrounds to align cutting-edge research with innovative practice: Rodolphe el-Khoury, Robert Levit, and Steven Fong. Because the practice ranges in the scale of its design activities from urban design to the details of architecture, KLF is able to envision and coordinate the synergies that occur across all scales of the built environment • The firm has gained international recognition for award-winning projects that balance the everyday needs of individuals with the collective identity and vision of institutions. The double commitment showcased in "Monuments + Bits," a solo exhibition at the Eric Arthur Gallery featuring projects that "operate at the real scale of urban culture, and help make it livable," as stated in John Bentley Mays' review in the Globe and Mail. The shared fundamental commitment of KLF's partners is to the communal aspects of architecture and to the role and potential of buildings and institutions in a wide social and cultural context. The partners' work in diverse urban environments from Los Angeles to Shanghai gives them a broad perspective on design possibilities; and they bring decades of experience to the development of award winning projects that capitalize on new technology as much as the environmental intelligence sedimented in traditional building types and construction techniques.

### Laurent de Carnière

Laurent de Carnière is a french architect based in Paris • After graduating with Honors in 2005 from the School of Architecture ISACF LA CAMBRE (Belgium), he gained his first experiences working with his teacher LHOAS & LHOAS, then with the Chinese architect HOU LIANG and META-FORM. In 2006, he moved to Australia where he worked with the firm LAVA in Sydney. In 2009, he returned to Paris, where he currently lives • Beside his current work at DOMINIQUE PERRAULT ARCHITECTURE, he is running his own architectural investigations through various creative projects, apartments, set designs, and competitions. In 2011, he designed ICI-MONTREUIL, the largest co-working space and fablab in France for creative people, which is now nearing completion. In 2013, he started a new artistic project called "AXO-NO-METRIC-CITY", a reflection on territories between street art and architectural drawing.

### Lederer Ragnarsdottir Oei

The office was founded in 1979 and currently has about 45 employees. Among the competitions won in recent years are the Historical Museum in Frankfurt, the Office and Business House Kaiserkarree in Karlsruhe, and the Municipal Museum in Stuttgart. Also the University of Cooperative Education in Lörrach, the Cloister Hegne Marianum in Allensbach, the Art Museum in Ravensburg, the Diocesan Curia and archive in Rottenburg and the Hospitalhof in Stuttgart are all important projects for us which were acquired by competitions. Since its founding, the firm has participated in 273 competitions, review procedures, and multiple assignments with over 128 works having been awarded with prizes.

## Loeb Sarli Architects

Loeb Sarli Architects is based in Basel and Miami. It was founded in 2009 by Tamar Loeb and Edgar Sarli. The firm's project-based research ranges from large scale urban interventions to a collection of portable furniture for contemporary nomadic urbanites. The office has won awards in Switzerland and Spain. Its work has been featured in AV, Domus web, and NZZ, and exhibited at the 2010 Architecture Biennale in Venice.

## Machado Silvetti

Machado Silvetti is an architecture and urban design firm known for creating distinctive spaces and unique works of architecture in the United States and abroad. Founders Rodolfo Machado and Jorge Silvetti have been in association since 1974. After more than three decades of steady, successful practice, its portfolio reflects the diverse scope, scale and breadth of the firm's experience, displaying special expertise in Art and Teaching Museums, Education and Institutional environments and facilities, conservation, cultural heritage, re-use, urban design and planning. Internationally recognized, the firm has worked in Berlin, Beirut, Buenos Aires, Seoul, Singapore, Rome, Dubai, Abu Dhabi, Malaysia, Vietnam and across the United States.

## MOS

If given the choice between staring blankly into space or reading architects' office statements on their websites, we choose the first. They all say the same thing: we're sustainable, responsible with budgets, experienced, award winning, etc.... The game seems to be how to say nothing in particular and comfort any worries of someone contemplating hiring you. After a few clicks, it's hard not to think that all this quote-unquote professionalism is very cold at its core • We can't tell you exactly when MOS started. We like to say it was 2003, but we did not have an office space then and our name was !@#?, which we quickly found was too difficult to use because 1. you couldn't pronounce it and 2. you couldn't get a web address. So, eventually, we drifted towards MOS- an acronym of our names and reflection of our shared desires to be horizontal and fuzzy, as opposed to tall and shiny. We began around an oversized table, a surface for collecting, gathering, and working through a range of design experiments- a make-believe of architectural fantasies, problems, and thoughts. As we've grown, we remain around a large table, working together on each project through playful experimentation and serious research.

## NADAAA

NADAAA is a Boston-based architecture and urban design firm led by principal designer Nader Tehrani, in collaboration with partners Katherine Faulkner and Daniel Gallagher. NADAAA's projects range in scale from furniture to architecture and urban design, with a focus on craft, construction, and digital fabrication. The office completed the first LEED gold-certified, multi-family housing building in Boston, the Macallen building, and the first LEED-rated gas station in the United States, Helios house. The firm has received the Cooper-Hewitt National Design Award in Architecture, the American Academy of Arts and Letters Architecture Award, the Harleston Parker award, the Hobson Award, numerous AIA awards, and 16 Progressive Architecture awards. Their work has been exhibited at institutions including the Museum of Modern Art, the Boston Institute of Contemporary Art and LA MOCA, and is part of the permanent exhibit at the Nasher and the CCA. Tehrani is currently Dean of the Copper Union School of Architecture and was formerly a Professor of Architecture at MIT, where he served as the head of the department from 2010-2014. In 2013 and 2014, NADAAA was ranked no. 1 in design for Architect magazine's top 50 firms in the United States.

## OFFICE Kersten Geers David Van Severen

Founded in 2002 by Kersten Geers and David Van Severen, OFFICE Kersten Geers David Van Severen is known for its idiosyncratic architecture. Kersten Geers graduated in Architecture and Urbanism from the University of Ghent, Belgium and at Esquela Tecnica Superior de Arquitectura in Madrid, Spain. He worked with Maxwan Architects and Urbanists and with Neutelings Riedijk Architects in Rotterdam. He was a professor at the University of Ghent, and a visiting professor at Columbia University, and the Academy of Architecture in Mendrisio, and is currently teaching at the EPFL, Lausanne. He is a founding member of the architecture magazine San Rocco • David Van Severen graduated in Architecture and Urbanism from the University of Ghent, Belgium and the Esquela Tecnica Superior de Arquitectura in Madrid, Spain. He worked with Stéphane Beel Architects, Xaveer De Geyter Architects and for Atelier Maarten Van Severen. He was a teacher and guest critic at the Academy of Amsterdam, the TU Delft, and the Berlage Institute in Rotterdam, and he is currently a guest tutor at the Architecture School of Versailles.

## Office of Adrian Phiffer

Office of Adrian Phiffer is practicing design. Its approach to the practice is rational and irrational, reasonable and unreasonable—a purely creative process. Every decision made is driven by instinct. We like it. We don't like it. We don't know. In that way, there are no predefined products. The outcome is completely unknown and it produces bizarre creatures that we often don't understand. But it's different. And authentic • Adrian Phiffer is originally from Romania. He received his Master of Architecture from the University of Architecture and Urbanism "Ion Mincu" in Bucharest, and a Master of Urban Design from University of Toronto. In 2001-2002 he studied at Ecole d'Architecture de Toulouse under a Socrates-Erasmus Scholarship offered by the European Union. He has worked with Baird Sampson Neuert Architects and Moriyama Teshima Architects in Toronto, and with Office for Metropolitan Architecture in Rotterdam. In parallel to Office of Adrian Phiffer, he directs The Flat Side of Design and teaches architecture and urbanism at University of Toronto - John H. Daniels Faculty of Architecture, Landscape, and Design.

### Pezo Von Ellrichshausen

Pezo Von Ellrichshausen is an art and architecture studio established in Concepcion, Southern Chile, in 2002 by Mauricio Pezo and Sofia Von Ellrichshausen. They have been the curators of the Chilean Pavilion at the 2008 Venice Biennale and teach regularly in Chile at the Universidad Catolica and in the USA at the Illinois Institute of Technology. They have been visiting professors at the University of Texas (Austin, 2011-14) and at Cornell University (New York, 2009). Their work has been distinguished with the Mies Crown Hall Americas Emerge Prize (Chicago, 2013), the Rice Design Alliance Prize (Houston, 2012), the V Iberoamerican Architecture Biennial Award (Montevideo, 2006), and the XV Chilean Architecture Biennial Award (Santiago, 2006). The work of the studio has been edited in Monographic issues of A+U (Tokyo, 2013) 2G (Barcelona, 2012) and ARQ (Santiago, 2007) and exhibited at the International Architecture exhibition at La Biennale di Venezia (Venice, 2010), at the Royal Academy of Arts (London, 2014), and as part of the permanent collection at the MOMA (New York, 2014) • Mauricio Pezo completed a Master in Architecture at the Universidad Catolica de Chile (Santiago, 1998) and a degree in Architecture at the Universidad del Bio-Bio (Concepcion, 1999). He has been awarded the Young Architect Prize by the Chilean Architects Association (Santiago, 2006) and the Municipal Art Prize by the Concepcion City Hall (Concepcion, 2013) • Sofia Von Ellrichshausen holds a degree in Architecture from the Universidad de Buenos Aires, 2002) where she was distinguished with the Fadu-Uba Honors Diploma.

### PRODUCTORA

PRODUCTORA is a Mexico City-based architectural studio, founded by four architects of different nationalities: Abel Perles from Argentina, Carlos Bedoya from Mexico, Victor Jaime from Mexico, and Wonne Ickx from Belgium. Currently the office is working on projects in Mexico and abroad, from residential projects to public and corporate buildings. Its work has been presented in the Architectural Biennales of Beijing and Venice, the National Art Museum of Beijing, the Victoria and Albert Museum in London, and in Italy, Spain and the USA. In 2008, the studio was selected by Herzog & de Meuron to participate in the Ordos100 Project to build a villa in Inner Mongolia, China. That same year, PRODUCTORA won, in collaboration with Lucio Muniain et al, the International Competition for the New CAF Headquarters in Caracas, Venezuela • PRODUCTORA has received awards from the Architectural League of New York's Young Architects Forum in 2007 and its Emerging Voices program in 2013. PRODUCTORA frequently operates in the contemporary art realm and has collaborated with artists such as Iñaki Bonillas, Marta Minujín, and David Lamelas. The studio has realized museographies at the Beaux Arts Palace of Brussels, the Cultural Centre Clavijero in Morelia, and the Tamayo Museum. In 2011 PRODUCTORA, alongside curator and art critic Ruth Estevez, founded LIGA—Space for Architecture—Mexico City, a platform that promotes emerging Latin-American architecture.

### R & R Studios / Roberto Behar & Rosario Marquardt

R & R Studios, the collaborative office of Roberto Behar and Rosario Marquardt, is a multidisciplinary practice weaving together visual arts, exhibition, design, architecture and urban design. The work of Rosario and Roberto has been published in over 200 publications worldwide, including Casabella of Milan, Wallpaper of London, and the New York Times. R & R's works has been presented in museums and galleries in the United States and abroad. Exhibition venues include solo exhibitions at the Museum of Contemporary Art in Denver, the Miami Art Museum (MAM) the Museum of Contemporary Art in North Miami (MOCA). They have also participated in group shows at The Palm Beach Institute of Contemporary Art, the Neuberger Museum of Art in Purchase, and the Center International Pour La Ville. Five books have been published on R&R Studios work: Here Comes the Sun, The Peace Project, M, The Living Room, and Museum Works. Notable works include Miami icon *The Living Room* and the visionary Opa-Locka Public Art Master Plan.

### Salottobuono

Salottobuono was an architectural office based in Milan founded by Matteo Ghidoni, Ludovico Centis, Marco Ferrari, Fabio Gigone, Michele Marchetti and Giovanni Piovene. It remained as a collaborative endeavor from 2006 until 2012. During those years, the office served as the editor of the "Instructions and Manuals" section for the magazine Abitare (2007-2010) and the creative director of Domus magazine (2011, 2012). The firm participated in the Venice Biennale of Architecture (2008, 2012), published the "Manual of Decolonization" (2010), and designed the Italian Pavilion for the Venice Biennale (2010). Since 2013, Matteo Ghidoni is the sole principal of the office.

## Sergison Bates architects

Established in 1996, Sergison Bates architects have earned a reputation as one of the UK's leading architectural practices by successfully engaging with all dimensions of architectural and urban design. The main office in London is international in outlook and staff composition, and in 2010 a second office was opened in Zürich. Both offices are currently involved in a wide range of international projects ranging from urban planning to regeneration, public buildings, housing, and private houses • Sergison Bates' projects are informed by a sensitive approach to place, the experiential potential of materials and construction and a concern for the environmental, social and economic aspects of sustainability. They aspire to create a design-led architecture that is contemporary and rooted in its context, at all scales, and are committed to a research-based approach supported by the partners' academic work • The practice has won numerous national and international awards – among them the Erich Schelling Prize, the Heinrich Tessenow Gold Medal and four RIBA Awards.

## UHO

UHO is an architecture studio led by Adrien Durrmeyer and Max Turnheim based in France, Paris. They recognize the possibility of a constant feedback between acts of emancipation in abstract and concrete space. UHO advocates the radical materiality of architecture as a means for potential modifications of the political structure. One of their first completed projects was in 2010, Stairs in a house, built in Rueil-Malmaison, France. The firm has participated in numerous worldwide competitions, including Albania where they won first prize for the City of Students Competition held in 2015.

# INDIVIDUALS

## Adib Cúre

Adib Cúre is an Assistant Professor in Practice at the University of Miami School of Architecture where his research focuses on the study of Latin American urbanism and architecture. He is also a principal of CÚRE & PENABAD, based in Miami. He has taught at a variety of institutions including the Boston Architectural Center and Northeastern University; and in 2013 was the Louis I Kahn Visiting Assistant Professor at Yale University with Carie Penabad.

## Carie Penabad

Carie Penabad is an Associate Professor and Director of Undergraduate studies at the University of Miami School of Architecture where her research focuses on the study of Latin American urbanism and architecture. She is also a principal of CÚRE & PENABAD, based in Miami. She has taught at a variety of institutions including the Boston Architectural Center and Northeastern University; and in 2013 was the Louis I Kahn Visiting Assistant Professor at Yale University with Adib Cúre. She is co-author of the book *Marion Manley: Miami's First Woman Architect* with historian Catherine Lynn (University of Georgia Press, 2010).

## Edgar Sarli

Edgar Sarli has been a faculty member at the University of Miami School of Architecture since 2009. Since 2014, he has been the co-Curator of exhibitions at the School. After collaborating in the office of Rafael Moneo for five years, he founded Loeb Sarli Architects. The firm's project-based research ranges from large - scale urban interventions to a collection of portable furniture for contemporary nomadic urbanites. The office has won awards in Switzerland and Spain. Its work has been featured in AV, Domus web, and NZZ, and exhibited at the 2010 Architecture Biennale in Venice.

## Esteban Salcedo Sánchez

Esteban Salcedo is an architect from the University of Granada. He has been awarded with scholarships at various universities including ENSA Marseille, Central University of Chile, and ETSA Madrid. He has received grants from different institutions for his postgraduate studies, most notably the Bancaja grant, Arquia European Internships and La Caixa Scholarships. He has worked in several architectural studios, including Architectures Torres Nadal in Murcia, Elisa Valero Architects in Granada, and Ateliers Jean Nouvel in Paris. He is currently the Design Director at Estudio Herreros Madrid. He has contributed to publications such as San Rocco Magazine and Desierto, and wrote for the recent monograph on Caño Roto. He has presented at the International Campus of Ultzama and the Spanish Ceramics Congress conferences. He has served as a visiting professor at ETSA Coruna, IED Madrid, and The Architectural Association. He is currently completing his Ph.D studies at the ETSA Madrid, where he is Assistant Professor of Postgraduate Studies and a member of the Emerging Practices in Architecture research group.

## Jean Francois Lejeune

Jean-François Lejeune is an architect and professor of architecture, urban design, and history at the University of Miami School of Architecture. He served as the Director of Graduate Studies from 2009 to 2014. He has been a visiting professor at the Universidade do Rio Grande du Sul, the University of Ferrara, the Università La Sapienza Roma, and the Universidad de Alcalá in Alcalá de Henares. His books include *The Making of Miami Beach 1933-1942* and *Modern Architecture and the Mediterranean*, which was commended for the 2011 CICA Bruno Zevi Book Award. He has published in Rassegna, Stadtbauwelt, Architektur Aktuell, The Journal of Decorative and Propaganda Arts, Journal of Architectural Education, and was one of the main contributors to the 2009 book *Miami Modern Metropolis*. He is a founding member and secretary of DoCOMOMO-US/Florida and was an Affiliated Fellow at the American Academy in Rome in 2007. In 2003 Lejeune curated in Brussels the exhibition *Cruelty and Utopia: Cities and Landscapes of Latin America*, whose catalogue won the Julius Posener CICA Award for Best Architecture Catalogue in 2005.

### Katherine Wheeler

Katherine J. Wheeler, Ph.D. is a Professor at the University of Miami School of Architecture. She received her Ph.D. in Architectural History, Theory and Criticism from MIT, a Masters in Architectural History from the University of Virginia School of Architecture, and a Bachelors of Architecture from the University of Tennessee. She has received several major fellowships for her research on the history of architectural drawing including the Huntington Library; the Institute for Historical Research, University of London; the Paul Mellon Centre for the Study of British Art; and the Renaissance Society of America. She is the author of the book *Victorian Perceptions of Renaissance Architecture*, 1851-1914.

### Matteo Ghidoni

Architect Matteo Ghidoni was a founding partner of the research agency Multiplicity from 2002 to 2006. His work with Multiplicity was exhibited at Kunstwerke in Berlin, the Venice Biennale, the Musée d'art moderne in Paris, the ZKM in Karlsruhe, and the Beijing Biennial. Ghidoni founded the architectural office Salottobuono in 2006. He has been a guest professor at the Istituto Universitario d'Architettura di Venezia, the Politecnico in Milan, the Royal Danish Academy of Arts in Copenhagen and the Pontificia Universidad Javeriana in Bogotà. He has given guest lectures at several schools and institutions including the Berlage Institute, the University of California Berkeley, and Columbia University. Ghidoni is founder and editor-in-chief of San Rocco International Magazine of Architecture.

### Nader Tehrani

Nader Tehrani is the Dean of the Irwin S. Chanin School of Architecture at the Cooper Union in New York. Nader Tehrani is also Principal of NADAAA, a practice dedicated to the advancement of design innovation, interdisciplinary collaboration, and an intensive dialogue with the construction industry. He was previously a professor of architecture at MIT, where he served as the Head of the Department from 2010-2014. As the principal and founder of Office dA, Tehrani's work has been recognized with notable awards, including the Cooper Hewitt National Design Award in Architecture, the United States Artists Fellowship in Architecture and Design, and the American Academy of Arts and Letters Award in Architecture. He has also received the Harleston Parker Award for the Northeastern University Multi-faith Spiritual Center and the Hobson Award for the Georgia Institute of Technology Hinman Research Building. Throughout his career, Tehrani has received sixteen Progressive Architecture Awards as well as numerous AIA, Boston Society of Architects, and ID awards. In 2013, 2014, and 2015 NADAAA has ranked No. 1 in design for Architect Magazine's Top 50 firms in the United States.

### Rodolphe el-Khoury

Rodolphe el-Khoury is Dean of the School of Architecture at the University of Miami. He was Canada Research Chair at the University of Toronto, Head of Architecture at California College of the Arts, and Associate Professor at Harvard Graduate School of Design. His current research focuses on applications of digital technology that aims for enhanced responsiveness and resilience in buildings and cities. Articles on his projects and research have appeared in the Wall Street Journal, The Globe and Mail, The Toronto Star and WIRED Magazine. He has also been featured online (Gizmodo, DeZeen, Fast Company, Domus, Reuters) and on television/radio shows (CBC, Space Channel, NBC, TFO, BBC World). el-Khoury is a partner at Khoury Levit Fong, an award winning professional practice based in Toronto.

### Steven Fett

Steven Fett is a full-time lecturer at the University of Miami School of Architecture and assistant director of the School's Center for Urban and Community Design. He received a Bachelor of Architecture from the University of Minnesota and a Master of Architecture and Master of Urban Design from the University of Miami. He is founder of the architectural design and planning firm, Steven Fett Architecture. Located in downtown Miami, the firm has won a number of awards including the Florida Redevelopment Association's President's Award and the American Public Works Association's, "Public Works Project of the Year." In 2011, Fett was featured in an exhibition titled, "13 Young Architects in Florida."

## BOOK CREDITS

Art Director: Oscar Riera Ojeda
Graphic Design: Lucía Bauzá
Copy Editor: Byron Hawes
Cover and End Papers Photographs: Julien Lanoo, Vitra Shaudepot, Weil am Rhein, Germany, Herzog & de Meuron Architects
Page 2: MAG Headquarters, CÚRE & PENABAD, Escuintla, Guatemala, 2015, Photograph by Carlos Domenech

OSCAR RIERA OJEDA
PUBLISHERS


ISBN 978-1-946226-14-3
Published by Oscar Riera Ojeda Publishers Limited
Printed in China

Oscar Riera Ojeda Publishers Limited
Unit 4-6 7/F.,
Far East Consortium Building,
121 Des Voeux Road Central, Hong Kong
T: +852-5311-1625

Production Offices | China
Suite 19, Shenyun Road,
Nanshan District, Shenzhen 518055
T:+86-182-0098-3774

www.oropublishers.com | www.oscarrieraojeda.com
oscar@oscarrieraojeda.com